TURNER **CLASSIC** MOVIES

HOLLYWOOD
VICTORY

THE MOVIES, STARS, AND STORIES OF
WORLD WAR II

CHRISTIAN BLAUVELT

FOREWORD BY **DR. ROBERT M. CITINO,**
of the National World War II Museum

RUNNING PRESS
PHILADELPHIA

Front-of-book endpapers: Marie Wilson, Betty Hutton, Greer Garson, Mickey Rooney, Judy Garland, and Lucille Ball stand in a military police jeep while on a war bond tour in September 1943. It was not long before Rooney himself was drafted. James Cagney can be glimpsed sitting in the jeep behind them.

Page vi: James Stewart and Clark Gable share a moment while in uniform. They both served in the Army Air Forces and flew daring bombing missions over Germany, with Stewart as a pilot and squadron commander and Gable as a documentary cameraman and gunner.

Back-of-book endpapers: Carole Landis hands out free tickets to servicemen for the Brooklyn Bond Bowl game at Ebbets Field. A popular pinup, she traveled 100,000 miles to entertain the troops during World War II.

Running Press
Hachette Book Group
1290 Avenue of the Americas, New York, NY 10104
www.runningpress.com
@Running_Press

Printed in China

First Edition: November 2021

Published by Running Press, an imprint of Perseus Books, LLC, a subsidiary of Hachette Book Group, Inc.
The Running Press name and logo is a trademark of the Hachette Book Group.

The Hachette Speakers Bureau provides a wide range of authors for speaking events.
To find out more, go to www.hachettespeakersbureau.com or call (866) 376-6591.

The publisher is not responsible for websites (or their content) that are not owned by the publisher.

All images courtesy of Turner Classic Movies, except: pages VIII, 10, 14, 27, 34, 40, 50, 57, 60, 64, 67, 70, 72, 73, 80, 81, 83, 85, 86, 88, 95, 97, 108 (Courtesy Photofest); pages 3, 5, 33, 36, 44, 47, 52, 53, 61, 71, 75, 78, 79, 80, 82, 87, 98, 122, 123, 124, 125, 126, 127, 128, 129, 131, 136, 137, 138, 142, 143, 144, 146, 152, 153, 154, 156, 157, 159, 160, 161, 162, 163, 164, 166, 167, 168, 169, 170, 171, 173, 174, 175, 176, 177, 178, 179, 180, 181, 182, 189, 190, 196, 197, 200 (Courtesy Everett Collection, Inc.)

Print book cover and interior design by Joshua McDonnell.

Library of Congress Control Number: 2021938238

ISBNs: 978-0-7624-9992-2 (hardcover), 978-0-7624-9990-8 (ebook)

RRD-S

10 9 8 7 6 5 4 3 2 1

TO MY MOM, MY QUARANTINE BUDDY,

FOR PUTTING UP WITH ME WHENEVER I'D SAY,

"NOT NOW, MY BRAIN IS IN 1942!"

CONTENTS

FOREWORD ---------------------- VII

INTRODUCTION -------------- IX

PART I
STORM CLOUDS (1933–1941)

Hollywood Opens Its Arms . . . ------- 1

. . . But Closes Its Mind --------- 4

Sounding the Alarm About Japan --- 8

Saving Her Homeland from Itself --- 11

"Quarantine Hitler" ----------- 13

Confessions of a Nazi Spy -------- 15

Turning Apathy into Engagement --- 20

The Great Dictator ----------- 23

Bombs, Bullets, and Bananas ----- 29

Down South American Way
    with Disney ------------- 32

Hollywood on Defense -------- 37

Jimmy Stewart Gets His Wings ---- 41

PART II
DAY OF INFAMY AND AFTERMATH
(1941–1942)

A Sunday in December --------- 45

Why We Fight ------------- 49

Mobilizing Star Power --------- 53

Carole Lombard: A Star Lost ----- 57

The War Oughta Be in Pictures ---- 61

Would America Be Invaded? ----- 63

Itchy Trigger Fingers --------- 66

Fighting for Freedom Abroad
    with None at Home -------- 69

Fifty Movie Stars Board a Train . . . - 73

PART III
TURNING POINTS (1942–1943)

Thanks for the Memories -------- 79

The Good Neighbor Policy vs.
    The Magnificent Ambersons --- 83

Victories Onscreen and at Sea ---- 89

Fleeing Nazis, Only to Play Nazis -- 95

How Chinese- and Korean-American
    Actors Fought Japan ------- 98

The Hollywood Canteen --------- 102

Hollywood's Rosies ----------- 107

Real-Life Refugees Give Casablanca
    Its Power ------------- 113

And May All Your Christmases
    Be White ------------- 120

PART IV
THE NEW NORMAL (1943–1944)

Stars in Uniform - - - - - - - - - - 123

Gable Finds Purpose, Howard
Becomes a Martyr - - - - - - - - - 127

Sherlock Holmes and
Lassie Go to War - - - - - - - - - 133

A *Why We Fight* for
African-Americans - - - - - - - - 140

New Stars Are Born, and
Old Ones Born Again - - - - - - - 146

How the Oscars Changed - - - - - - 153

The Rise of Youth Culture . . .
and the Pinup - - - - - - - - - - 156

Drawing Up Propaganda - - - - - - 161

Hollywood Was There on D-Day - - - 164

PART V
A NEW WORLD, A NEW
HOLLYWOOD (1944–)

Raising Money, Raising Hopes - - - - 169

Frontline Entertainment - - - - - - 173

Black Excellence - - - - - - - - - 180

Victory - - - - - - - - - - - - - 184

Coming Home to New Battles - - - - 190

Hollywood's Cold War Retreat - - - - 196

ACKNOWLEDGMENTS - - - - - - 203

NOTES - - - - - - - - - - - - - - 205

BIBLIOGRAPHY - - - - - - - - - 215

INDEX - - - - - - - - - - - - - - 217

FOREWORD

We have all experienced dramatic moments in our lives, events that seem so unbelievable we cannot process them at first. "This isn't happening," we say to ourselves. "I must be dreaming." And there's one other thing that Americans invariably say when they see something shocking:

"I thought someone was filming a movie."

That's the way it was with the surprise Japanese attack on Pearl Harbor on December 7, 1941. The sudden strike on Pearl was a bewildering event. Every single survivor account emphasized the sheer shock of the attack: strange aircraft appearing out of nowhere, big red circle on the wings, coming on so suddenly that many US sailors thought they were witnessing an exercise, a simulation of an attack, or even a movie being filmed.

Of course, it wasn't a movie. The country was at war, as President Franklin Roosevelt informed the American people the next day, and the road ahead was going to be hard and bloody.

Hollywood would be there every step of the way. We have so many sources of music and entertainment today—a bewildering assortment, in fact—that it's difficult to conjure a time when movies so clearly dominated American culture. The average US citizen went to the theater at least twice a week during wartime. Double and triple features and newsreels relayed events from the front, shaped public opinion, and molded America into a wartime community determined to avenge Pearl Harbor, defeat the Axis, and build a better world based on Roosevelt's "Four Freedoms": freedom of speech and worship, freedom from want and fear. A savvy operator if ever there was one, FDR understood the power of Hollywood. "Entertainment is always a national asset," he once proclaimed. "Invaluable in time of peace, it is indispensable in wartime."

In *Hollywood Victory*, Christian Blauvelt tells the unforgettable story of wartime cinema. You'll thrill to what Hollywood used to call a "cavalcade of stars," all doing their bit for the war effort. Charlie Chaplin and the Three Stooges skewered the Axis dictators of "Tomania" and "Moronika," respectively. Carmen Miranda put her outsize persona to work for US-Latin American friendship. The Duke led the American Volunteer Group of fliers—you know them better as the "Flying Tigers"—into action in the skies over China on screen. Director John Ford did a little surreptitious spy action for navy intelligence on a voyage around the Baja. Many stars fought. Jimmy Stewart enlisted at age thirty-two and wound up commanding a bomber squadron in air raids over Fortress Europe. And some—like Carole Lombard and Leslie Howard—gave their lives for the cause.

While many wartime movies could reasonably be described as escapist, Hollywood also waged war on the ideological front. Frank Capra's series *Why We Fight*, for example, explained the war in stark terms. Two worlds were in conflict, Capra told his audience: a world of darkness and a world of light. The stakes were high, and defeat would mean the end of human freedom. But he also made another remarkable film, *The Negro Soldier*, portraying the equally grim reality of millions of Americans who were willing to fight and die for the cause of freedom abroad while systematically being denied it at home, a battle that continues into our own day.

As I absorbed Blauvelt's remarkable book, I couldn't help but think that perhaps those sailors under attack at Pearl Harbor were right after all, in a way that they couldn't have known at the time. There really was a movie being filmed—an American film for the ages.

Dr. Robert M. Citino

Senior Historian, The National World War II Museum

INTRODUCTION

Legend has it that Emil Jannings brought an Oscar to a gunfight.

He had been the first performer ever to win Best Actor at the Academy Awards—in fact, his statuette was the first Oscar ever awarded, period. In the years that followed that first ceremony in 1929, Jannings had become an enthusiastic supporter of the Nazi regime, even being named "Artist of the State" by Joseph Goebbels. The story goes that while the Third Reich fell in 1945, the German actor shakily approached American troops, clutching that little gold knight as if it would protect him from an itchy trigger finger: "I have Oscar!"

It worked. Movies loomed so large in the ordinary American soldier's mind that even an actor who hadn't been in a Hollywood film for seventeen years but possessed the industry's highest achievement—the Academy Award statuette—commanded respect. "The Americans have behaved extraordinarily fair and decent," Jannings said a few weeks later. Looking back, it is remarkable but not surprising that anyone involved behaved the way they did:

- -

OPPOSITE: "The US officers who came to take residence at Emil Jannings's estate couldn't believe their eyes," according to Jannings biographer Frank Noack. "Right in front of them, in the entry hall of the main building, stood a small golden statuette which in their home country was called Oscar, or more formally, Academy Award. And it turned out that the owner of this house himself had won the award. Such a man, they decided, had to be treated royally, and they didn't expect him to provide them with more rooms than necessary."

at that moment in 1945, Hollywood's cultural power was the greatest it had ever been—and even someone who'd spent years making films for the Nazis would have known it.

For the twelve million American soldiers then in uniform, movies had been a lifeline to the homeland they left behind. Those flickering images on the screen simultaneously reflected their harsh experiences and gave them inspiration to keep going. And many of the Hollywood talents who made the movies had just spent four years fighting the war themselves, wagering their careers—and sometimes their lives.

In the early morning of December 7, 1941, the talk of Hollywood was the scandal around Greta Garbo's latest, and last, movie: *Two-Faced Woman* (1941), excoriated by the Catholic Legion of Decency for the charge of libertinism. At 11:25 a.m. Pacific Time, that furor was extinguished forever. At that moment, radio announcers broke into their regularly scheduled programming to announce that Imperial Japan had attacked Pearl Harbor. Suddenly, the moguls who ran all of Hollywood's studios—and the stars and filmmakers who had made them rich in the first place—had a purpose beyond the pursuit of profit. In fact, they had a mission from the government: to depict the devastation Fascism was unleashing in Europe and Asia, and empower viewers, whether soldiers on the battlefield or civilians on the home front, to aid in this battle themselves. Hollywood movies had been a lifeline of escapist entertainment to audiences during the Depression. Now the industry needed to confront reality.

The ways in which Hollywood contributed to the war effort were manifold: from actors selling war

as part of the industry's effort to reinforce the Roosevelt administration's Good Neighbor Policy, which aimed to improve relations with Central and South America (lest those countries become Axis allies). The industry also tried courting the African-American audience like never before— prominent Black entertainers had often appeared in only one scene in a movie (for that scene to be easily cut out for cinemas playing it in the South), but now there were major studio films like *Cabin in the Sky* (1943) and *Stormy Weather* (1943) with all-African-American casts, all the better for stars like Lena Horne to stir up enthusiasm for the war effort among the Black audience.

And there were a number of Hollywood stars who served in uniform, and saw action, themselves: Jimmy Stewart, who joined up nine months before Pearl Harbor and became one of the few enlisted men ever to rise from private to colonel in the span of four years, due to twenty daring bombing raids he commanded over occupied Europe; Henry Fonda, who dodged kamikaze fighters while serving with Naval Intelligence in the Pacific; and Clark Gable, who pushed through grief over the death of his wife, Carole Lombard, to fly in bombers as a gunner and documentary filmmaker. Lombard, who died in a plane crash outside Las Vegas while on a cross-country war bonds fundraising tour, wasn't the only star who died while serving the cause: *Gone with the Wind* (1939) actor Leslie Howard's commercial airplane was shot down by the Luftwaffe over the Bay of Biscay.

bonds to the creation of the Hollywood Canteen, which democratized Hollywood like never before by allowing ordinary soldiers to mingle with top stars. The studios helped write a first draft of history by making war films that depicted battles and campaigns that had just occurred mere months before. Escape took a back seat to engagement in the movies that emerged from 1941 to 1945. And by the end of the war, motion pictures, having become the voice of the nation, would end up as the defining American art form—America's great cultural export to the world.

Even films that weren't about the war subtly underscored actions viewers could take to help with the war effort: women's fashions and hairstyles onscreen suddenly hued toward more professional attire to encourage women to take up jobs the men had left behind. There was also an explosion of films depicting Latin America and its entertainers

A New Play by WILLIAM GIBSON
Directed by ARTHUR PENN
Scenery and Lighting by GEORGE JENKINS
Costumes by VIRGINIA VOLLAND

AIR-CONDITIONED
BOOTH THEATRE
45ᵀᴴ St. West

The United States was never as, well, *united* as it was during World War II. Hollywood was not only a reflection of that unity but a primary engine of it. All the more remarkable when you consider that many of the moguls who ran Tinseltown shared the nation's widespread isolationist feeling in the lead-up to Pearl Harbor. They had been much like Rick Blaine in *Casablanca* (1942): unwilling to risk what they had in what seemed like someone else's fight ("I stick my neck out for nobody") until realizing that it was their fight after all. The future of freedom itself depended on this fight.

Before it was over, even Lassie would battle Nazis onscreen.

Many of the stars who entertained the troops during the war continued reach-out efforts to Armed Forces personnel for the rest of their careers, as Lena Horne did here, with Ricardo Montalbán, for crewmembers of the USS Nautilus in 1958.

PART I STORM CLOUDS

1933– 1941

Lithuanian-Jewish director Anatole Litvak and the star of his French-language hit <u>Mayerling</u> (1936), Charles Boyer, cross the Atlantic aboard the <u>Normandie</u> in 1937 to make it big in Hollywood. Litvak would become one of Hollywood's leading anti-Nazi voices. The <u>Normandie</u>, then the world's biggest ocean liner, was often the vessel refugees used to make their way from Europe to America during the 1930s.

HOLLYWOOD OPENS ITS ARMS . . .

"**B**illy—What kinda name is that for an Austrian?" Columbia executive Samuel Briskin was skeptical when Billy Wilder stood before him in his Hollywood office. It was 1934, the year after the Nazis had taken power in Germany, causing many Jewish writers and directors who had made their names in the German film industry to flee for Los Angeles. And the boorishness of Briskin notwithstanding, Hollywood was welcoming. From 1933 to 1941, more than ten thousand refugees from Germany and Austria settled in Los Angeles, in what California historian Kevin Starr called "the most complete migration of artists and intellectuals in European history." Among those, over 750 had been film industry professionals in their former homelands. This was the first stand the American motion picture business took against the Nazis—even if for years, the moguls would claim they simply cared about people, not politics.

Hollywood's embrace of these émigré filmmakers was not purely altruistic: if there's one thing the industry knew how to do, it was identify talent. For the next six months, Briskin put Wilder to work at a desk in a bungalow that had become the studio's writers bullpen. One of his Columbia coworkers was the budding screenwriter and novelist James M. Cain, who told Wilder they didn't have to start clacking away at their typewriters until 11:45 in the morning or so—studio boss Harry Cohn never showed up until noon. Ten years later Wilder adapted Cain's novel *Double Indemnity* (1944) into as perfect a film noir as had then been made.

The intervening years would be difficult for Wilder. When his six-month contract was up, so was his work visa. In order to apply for an immigration visa, Wilder had to leave the country. So he crossed the border into Mexicali, Mexico, where he waited a few days for the US Immigration and Naturalization Service to approve his request. In his acceptance speech for the Irving G. Thalberg Memorial Award at the 1988 Oscars, Wilder said that the American consul in Mexicali took pity on him. This man held his life in his hands. Wilder told him he wrote movies for a living. "Write some good ones," the consul said, stamping his passport and letting him stay in America for good. But having to leave the US so he'd be allowed to return permanently left a mark—he immortalized the experience in his screenplay for Mitchell Leisen's *Hold Back the Dawn* (1941) a few years later.

Wilder must have felt extraordinary uncertainty in Mexico, and in the months ahead when he lived in a small room overlooking a back alley at the Chateau Marmont. It was a far cry from his Viennese upbringing.

Born Samuel Wilder in 1906, his mother, Eugenia, nicknamed him "Billy" because she had grown up in New York City and was mesmerized with stories about Buffalo Bill. He had cut his teeth in film at the legendary studio UFA, near Berlin, where he met future Hollywood directors, and fellow Jews, Fred Zinnemann and Robert Siodmak. Zinnemann did not end up a refugee: he left for Hollywood in 1929 when a Nazi takeover of Germany still seemed a distant possibility.

What was going through Wilder's mind while hunched over his hot plate at the Chateau Marmont? He'd only have two credits in the entirety of 1934 and 1935: the screenplays for *Music in the Air* (1934) and *Lottery Lover* (1935). But he'd connected with the author of what would be his breakout directorial effort (*Double Indemnity*), gathered inspiration for *Hold Back the Dawn*, and become friends with the star of *Music in the Air*, Gloria Swanson. He had found a home in Hollywood, but those harsh early experiences in Tinseltown left their mark on the industry forever.

———

A different kind of fate awaited Hedwig Kiesler. Born in 1914 to haute bourgeoisie Jewish parents in Vienna, she was married at nineteen to Fritz Mandl, fourteen years her senior and a munitions manufacturer who was allied with the Nazis. She'd caught his eye after appearing in the erotically charged Czech film *Ecstasy* (1933), thought to be the first mainstream film to depict an orgasm. The couple lived in the Austrian countryside in Castle Schwarzau, with twenty-five guest rooms. She was his armpiece for all the soirees he threw for top military brass in the German and Italian armed forces. Hitler never wanted to be seen with Herr Mandl, because by

TOP: Long hours at typewriters in close quarters was the norm for Hollywood screenwriters in the 1930s and '40s, such as for Billy Wilder and Charles Brackett, here tweaking the script for <u>The Major and the Minor</u> (1942). **BOTTOM:** Fritz Lang, pictured in 1937 after making his first two movies in Hollywood, engaged in a bit of mythmaking about the abrupt nature of his departure from Germany following the Nazi takeover. He said that he left the country the very night Joseph Goebbels had summoned him to take over the German film industry. "I'll decide who's Jewish!" Lang claims the Nazi propaganda minister said when the director told him about his Jewish ancestry. In reality, Lang's passport showed he went back and forth from Germany several times over the next months.

Nazi standards he was Jewish, but Mussolini was at their dinner parties. The husband was fanatically jealous, and even tried to buy up all existing prints of *Ecstasy*—made easier when Hitler banned the film because Kiesler was Jewish—and had maids listen in on her phone calls. Her father was so worried about all this that he died suddenly from a heart attack. That seems to have been a turning point for Hedwig.

One night at a dinner party in 1937, months before the Anschluss (when Austria was officially incorporated into the German Reich), she gave a maid who looked like her a sleeping potion, took her uniform, sewed her jewels into its lining, and hopped on her bicycle to escape from her husband's estate. She went to London, immediately got a film agent, and before long met Hollywood's most powerful man, Louis B. Mayer. Kiesler had already seen the MGM lion before a movie and said, "Oh, I want to be in that." He offered her $125 a week and said she had to keep her clothes on—a not-so-subtle dig at *Ecstasy*.

She turned Mayer down but booked passage on the *Normandie*, knowing that the studio boss would be aboard on her first journey to America too. She made certain Mayer saw what a stir she caused all around the ship, to convince him that she was worth that much more. Mayer upped the offer to $500 a week while still on the voyage. By the time the *Normandie* docked in New York City, photographers were waiting at the gangplank to snap pictures of MGM's latest discovery. Hedwig Kiesler had a new life ahead of her, and a new name that Mayer and his wife had helped her select: Hedy Lamarr.

A new life of big-screen glamour awaited Hedy Lamarr—but at the cost of completely erasing her Jewish heritage and dooming herself to be defined by her beauty, not her brains, for the rest of her life. Even despite a revolutionary invention she patented that could have helped the Allies in the coming war.

ABOVE: Ecstasy was a sensation for the eighteen-year-old actress who'd one day be known as Hedy Lamarr. Her costar, Aribert Mog, called up to serve in the Wehrmacht, died on the eastern front in October 1941 at age thirty-seven. **BELOW:** A portrait of Hedy Lamarr by Robert Coburn taken to promote the film Algiers (1938), her first Hollywood feature. She starred opposite Charles Boyer, who had also left Europe as the specter of Fascism began to hover over the continent.

. . . BUT CLOSES ITS MIND

edy Lamarr's desire to ignore her Jewish heritage was shared by the moguls who ran Hollywood in the late 1930s. Except for 20th Century Fox head Darryl F. Zanuck, all of the "Big Five" studio chiefs were Jewish—Samuel Briskin and Pan Berman of RKO, Harry and Jack Warner of Warner Bros., Adolph Zukor of Paramount, and the most powerful of all, Louis B. Mayer of MGM—and had either immigrated to the United States or been born to immigrants. Jews more than any other group had created the Hollywood studios, in part because Jews were excluded from most so-called legitimate businesses in American life due to discriminatory hiring policies and university quotas. They had few opportunities, so they created their own. Now they were in charge of the most popular art form in America, yet the desire to prove that they were, in fact, Americans was still overwhelming for them.

"I think one of the most important things for these Jews who came to this country, not just the moguls but for an entire generation or two of Jewish immigrants, was to assimilate," said Samuel Goldwyn biographer A. Scott Berg. "And part of that was not necessarily to deny being Jewish, but it was just not to broadcast it either. That was certainly the case here in Hollywood where they were producing this all-American art."

Americana was the order of the day for many of the movies of the late 1930s. If the films in the earlier part of the decade, when the Depression had

Sidney Miller, right, with young Bobs Watson on his shoulders, played one of the few overtly Jewish characters in a Hollywood film of the 1930s, in MGM's Boys Town.

Thousands of American Nazis, affiliated with the German American Bund, packed Madison Square Garden for a rally in 1939. The incident became the subject of the documentary A Night at the Garden, which was nominated for Best Documentary Short at the 2019 Academy Awards.

been at its worst, provided urbane, witty, escapist fantasies—Fred Astaire in white tie and tails and Ginger Rogers in a glittering gown—the idealization of small-town life became the new trend. "He had this idea of, 'I want to create the America that I want to see on the screen,'" Daniel Mayer Selznick said of his grandfather, MGM head Louis B. Mayer. And thus, the Andy Hardy series was launched in February 1937 with *A Family Affair*, with fifteen more films to follow. It was an ethos that carried over into many other films: watch MGM's *Boys Town* (1938) and you'll find a young Jewish boy at Father Flanagan's orphanage saying a prayer in Hebrew, while the Christian kids say grace before a dinner overseen by Spencer Tracy's Catholic priest.

To prove they were as American as anybody, the moguls felt it was important to reflect American beliefs, as well as create a vision of Americana—and

in November 1936, 95 percent of Americans polled said they were opposed to another European war. World War I had ended less than twenty years earlier, and memories of the over 116,000 American soldiers who had died were fresh. It didn't mean that the general public was sympathetic to Hitler—reports of the Nuremberg Laws, and the government-sanctioned violence against Jews that culminated in November 1938's brutal Kristallnacht, horrified many Americans. But their sympathy for persecuted Jews had limits—and going to war to oppose Hitler's attacks on human rights and democracy was out of the question. As such, there are no Hollywood films before 1939 in which Nazism is criticized or any intervention is called for. And absolutely no persecution of Jews by Nazis was to be depicted.

It's also undeniable that anti-Semitism in

the United States had steadily grown since Jewish migration to America from eastern Europe had begun in earnest in the 1870s. Throughout the 1930s, Father Charles Coughlin broadcast anti-Semitic rants to millions of radio listeners, continually suggesting that Judaism and Communism went hand in hand. The Nazi-aligned German American Bund counted twenty-five thousand members, many of whom attended a swastika-draped rally at New York City's Madison Square Garden on February 20, 1939. The anti-Semitic organization known as the Silver Legion of America, or the "Silver Shirts," began building their fortified headquarters on the fifty-five-acre Murphy Ranch in the Santa Monica Mountains, just north of Pacific Palisades, in 1935; they planned for it to be a place where they could hole up until Fascism had taken over the world. "The Silver Shirts and the Bundists and all the rest of these hoods are marching in Los Angeles right now," said Jack Warner in 1938. "There are high school kids with swastikas on their sleeves a few crummy blocks from our studios." America's sweetheart of the silent era, Mary Pickford, offered a different view. "Italy has always produced great men and when she needed one most Mussolini was there. Viva Fascismo! Viva Il Duce!" she said. Of Hitler, Pickford added, "He seems to be a very great fellow too, for the German people. Things look much better over there."

The view from Washington wasn't much more favorable. From May 1938, Texas Democratic congressman Martin Dies led the newly formed House Un-American Activities Committee and began inquiries into foreign subversion in Hollywood. It ended up spending an inordinate amount of time parsing Hollywood films for prowar sentiments: evidence the Jewish moguls were seeking to influence American foreign policy and calling for action against Hitler. Joseph P. Kennedy, then ambassador to Great Britain and an ardent supporter of Prime Minister Neville Chamberlain's attempts at appeasing Hitler, even called a meeting with the studio heads, in which he encouraged them to remove all Jewish names from the credits of their films. The idea was that Hitler, an ardent film watcher, would then have no problem with America or American films.

In fact, Warner Bros. was the one and only Hollywood studio to take a stand against Hitler throughout the 1930s. In 1934, the company closed its office in Berlin and suspended all business operations in Germany, after the new government demanded that the studio refuse to hire any of the German Jewish émigrés who had settled in Los Angeles. The manager of the studio's Berlin branch, Phil Kaufman, had even been beaten up in the street by Nazis. Warner Bros. cut off business with Austria as well, following the Anschluss, in 1938, with Jack Warner hosting a Hollywood dinner for one of the most outspoken anti-Nazi voices in the world that spring: author Thomas Mann, who had been stripped of his German citizenship.

For all the other studios, Germany remained one of the largest markets for Hollywood film outside the United States, and alienating the nation meant cutting off a major revenue stream. "They were very wary of rocking the boat because they were still making money in Germany, they were making money in Italy," said legendary Hollywood screenwriter Budd Schulberg, who assembled film evidence for the Nuremberg trials after the war. "The bottom line was profit and really not principle." The prevailing view was summed up by MGM production chief Irving Thalberg to Mayer in 1934, after Thalberg had visited Germany: "A lot of Jews will lose their lives" but "Hitler and Hitlerism will pass; the Jews will still be there."

Carl Laemmle, head of Universal, which was then considered one of the "Little Three" studios (primarily because it didn't own as many theaters as the Big Five) alongside Columbia and United

MGM studio head Louis B. Mayer was one of the moguls most concerned with losing the German market. Budd Schulberg claimed Mayer "would run those films by the Nazi German consul and was willing to take out things that the consul, the Nazi, objected to."

Artists, actually did fight Hitler's government in the mid-1930s too—but in his own way. Born in the village of Laupheim in the Kingdom of Württemberg in 1867, four years before the unification of Germany, Laemmle returned to his homeland for a nostalgic visit every year. As a Jew, that had been complicated greatly with Hitler's rise to power. The mogul pivoted, and he started to use his money and influence with Secretary of State Cordell Hull to send for four hundred to five hundred Jewish families who lived in Germany, helping them resettle in the United States.

Once a major silent screen star, Gloria Swanson followed in Laemmle's footsteps with her own resettlement work. With her film career on a perpetual wane since the introduction of talkies, she decided the best way to help refugees was via entrepreneurship.

Swanson had an inventor's mind—in the late twenties she claimed she had an idea for a wireless communication device, but someone else patented it first—and, concerned about what she had heard was happening in Germany with Jewish scientists and engineers, she figured she could help save as many as she could if she founded a company to hire them so they'd get work visas to live in the United States. Metallurgists, chemists, plastics experts, and acoustical engineers were among those she brought to America. It's unclear exactly how many Jews she saved, but from their office in New York City's Rockefeller Center and their factory in Queens, they created inventions (and were issued patents) with applications for everything from automobiles to musical instruments to home appliances.

Swanson understood that reinvention was the key to survival. Soon, all of Hollywood would realize it.

SOUNDING THE ALARM ABOUT JAPAN

I f the power brokers of Hollywood were unwilling to take a stand against Hitler beyond the basic human decency of welcoming artists into their ranks, several stars and filmmakers were willing to make bold, public declarations against global Fascism.

Paul Robeson had left the United States after finishing *Show Boat* (1936), in which he sang the classic "Ol' Man River." His departure in early 1936 was motivated, in part, by the desire to seek better roles in Britain and so his son could attend school there, avoiding the kind of prejudice they faced in a still deeply segregated America. But settling in London also meant he could support the Republican cause in the Spanish Civil War against the Rebellion by Francisco Franco's Fascists. "The artist must take sides," he said. "He must elect to fight for freedom or slavery. I have made my choice. I had no alternative." Throughout 1937, he donated the proceeds of his concerts to the Republican forces, and visited a soldiers hospital in the Spanish coastal town of Benicàssim.

Robeson was also one of the most visible early supporters of China's fight against Japan. World War II in Asia was raging for more than two years before the conflict in the European theater began, and four years before the United States got involved. Japan's invasion of China began with the Marco Polo Bridge incident that took place from July 7 to 9, 1937, in which an attack was made on Beijing. Over the next eight years, ten to twenty-five million Chinese civilians and another estimated four million Chinese military personnel would be killed. In 1940, after he'd returned to the United States, Robeson worked with the Chinese activist Liu Liangmo to

Paul Robeson in 1935, right before he was to start shooting Show Boat.

record "Chee Lai (Arise!)," a patriotic song also known as the "March of the Volunteers," a stirring tribute to Chinese sovereignty. He debuted the song at City College's Lewisohn Stadium in New York, to a packed crowd, and spent much of the next year before America's entry into the war trying to raise awareness in the United States of how China was in the fight for its life. With the blessing of Eleanor Roosevelt, Robeson performed the song at a massive rally in Washington, DC, at Uline Arena in April 1941; after the performance, donations soared to United China Relief and the China Aid Council.

The other major voice beating the drum about China's suffering was Anna May Wong, who had

Anna May Wong, pictured in 1929, came from a family that had lived in California since the 1850s, when they emigrated from China.

----

appeared in Hollywood movies since she was fourteen in the late 1910s. Her star rose throughout the 1920s, and she was presented as a sex symbol. Wong spoke out after Japan's first overwhelming act of aggression against China: in 1931, the increasingly militarist Japanese, embodying an expansionist, ethnocentric ethos that made it virtually indistinguishable from European Fascism, invaded Manchuria, taking over the entire northeast region of China. War between the rest of China and Japan did not then erupt—not for another six

years—but the move was seen as being every bit as aggressive and threatening as Germany's later incursions against Austria and Czechoslovakia.

The invasion of Manchuria was not something that captured a great deal of Hollywood's attention, however. So Wong felt it was her duty to educate the public as much as she could: she published a lengthy editorial in the *Beverly Hills Script* to try to wake up the industry to what was at stake for China.

Wong saw that the most important step she could take to raise awareness about China's struggle against Japan, apparent even before open war broke out in 1937, was to portray better images of the nation. Hollywood's take on China had always been tinged by Orientalism and vacillated between images of its people as exotic and as a threat, often with white actors playing Chinese roles. In 1933, Wong gave an interview to *Film Weekly*, titled "I Protest," in which she did just that: "Why is it that the screen Chinese is always the villain? And so crude a villain—murderous, treacherous, a snake in the grass! We are not like that."

Today, issues of representation are front of mind in Hollywood; ahead of her time, Wong anticipated contemporary discourse by fighting for better parts. When Irving Thalberg offered her a role in MGM's *The Good Earth* (1937), a tearjerker about Chinese peasants clinging to their humanity despite endless hardships, he didn't offer her the lead. The Production Code, a set of content guidelines industry leaders had agreed upon to avoid accusations of immorality, had anti-miscegenation rules, which prevented her from playing *The Good Earth*'s heroine, O-Lan. Playing her meant Wong would have starred opposite Paul Muni (a white actor playing a Chinese character) as her love interest. White actors playing Asian leads was the norm then for films with an Asian setting, while actual Asian actors were only allowed to play supporting characters in such films. Thalberg, who had helped write the Production Code, offered Wong the part of a villain who seduces O-Lan's oldest son and sunders the family. "If you let me play O-Lan, I will be very glad," she told Thalberg. "But you're asking me—with Chinese blood—to do the only unsympathetic role in the picture featuring an all-American cast portraying Chinese characters." She turned the film down. The B-movies she chose to make instead, for Paramount, would not earn awards, but with their small budgets she could have control.

The very first Hollywood film overtly advocating for America's armed intervention in the brewing war abroad was not about the Nazis in Europe. It was *King of Chinatown* (1939), directed by Nick Grinde for Paramount, and starring Wong as a surgeon who, after getting caught in the middle of gang warfare—she heals a gangster who, in gratitude, donates his fortune to China war relief—turns her back on a lucrative promotion so she can instead help China's fight against Japan. (In real life, Wong had held an auction for her movie costumes in 1938 to raise money for United China Relief herself.) The film ends with her leaving America behind and flying, with her husband, played by Korean-American actor Philip Ahn, to China to deliver medical equipment for the war effort. It debuted March 17, 1939. And in many ways, it was Hollywood's first World War II film.

Wong starred opposite Korean-American actor Philip Ahn in <u>Daughter of Shanghai</u> (1937), a film she deliberately intended to present a more well-rounded, less stereotypical image of Chinese-Americans. Ahn also played her husband two years later in <u>King of Chinatown</u>.

SAVING HER HOMELAND FROM ITSELF

Just like Paul Robeson and Anna May Wong had raised money for Republican Spain and China, Marlene Dietrich's approach to fighting Fascism was to put her money where her mouth was. Born in Berlin and an up-and-coming star in its smoke-filled cabarets during the decadent Weimar twenties, she loathed the Nazis, who had forever destroyed that heady milieu in which anything went and everyone was accepted. Dietrich had immortalized that era in her breakout film, *The Blue Angel* (1930), in which she played a cabaret singer who leads a fastidious professor (Emil Jannings) to disgrace and moral degradation simply through her sex appeal.

Jannings, of course, became a prominent supporter of the Third Reich, which persecuted many denizens of the Berlin cabaret scene: artists and performers who were Jewish, Communist, homosexual, or otherwise given over to the libertine. Dietrich herself was bisexual, and cultivated an aura of androgeneity. *The Blue Angel* had been made by Berlin's biggest film producer, UFA, which was a partner studio to Paramount in the United States, so it was a cinch for her and the film's director, Josef von Sternberg, to pursue Hollywood glory next. In her first Paramount film, released just seven months later in 1930, Dietrich would wear a top hat, tux, and tails—if she'd wear men's clothing, "What else was she capable of?" puritanical American viewers wondered—and kiss a woman on the lips. Complaints over her films, as well as many others in what's referred to as the Pre-Code era, led to enforcement of the Production Code starting in 1934. The Nazis shook their heads at Dietrich's films as well. In late 1933 the new government declared that any so-called Aryan Germans working abroad must return to Germany or else they would reveal "they are not interested in the great cultural upbringing of Germany or are even sabotaging it," and are "economic and ideological traitors." Dietrich was particularly targeted for the "prostitute roles in America" she had played, such as in *Shanghai Express* (1932) opposite Anna May Wong as her friend and fellow woman of the night. Her roles gave "a thoroughly false and unrealistic picture of Germany," the Nazis said. This on its own may not have concerned Dietrich, but her mother and sister still lived in Germany, and the Nazi government was known to target the families of its enemies. She returned to Berlin in late 1934 to see if reconciliation was possible. She donated a considerable sum to the German national film fund, yet Goebbels still banned her new film *The Song of Songs* (1933), anyway. The Nazis did not reject her citizenship, however, as they had done with Thomas Mann and others they felt opposed them; they believed that she could still be courted to serve the Reich. Goebbels had criticized her choice of roles in Hollywood, but he would gladly have welcomed her back into the German film industry as its top star. She was Hitler's favorite actress after all, and the Führer was known to host private screenings of her films in his mountain stronghold at Berchtesgaden while his ministers condemned them publicly. Later on, she'd fantasize about what could have happened if she had let Hitler indulge his infatuation with her. If she had slept with him, she could have been in a position to assassinate him—maybe with a poisoned hairpin? "I sometimes wonder," she said, "if I just might have been the one person in the world who could have prevented the war and saved millions of lives." Dietrich must have sensed the public relations extortion campaign the Nazis were waging against her, so she left Berlin after that 1934 visit and didn't return again until after the war had ended. But that didn't mean the Nazis ceased pursuing her in the meantime. At Christmas 1936, while celebrating the holiday at her lavish London flat with then beau Douglas Fairbanks Jr., Rudolf Hess showed up at her door. He basically offered her a blank check to return to Germany and be the leading light of its film industry. Emil Jannings alone wasn't cutting it.

It had to have been a blank check too, because earlier in 1936, Dietrich had been lured away from Hollywood by producer Alexander Korda to make a film in Britain with the highest salary ever offered a female movie star: $450,000. Hess assumed that if loyalty to Germany wouldn't sway Dietrich, money would. Instead, Dietrich not only turned down the Nazis' extravagant offer, she donated the entire $450,000 salary for *Knight Without Armour* (1937) to a fund she'd created with Billy Wilder to help Jews and dissidents escape Germany. On March 6, 1937, she applied for US citizenship at the Federal Building in downtown Los Angeles. But in a way, that was only a formality. She'd told the Nazis once and for all what she thought of them by letting her money do the talking. In the years ahead, she'd do that and so much more.

Dietrich in <u>Knight Without Armour</u>, for which she received the highest salary ever offered to a female star at that point. She donated it in its entirety to help Jews and other oppressed groups to leave Germany.

"QUARANTINE HITLER"

In October 1938, shortly before he was to begin filming *Stagecoach* (1939), John Ford mounted the stage at the Shrine Auditorium at a gathering of the Hollywood Anti-Nazi League (HANL). It was the largest and most visible such organization in the industry at the time. In his typically direct way, Ford said, "May I express my whole-hearted desire to cooperate to the utmost of my ability with the Hollywood Anti-Nazi League. If this be Communism, count me in."

As the thirties wore on, those in Hollywood with a conscience realized they had to raise their voices. But the HANL, founded in 1936 and already boasting five thousand members by the time of Ford's speech—Harry Warner urged his entire staff to join up—had already come under the investigation of Martin Dies and his House Un-American Activities Committee. Dies's work had not had an auspicious beginning. He had overseen a hearing that named ten-year-old Shirley Temple as an example of someone spreading Communist ideology in Hollywood. That had drawn international indignation, with even the speaker of the Finnish parliament issuing a decree that said, "America's main cultural influence in Finland unfortunately still rests on the shoulders of that little girl, and your mouse." But the others that Dies named took the allegations seriously and felt it was necessary to respond, among them Robert Taylor, Clark Gable, and James Cagney, who'd feel such heat from Dies in the next couple of years that he'd make *Yankee Doodle Dandy* (1942), in part, just to prove his patriotism.

The HANL protested the November 1938 visit of Leni Riefenstahl to Los Angeles, as they had done with the earlier visit of Benito Mussolini's son Vittorio, a film producer himself. Most of the major studios refused to give Hitler's favorite filmmaker a tour, and she was turned away from multiple nightclubs. Walt Disney did roll out the red carpet for Riefenstahl at his studio, however, and shared concept art from the forthcoming *Fantasia* (1940) with her and hosted a screening of her documentary *Olympia* (1938), about the Berlin Olympics. The move furthered the management-labor divide at the Disney studio, though it should be acknowledged Walt had welcomed Soviet filmmaker Sergei Eisenstein on a separate occasion. (Hal Roach was the one other producer who welcomed Riefenstahl.)

Kristallnacht, the government-sanctioned pogrom against German Jews that once and for all laid bare the violence Hitler intended for all Jewish people, occurred just before Riefenstahl's Hollywood arrival. After this, it was impossible to deny Hitler's monstrosity, unless you were an anti-Semite or absurdly ill-informed. Frank Capra, despite being offered by Mussolini to direct his life story, had turned so far against Fascism that he spoke at the HANL's "Quarantine Hitler" rally. Taking the microphone at the November 1938 event at L.A.'s Philharmonic Auditorium, just a week after Kristallnacht, he said that anything less than a trade boycott of Germany was "capitulation to Hitler," which "meant barbarism and terror."

Among actors, one of the most powerful voices in the HANL was Edward G. Robinson. Best known for playing Little Caesar in the 1931 film of the same name and for a rogues' gallery of other

Edward G. Robinson, center, on the set of <u>The Amazing Dr. Clitterhouse</u> (1938) with its director Anatole Litvak (at right), reunited with the Lithuanian-Jewish director to make <u>Confessions of a Nazi Spy</u> (1939).

gangsters and sadists, he leveraged his screen persona into his plea at a December 9 rally that also called upon Congress to initiate a total boycott of German goods following Kristallnacht: "The world is faced with the menace of gangsters," he said, "who are much more dangerous than any we have ever known." The idea being that, given his history of playing gangsters, Robinson should know. He followed Capra and Ford in his activism, but he was the biggest star to date to criticize Hitler, and the backlash against him, including death threats from American anti-Semites, was fierce. Despite this, he'd be the first to put his anti-Nazi activism on the big screen too.

CONFESSIONS OF A NAZI SPY

The time had come to attack Nazi Germany itself onscreen. But how? Jack Warner was committed to the idea that his studio would "strive for pictures that provide something more than a mere idle hour or two of entertainment." Warner Bros. had attacked white supremacy in the movie *Black Legion* (1937), about a Detroit-based splinter group of the Ku Klux Klan. And the studio had criticized European imperialism via *Juarez* (1939), about the famed Indigenous Mexican president's resistance to the French-Hapsburg invasion of his country in the 1860s. For that film, screenwriters John Huston and Wolfgang Reinhardt—son of exiled German theater impresario Max, who had given many of the new refugees in Hollywood their first jobs back home—self-consciously cast Claude Rains's Emperor Napoleon III as a Hitler type who talks about spurious notions of racial superiority.

Harry and Jack Warner realized that metaphor wasn't enough; they needed to show goose-stepping brownshirts Sieg-Heiling Hitler outright. Luckily enough, the story they wanted to tell fell right into their laps.

Guenther Gustave Maria Rumrich, a German immigrant to the United States, was arrested in February 1938 as a Nazi spy. An amateur keen to prove his devotion to the Führer, he drew suspicion and was caught easily enough after he tried to arrange for fifty American passports to be issued from the New York City passport office for future use by German intelligence. Warner Bros. sent its contract writer Milton Krims to cover the trial in New York City. It lasted just four days, from November 29 to December 2, but the screenwriter quickly turned the basics of the case into a film treatment.

Almost immediately, Georg Gyssling, the German consul in Los Angeles, appealed to Joseph Breen's Production Code Administration (PCA) to stop this film from being made. Charlie Chaplin had been planning to make a satire of Hitler himself, but it seemed like that production was shelved at the moment, in part because the UK government, desperate to appease the Nazis under Prime Minister Chamberlain, had preemptively announced they would ban it. The Paramount foreign office made note of Chaplin's picture halting preproduction when they wrote the PCA to say that making a film of the Rumrich case was simply too dangerous. The Warners would have "on their hands the blood of a great many Jews in Germany," the Paramount letter said. Breen, Hollywood's moral arbiter and enforcer of the dreaded Code since 1934, was generally thought to be an anti-Semite. He had referred to "the Jews" as being purveyors of immorality in his letters of the early 1930s—though by the end of the decade he had evolved enough to take a stand against Father Coughlin's radio broadcasts. The members of Breen's PCA office were not sympathetic to Warner Bros.' film, however, now titled *Confessions of a Nazi Spy*. After reading Krims's script on January 22, 1939, one PCA official, Karl Lischka, wrote that the film violated the Code because it was propaganda presenting Hitler as "a screaming madman and a bloodthirsty persecutor." Lischka felt that was untrue, writing that Hitler had "a phenomenal public career" with "unchallenged political and social achievements." Moreover, putting out a negative view of Hitler could spark a riot. The Dies committee rushed to Germany's defense as well, advising Warner Bros. "against slurring a friendly country."

Confessions of a Nazi Spy (1939) re-created a German American Bund meeting like those that had been popping up around the country the past few years.

In order to get the film made, Warner Bros. had to present the film in as objective a manner as possible. That meant giving it a semi-documentary style, with montage sequences built around newsreel footage featuring a narrator.

So long as the film was rooted enough in the facts, even the PCA couldn't block *Confessions of a Nazi Spy*. Warner Bros. hired Edward G. Robinson to play the lead investigator. The actor had lobbied hard for the role, saying he would "gladly work as first assistant to the prop boy if it would help him get a crack at Adolf Hitler," and "I am serving my country just as effectively as if I shouldered a gun and marched away to war."

Confessions of a Nazi Spy was dismissed in later years for being either war propaganda or a B-movie crime-thriller treatment of its subject. But it's a fresh, fast-moving film, with its journalistic tone anticipating the metafictional "News on the March" sequence in *Citizen Kane* (1941). In content, the voiceover by narrator John Deering could not be more direct: as graphics produced by Warner Bros.' animation department show the spread of Nazi pamphlets, he calls it "a deluge of vitriolic, scurrilous propaganda, circulated by the Nazis and certain American sympathizers ready to violate the basic principles of their American citizenship." He then adds, "Aided by the disgruntled, the dishonest,

Francis Lederer and Edward G. Robinson play a game of cat-and-mouse in <u>Confessions of a Nazi Spy</u>.

and the disloyal, an intensive campaign is launched to create mass sympathy for the doctrines glorifying hatred and brute force." The propagandistic documentaries made during the war a few years later, such as Frank Capra's *Why We Fight* series (1942–1945)—several of which *Confessions* director Anatole Litvak helped direct himself—were only a little more direct.

What really distinguishes *Confessions of a Nazi Spy*, though, is that for all its documentary-style info-dumps, it's a potent character study about why Nazism held so many in its thrall: there's no one onscreen here who looks anything like Hitler's Aryan Superman. Francis Lederer, himself a Jew from Prague who'd chosen to stay in America after acting in the country for several years, played the Rumrich stand-in: one of Hitler's true believers. But he's a frustrated, emasculated man who seems to have shunned responsibility for much of his life. He has no career prospects and feels stifled in his marriage. So he tries to glean US military secrets from a friend who works at a nearby army base and then sell them for cash to German intelligence. "It will be very daring," he says. Being a spy is a way to puff himself up, a way for him to feel like more of a man. And the same goes for the German American Bund leader played by Paul Lukas, a neurotic doctor, sweaty and stressed, who thinks Nazism is his path to fulfillment. The implication is clear: Hitler's ideology was like a "get strong quick" elixir marketed to the weak-willed and feeble-minded, who'd find in it a brotherhood and sense of belonging they'd never felt before.

Far more about the venality of its villains than the heroism of Robinson's FBI agent, *Confessions of a Nazi Spy* is as much a clinical diagnosis of Nazism as any film Hollywood produced once America actually entered the war. And that might be why its production and release were so acutely fraught. To direct, Warner Bros. brought in Litvak, the Kiev-born director making his fifth Hollywood movie after helming an international sensation with the French film *Mayerling* (1936), which catapulted both Charles Boyer and Danielle Darrieux to stardom. *Confessions of a Nazi Spy* was personal for Litvak. Jewish himself, he had also fled Berlin in 1933, where he had been working in the film industry for a few years. An unprecedented level of security was required for the seven-week *Confessions of a Nazi Spy* shoot from February 1 to March 18, 1939. Studio policemen guarded each entrance of its soundstages. Some of the cast in small roles—about a dozen in total who were refugees from Germany and Austria in real life—lived at the studio for the duration of the production for fear they might be targeted by Nazis or their sympathizers at home. A few others used pseudonyms. To keep any of the film's more devastating critiques of Nazism under wraps, only ten copies of the script were mimeographed, and the actors weren't given their lines until right before shooting. The thinking was that the more that leaked about the story or dialogue, the more actual Nazis might have to get upset about, with violence against people working on the film a possible result. One day an overhead light came crashing down on the set, barely missing several of the cast and crew. Litvak suspected sabotage, though it was never proven.

The real-life German American Bund leader Fritz J. Kuhn—for whom Paul Lukas's character was a rough analogue—filed a $5 million libel suit against Warner Bros., which he thought would prevent the film's exhibition. But *Confessions of a Nazi Spy* was released anyway. At the April 27 premiere at the Beverly Hills Theater, it was reported that the crowd was made up of as many plainclothes policemen as actual guests. This was in the era before wide releases, with studios opting for slower-burn rollouts over time, so Warner Bros. only answered Kuhn's suit in September, at which point they requested a jury trial so they could present their evidence that the Bund was an "active militant propaganda agency" doing Nazi Germany's bidding in the United States and "abusing the rights and privileges of American citizens."

Goebbels was so outraged by the existence of *Confessions of a Nazi Spy* that he banned all Warner Bros. films from ever again playing in the Reich and vowed to make his own series of documentaries illuminating problems in the United States, such as organized crime and institutional corruption. An item in *The Hollywood Reporter* that August told the story of how five citizens of the Nazi-aligned Free City of Danzig, a semi-autonomous city-state on the Baltic Sea, were arrested after they traveled to Gdynia, Poland, to see the film. After Germany invaded Poland in September, the gestapo rounded up seven cinema owners who had screened *Confessions of a Nazi Spy* and hanged them. The film was subsequently banned in Japan and eighteen European and Latin American nations, including Ireland, Italy, Denmark, Norway, Argentina, Costa Rica, Sweden, Belgium, Switzerland, and Brazil. Harry Warner reached out to the Brazilian government directly and offered to donate all the box-office grosses from any Brazilian run of the film to the Red Cross. It still didn't play.

Part of why the film was so particularly incendiary was because it didn't just elaborate on the threat of Nazism in Germany: it suggested that a homegrown version of Nazism could take root by latching on to America's own history of racism and anti-immigrant sentiment. The film's version of Goebbels tells Lukas's Bund leader that "National Socialism in the United States must dress itself in the American flag. It must appear to be a defense of Americanism. Class hatreds must be encouraged in such a way that labor and the middle classes will become confused and antagonistic. In the ensuing chaos, we will be able to take control

<u>Confessions of a Nazi Spy</u> captures how the German American Bund and other US-based Fascist groups organized part of their membership into armed militias.

. . . From now on, your watchword will be 'America for Americans.'" Including that bit of dialogue was Warner Bros.' dig at the America First movement, which encouraged isolationism; one of its leaders, aviation hero Charles Lindbergh, was a known anti-Semite who as late as September 1941 railed against Jews as being among those "pressing this country toward war." And though the film never actually uses the word "Jew" to describe who Hitler is oppressing—the closest it comes is Lukas's Nazi ranting against "an international conspiracy of subhumans"—and doesn't emphasize the plight of its victims, it is a 35-mm cannonade into Nazism itself. Not to mention, a flash-bang condemnation of isolationist Americans who'd rather look the other way.

TURNING APATHY INTO ENGAGEMENT

Confessions of a Nazi Spy was a moderate box-office success and inspired a number of similar films in its wake. But none were quite as full-throated an endorsement of armed intervention. Louis B. Mayer considered adapting Sinclair Lewis's 1935 novel *It Can't Happen Here*, about how a Fascist takeover could take place in the United States, but he shelved the project after seeing the controversy around *Confessions*. Box office wasn't worth that backlash. Instead he greenlit an adaptation of Phyllis Bottome's 1937 novel *The Mortal Storm* and paired Jimmy Stewart and Margaret Sullivan, who had just played opposite each other in an extremely different European-set film, *The Shop Around the Corner* (1940). This film would be a stirring cry of humanity whereas *Shop* had been witty and romantic. *The Mortal Storm* (1940), set in the Bavarian Alps, told a story of the early days of the Third Reich and the sweeping changes to Germany that Hitler enacted in the fateful months after he took power on January 30, 1933. Where *Confessions* had dissected the Nazi mindset, *The Mortal Storm*, released in June 1940, appealed to the heart and made you feel for the regime's victims. The calculus had also changed ever so slightly in America: Britain and France had gone to war with Germany at the start of September

Jimmy Stewart stares down a group of Nazis in his Bavarian town in <u>The Mortal Storm</u>, a moving drama about staying true to one's individual identity in the face of overwhelming pressure to conform.

1939. But America remained resolutely neutral—even after Dunkirk, the fall of France, and the Blitz in the year to come, by June 1941, a Gallup poll found 79 percent of the American public remained opposed to entering the war. The triumph of *The Mortal Storm*, directed by Frank Borzage with his trademark style of deeply felt humanism, is twofold: it shows how even otherwise good people could be corrupted and even become Nazis, and it shows how impossible it is to remain neutral in the face of such a rising evil. "We are a very united family," says Professor Roth (Frank Morgan) about the mixed brood he married into, some of whom will become Nazis, others Nazism's victims. His family is meant to symbolize the all-embracing attitude of the Weimar era, full of hope and creativity, but containing the seeds of its own destruction. "We pride ourselves on our tolerance and our sense of humor. May our happiness continue as long as we live." It does not.

The most heartbreaking sequence is when we see Professor Roth in a concentration camp, saying a last goodbye to his wife, who doesn't know it will be the last time she'll ever see him—but he does. Despite his surname, Roth is never explicitly identified as a Jew in the film until this moment. He's just labeled a "non-Aryan." And an SS operative earlier says, "Roth . . . your name doesn't sound very well to German ears." But now, as Professor Roth sees his wife for the last time, he wears an armband bearing the letter "J." The meaning is clear, even if it's not as explicit as it could be. But there was reason to tread lightly: an April 1938 Gallup poll had shown that 54 percent of Americans had felt "the persecution of Jews in Europe has been partly their own fault," with 11 percent saying it was "entirely" their own fault. Right after Kristallnacht in November 1938, 72 percent of Americans polled replied "no" to the question, "Should we allow a larger number of Jewish exiles from Germany to come to the United States to live?" Sixty-seven percent said that even Jewish child refugees should be refused admittance. Being anti-Nazi definitely did not mean being sympathetic to Jews in the late 1930s, and, clearly, Louis B. Mayer didn't want to suggest that one meant the other. Not entirely devoid of humanitarian empathy for the victims of Nazi persecution, however, Mayer did let actor Robert Montgomery hold a rally for the American Red Cross's war relief efforts on the MGM lot the month after *The Mortal Storm*'s release.

———

Two months after *The Mortal Storm*, 20th Century Fox directly referenced Jews in their own first major attack on Hitler: *The Man I Married* (1940), a riveting domestic drama that should be far better known and, one suspects, may have been overlooked by many critics because it's "a woman's picture." A New York City career woman, played by Joan Bennett, has been married to a German immigrant (Francis Lederer, returning to *Confessions of a Nazi Spy* territory) for eight years. They have a seven-year-old son. As Hitler's power begins to threaten Europe, Lederer's character gradually buys into Nazi ideology, and his zeal only grows when he takes his wife and son on a trip to Germany. There, Bennett is appalled at the abuses of power she sees, with "undesirables" degraded in the streets. But her husband looks on approvingly. He eventually falls in love with a woman who is a member of the Nazi Party, and wishes to divorce his wife. He can present as grounds for divorce to the Nazi court that his wife made jokes about the Führer, and he knows he'll be granted full custody of his son. The most chilling moment comes when she overhears her son, changed himself by his time in Germany, answer a stern paternal directive with "Ja, Vater!" No self-respecting American woman would put up with that! It all seems like it's headed for an explosion

Francis Lederer's fervent Nazi supporter has just learned he's Jewish in <u>The Man I Married</u>, originally titled <u>I Married a Nazi</u>, dashing his Party Member dreams. His wife, played by Joan Bennett, looks on with pity but also relief to be done with a husband who was so easily seduced by Hitler. She escapes Germany without him. This is a film that very much endorses divorce, if your husband becomes a Nazi.

of "woman in peril" suspense when the Lederer character's father, played by Otto Kruger, reveals that Lederer's mother had been a Jewish woman. Lederer realizes, to his horror, that this means the Nazi state will consider him Jewish too. His Nazi girlfriend, there for the revelation, immediately shrinks away. "Juden," Lederer's character, sobbing, keeps repeating. "Juden."

20th Century Fox head Darryl F. Zanuck had already developed a reputation for being able to shepherd movies past the Production Code Administration, especially with *The Grapes of Wrath* (1940) earlier in the year. In that film, Henry Fonda's Tom Joad even criticizes "red panic" fearmongering. It was an about-face from a few years earlier when Zanuck had passed on making John Ford's *The Informer* (1935), for which the director

won his first of four Best Director Oscars after taking it to RKO. And he then turned down a proposed remake of *La Grande Illusion* (1937) by Ford as well. By the time of *The Man I Married*'s August 1940 release, though, Zanuck, the only gentile to run one of the Big Five studios—which possibly made him less self-conscious about referencing Judaism in the film—was convinced that America's entry into the war was inevitable. Perhaps because he helped director Irving Pichel turn *The Man I Married* into a seventy-seven-minute "woman's picture," he ensured those genre trappings meant the Production Code wouldn't take quite as close a look.

Jewish identity in *The Man I Married* was something used more or less as a plot contrivance, however—a way to have a clever final reveal. It took the world's most beloved comedian to go deeper.

THE GREAT DICTATOR

Sometime in the mid-1930s, Charlie Chaplin, accompanied by René Clair and Luis Buñuel, went to see *Triumph of the Will* (1935) at New York City's Museum of Modern Art. Buñuel reports that Clair was terrified by Leni Riefenstahl's propaganda—so much so that he thought it should never be shown or the West would surely fall. He felt the unity of purpose that had coalesced around Hitler was too much to break through, and more than a few in America, Britain, and France would be attracted to Riefenstahl's Nazi vision outright.

Chaplin's response to the film? Howling laughter. He thought the whole thing—two hours of ranting Hitler speeches at his 1934 Nazi Party Congress in Nuremberg intercut with goose-steppers marching around carrying paraphernalia—was ludicrous, self-evidently without merit. And yet somehow this nonsense held an entire nation under its thrall. It must have been all the more remarkable for Chaplin to have watched *Triumph of the Will* for the first time, given the commonalities he had with Hitler.

They were born within four days of each other in 1889, had both risen out of poverty—Chaplin first played The Tramp in 1914, while for much of the five previous years Hitler had been a tramp in Vienna, living in a men's dormitory among other homeless shelters—and, of course, they shared that toothbrush moustache. Did Hitler steal his look

from Chaplin? There's been a popular belief that he did, since Chaplin was the most famous man in the world by the end of the 1910s. If so, that surely constitutes the most outrageous trademark theft of all time. It must also be acknowledged that toothbrush moustaches had become increasingly popular among members of the German military at the start of the twentieth century. A British song from 1938, titled "Who Is This Man? (Who Looks Like Charlie Chaplin)," played up their physical resemblance, while *The New York Times* wistfully noted, upon Chaplin's announcement he was retiring The Tramp following *Modern Times* (1936), that "it is an ironical thought the mustached face of Adolf Hitler will be the only living reminder of the little clown. Goodbye, Charlot. Pleasant dreams." After the triumph of

Chaplin stayed in the uniform of his character, Adenoid Hynkel, while behind the camera making The Great Dictator (1940)—and had some fun mugging for an over-the-top publicity photo shoot while on set.

One of the funniest sequences in <u>The Great Dictator</u> is the visit of rival Fascist dictator Benzino Napaloni (Jack Oakie), a parody of Mussolini that imagines the two autocrats jockeying to one-up each other in increasingly petty ways—such as Hynkel relegating Napaloni to a chair that's very low indeed.

Modern Times, three things likely catalyzed Chaplin's choice to make a film about Hitler: he had been appalled by Fascism when he first encountered its adherents while traveling through Germany, before the Nazis had even officially come to power, during the promotional tour for *City Lights* (1931); British film producer Alexander Korda remarked Chaplin's resemblance to Hitler could lend itself to a comedic tale of mistaken identity; and finally, his friend Ivor Montagu had presented him with an astonishingly hateful bit of Nazi propaganda in which Chaplin had been featured. It was a 1934 book the party had published called *Jews Are Looking at You* and served as a Nazi index of prominent Jews in various walks of life. Of Chaplin it remarked, "This little Jewish

tumbler, as disgusting as he is boring."

Chaplin was not Jewish, but the Nazis were convinced that he was. As such, throughout the 1930s, when he'd be asked about whether he had a Jewish background, Chaplin always demurred: he felt that answering in the affirmative or the negative could play into anti-Semites' hands. He felt no fear of the Nazis the way others in Hollywood had: thinking he was Jewish, Germany and Italy had banned his films anyway. Therefore on October 18, 1938, gossip columnist Louella Parsons announced to the world, "The Hitler-like moustache that Charlie Chaplin has always worn in his comedies will be doubly important in his next picture." *The Great Dictator* was going ahead. But within a couple of months, a wall of doubts hit Chaplin. The movie had been preemptively banned in appeasement-minded Britain, but it was the alarm signaled by the moguls that especially shook his confidence. Chaplin's then assistant Dan James said, "A lot of the [Jewish moguls] said, 'Look, Charlie, you're going to make it terribly hard for our people over there. This will make Hitler furious.' And Charlie said, 'He can't be any worse than he is, can he?' . . . So Charlie was beginning to get a little scared." He was even considering shelving the film altogether, which the head of Paramount's foreign office noted to Warner Bros. as an argument for nixing *Confessions of a Nazi Spy*. But Chaplin, as someone who had full control of the production of his movies and had them distributed through United Artists, didn't have to answer to anyone, unlike directors working for the major studios.

A presidential intervention may have recommitted Chaplin. President Roosevelt himself loved the idea of *The Great Dictator* and thought it was an essential expression of democracy for Chaplin to make it. He sent Secretary of Commerce Harry Hopkins to visit the comedian and reassure him about the project. With FDR's support, Chaplin was all in. He spent the first eight months of 1939 feverishly perfecting the script, sticking close to Los Angeles but taking a break from work on Saturdays to attend the races at Santa Anita, at least once with Walt Disney as his guest. By the time he began shooting on September 9, his film had become more relevant than ever. Just six days before the cameras rolled, Britain and France declared war on Germany, following Hitler's invasion of Poland. World War II in Europe had begun.

While most anti-Nazi films to this point refused even to mention Jews by name, Chaplin was determined that *The Great Dictator* would be made "for the Jews of the world." It features several multidimensional Jewish characters, including Mr. Jaeckel (Maurice Moscovich, a Yiddish theater legend), who rents a room in his apartment to Hannah (Paulette Goddard, half-Jewish herself). They've been living in the confines of the ghetto in the fictional Tomania's capital city ever since the rise of Adenoid Hynkel (Chaplin), the "Phooey" of a Fascist party, who whips up anti-Semitic fervor to distract his followers from the hardships of their own lives. Drawing from the comedy of mistaken identity that Korda first suggested, Chaplin plays a second character, a Jewish barber, who bears an uncanny likeness to the dictator. He returns to the ghetto after fifteen years in a hospital, having lost his memory during World War I and his entire sense of the passage of time since. Needless to say, he's in for a shock. He had served his country as a soldier and now he's not only not considered a citizen of Tomania, he's labeled "subhuman." Almost from the start he's threatened with horrible violence: having resisted a couple stormtroopers earlier, a larger pack of brownshirts catch him, place a noose around his neck, and are literally going to lynch him from a lamppost in front of his own barber shop. Chaplin doesn't hold back from the brutality here. He's ultimately saved, but it's become clear that, under Fascism, his fate is not his own. What's so impressive is that *The Great Dictator* doesn't just show the violence being inflicted on Jews—the word "Jew" is painted on his barber shop, stormtroopers randomly smash windows and harass the denizens of the ghetto—it accomplishes something Holocaust films ever since have struggled with: Jews aren't simply depicted as victims, but as complex human beings, full of dreams and passions and fears and shames, just like everyone else. *The Great Dictator* doesn't shy away from the perils of Jewish life at this time, but it doesn't obsessively linger on them either so that these human beings just become symbols.

Confessions of a Nazi Spy may be the stronger dissection of the Nazi mindset, but *The Great*

Dictator does a better job of showing how exactly Hitler mobilized the tools of mass media to hold such sway. When playing Hynkel, Chaplin borrows heavily from *Triumph of the Will*—which he studied closely upon multiple viewings after that first MoMA screening—incorporating Hitler's uniquely twitchy body language. The very first time we're introduced to Hynkel, he's giving a speech that, if delivered in German and not via nonsense words, more or less could have been delivered by Hitler himself. The Führer had been defined by the very thing that Chaplin had always left out of his own persona: his voice. Hitler had deployed his highly emotive rhetorical style over the radio, and a nation became transfixed. Hitler had had his say. Now Chaplin, who still made silent movies in *City Lights* and *Modern Times* well after the end of the silent era, was to have his first all-talking picture. Chaplin himself would finally speak. If there was ever a moment to, it was this. "Leaders with tenth-rate minds have captured the new instruments of propaganda and are using these instruments to destroy good, civilized, kind behavior," he said. "I'm the clown, and what can I do that is more effective than to laugh at those fellows who are putting humanity to the goose-step?"

Mission accomplished. *The Great Dictator* inaugurates the cinematic conceit of weaponized parody: it was the first big-screen satire to use laughter in an attempt to rob a real-life autocrat of some power, by poking holes in his image. The closest previous example arrived a few months before *The Great Dictator*'s October 15, 1940, premiere—the Three Stooges had unleashed their own parody of Nazism with *You Nazty Spy!* (1940), a two-reel comedy of

errors set in a fictional Fascist country with a name no less funny than Tomania: Moronika. Director Ernst Lubitsch followed suit in two years with *To Be or Not to Be* (1942) and Mel Brooks gave his Nazi parody a musical setting in *The Producers* (1968) nearly three decades later, but it's hard to see how either of these would have been possible without *The Great Dictator*. The particular balancing act Chaplin pulled off is that he managed to convey that Hitler should be both ridiculed and feared at the same time. Laughing at the tyrant doesn't mean he isn't a threat—our Jewish barber hero almost being strung up surely proves that.

"Had I known of the actual horrors of the German concentration camps, I could not have made *The Great Dictator*," Chaplin said in 1964. "I could not have made fun of the homicidal insanity of the Nazis." Whatever regrets he had about the film later in life, in 1940 Chaplin had struck a major cinematic blow. It was the third-biggest box-office success of the year—ahead of *The Grapes of Wrath* and *The Philadelphia Story*—and it moved the audience to think scornfully of Hitler while empathizing with his victims. A potent combination, and one that the

Having to kiss babies is one of Hynkel's least favorite things about his job. But a Phooey's got to do what a Phooey's got to do.

Columbia attached the short <u>You Nazty Spy!</u> to their features starting January 19, 1940. Nine whole months before <u>The Great Dictator</u>, the Three Stooges offered up this comedic takedown of Hitler, which Moe Howard and Larry Fine later called their favorite short they ever made. Several subsequent wartime Stooges shorts were set in the fictional Moronika, whose Fascist dictator rose to power on the rousing slogan "Moronika for Morons!"

Nazis feared. Seventeen-year-old future filmmaker Nikola Radosevic played a prank using the film in his hometown, Belgrade, Serbia, then occupied by the Wehrmacht. He swapped in *The Great Dictator* for a different film a group of German soldiers was supposed to see. "At the start of the show people didn't immediately realize what was going on," he said. "But after forty minutes an SS man pulled out his gun and shot at the screen. All the others rushed out of the hall because something was happening against Hitler."

Did Hitler actually see *The Great Dictator*? A couple different sources—including Budd Schulberg, then working to gather evidence for the Nuremberg trials—say that he did. Schulberg said he saw Hitler's movie log, which indicated what films were ordered when. He said Hitler not only ordered *The Great Dictator* to watch by himself, he ordered it to watch again the next night.

The smash success of *The Great Dictator* changed Hollywood. It showed that being anti-Nazi could mean big business. Eighteen months before its release, twenty-five thousand American Nazis had held a rally in Madison Square Garden. Now, mocking that ideology meant box-office success— the biggest of Chaplin's illustrious career—and five Academy Award nominations. With the war in Europe fully raging, much of the filmgoing market there was closed to Hollywood, which further freed up what kind of statements about the conflict the moguls allowed onscreen. And *The Great Dictator* had been the torchbearer: Americans still might not have been ready for war, but now at least they had no doubt about who the enemy was.

BOMBS, BULLETS, AND BANANAS

A s 1940 wore on, it started to become more and more clear to Americans in positions of power that war with Germany and Japan might be inevitable. France had fallen to the Wehrmacht's blitzkrieg, as had the Netherlands, Belgium, Denmark, and Norway. China entered the fourth year of the fight for its life against Japan. In June, Italy declared war on France and Britain, annexed British Somaliland, and prepared its invasion of Egypt to control both ends of the Red Sea. From their base in Albania, which they had conquered the year before, Mussolini's forces prepared to invade Greece. And from September 7, the German air force, the Luftwaffe, began its terror bombings of London known as the Blitz. For fifty-six out of the next fifty-seven nights, German bombs fell from the sky as civilians clustered in London Tube stations. The feeling of the Blitz, of courage despite the possibility of death at any moment, was captured in Alfred Hitchcock's *Foreign Correspondent* (1940), which ends with American journalist Johnny Jones (Joel McCrea) giving an impassioned radio broadcast of how he had seen British resolve in the face of the ordeal.

"Hello, America," he begins. "I've been watching a part of the world being blown to pieces. A part of the world as nice as Vermont and Ohio and Virginia and California and Illinois lies ripped up bleeding like a steer in a slaughterhouse." Then bombs start

falling in the middle of his broadcast, and a producer suggests he take refuge in an underground shelter. He turns to his fiancée Carol (Laraine Day) about what to do. "How about it, Carol?" "They're listening in America, Johnny." Of course he soldiers on. "It's as if the lights were all out everywhere. Except in America. Keep those lights burning there. Cover them with steel, ring them with guns, build a canopy of battleships and bombing planes around them. Hello, America! Hang on to your lights! They're the only lights left in the world." Then "The Star-Spangled Banner" swells and the film ends—about as much a warning to prepare for war as you can get. All the more remarkable because when *Foreign Correspondent* premiered on August 16, 1940, the Blitz hadn't yet actually begun. But Hitchcock, and most close observers, knew that it was coming. American viewers were starting to realize that it might very well happen in the United States too. Pray for peace and prepare for war. Yes, the 79 percent of Americans in that June 1941 Gallup poll who still didn't want the US to enter the war hoped

OPPOSITE: Carmen Miranda was the muse of the Good Neighbor Policy. **RIGHT:** Alfred Hitchcock directing Joel McCrea and Herbert Marshall on the set of <u>Foreign Correspondent</u>.

the nation wouldn't be drawn into the conflict—that didn't mean they didn't want to be prepared. As much as ordinary Americans dreaded it, war was becoming ever more likely.

On September 16, 1940, President Roosevelt signed into law the first-ever peacetime draft. The Selective Training and Service Act required all men between the ages of twenty-one and forty-five to register with their local draft boards, to bolster what had been a small peacetime military with new twelve-month conscriptions (later expanded to thirty months). A few weeks before, Roosevelt did something else that had a profound effect on US foreign policy. Since he took office in 1933, he had talked about the United States being a "good neighbor" to the countries in Latin America, after several decades of a more interventionist agenda. He immediately ended the US Marines' occupation of Nicaragua that year, and pulled out of Haiti the next. Memories of those American incursions brought fear to the leaders of many other countries in the region, and a belief by some that they needed to make strong allies in Europe to counteract US influence: namely, Germany and Italy.

To reset relations via a new soft-power campaign of cultural diplomacy, Roosevelt created the Office of the Coordinator of Inter-American Affairs (OCIAA) in August 1940. Nelson Rockefeller served as its head, while John Hay Whitney led its Motion Picture Division, in recognition of the unique importance of using movies to reshape the ideas Americans had about Latin Americans—debunking harmful stereotypes included—and vice versa. The OCIAA urged Hollywood studios to hire actual Latin American performers, not just have white actors play Latin Americans. According to historian Brian O'Neil, Whitney, one of the founding investors of Selznick International Pictures, believed there was "power that Hollywood films could exert in the two-pronged campaign to win the hearts and minds of Latin Americans and to convince Americans of the benefits of Pan-American friendship." Better representation onscreen wasn't just the right thing to do: it could result in a recognition among the various cultures of the western hemisphere of what we all share—and need to defend.

———

Carmen Miranda was actually born in Portugal before moving to the Americas at an early age. Rio de Janeiro was where she grew up and first began to forge her singular identity as a sex symbol, a camp figure, and a national icon of Brazil. She couldn't have dreamed, as a teenager working in a hat shop, that she'd one day have an entire museum devoted to her in Rio. Or maybe she could. Miranda had a singular ability to channel her life experiences and synthesize the culture around her into a pop persona all her own. That hat shop experience? Invaluable for creating the elaborate fruit-based chapeaus that became her trademark. She made her first recording at the age of twenty in 1929 and quickly became a symbol of Rio's annual Carnaval each February, parlaying her samba moves and rapid-fire singing into performances on the radio, at Rio nightclubs—including the city's most glamorous, the Cassino da Urca—and in Brazilian movies. Much of her look, with a head scarf or fruit hat, giant hoop earrings, and long skirt draping from a bare midriff, actually came from the Afro-Brazilian community, the cultural heart of which is the northeastern Brazilian state Bahia. What became her signature look was not what was on trend in Rio. It was an example of a white artist appropriating Black culture to present an exotic image. But when Broadway producer Lee Shubert, of the Shubert organization that still owns many Broadway theaters to this day, saw her perform at the Urca, he was captivated: this was an exotic fantasy he wanted to bring back with him to New York. He offered her an eight-week contract

Carmen Miranda, relaxing in the usual get-up she'd wear around the house. By the end of 1941 her superstardom was so intense even Mickey Rooney dressed up as her to perform "Mamãe Eu Quero" in Babes on Broadway.

in his show *The Streets of Paris*, which she accepted.

Twenty-four years before the Beatles led the British Invasion, Miranda spearheaded the Brazilian Invasion. America didn't know what hit it. She made such an impression in *The Streets of Paris* that she was quickly put on the radio and then recorded two back-to-back hits: "South American Way" and "Mamãe Eu Quero," both of which featured in her debut Hollywood film, *Down Argentine Way* (1940). She played herself in the 20th Century Fox production, which opened on October 11, 1940, four days before the premiere of *The Great Dictator*. It grossed $2 million at the box office, making it one of the top ten films of the year, and Miranda herself made such

an impression she was voted the third most popular star of 1940 and was invited to perform for President Roosevelt himself. In Miranda, Roosevelt saw the perfect symbol for his Good Neighbor Policy: an appealing personality who'd expand Americans' awareness of their neighbors to the south and provide a case study in how much opportunity anyone from Latin America could find in the United States. As a mark of how important Miranda was to the outreach effort—and a sign that Brazil was the country the United States most wanted to ensure stayed on its side in the conflict to come—Roosevelt even had Nelson Rockefeller establish the headquarters of the newly created OCIAA in Rio.

DOWN SOUTH AMERICAN WAY WITH DISNEY

Miranda had come to Hollywood from Brazil, but who would go to Brazil from Hollywood? Call it Donald Duck Diplomacy, because the person charged with this task was Walt Disney. "I was asked by the government to go to South America and do a cultural thing during those Nazi days," Walt Disney said. "They first wanted me to go on a handshaking goodwill tour, and I said, 'I don't go for that. I'm not a good handshaker, and everything.' And then they said, 'Why don't you go down and make some films about these countries?' I said, 'Well that's my business. I can do that.'" Disney assembled a group of eighteen artists, musicians, and writers to accompany him on a two-and-a-half-month trip around South America to act as cultural ambassadors of the United States and gather material for films. It couldn't have come at a better time. Disney needed to hit the reset button. His studio was on the verge of bankruptcy, despite having scored the second-biggest box-office success of all time at that point with *Snow White and the Seven Dwarfs* (1937)—only *Gone with the Wind* (1939) made more money. Disney had invested his profits from the film into building a massive new studio campus in Burbank, which remains the Disney studio headquarters to this day. Yet there was no consistent influx of profits to pay the remaining costs of the new studio: Snow White's follow-up, *Pinocchio*

(1940), was a box-office bomb, in part because the closure of the European market due to the war meant a loss of 45 percent of its revenue potential. The next film later that year, *Fantasia*, which required a unique Fantasound road show setup, was an even bigger loss. But despite its extraordinary production and exhibition costs, Disney still donated the entire proceeds from the film's November 13 premiere to the British War Relief Society.

Animators at work in 1931 at the old Disney studio on Hyperion Avenue in Los Angeles.

1941 was a year of unprecedented crisis for the Disney studio. It started the year $4.5 million in debt, resulting in salary reductions and the looming threat of layoffs. But Disney's top animators, such as Frank Thomas and Ollie Johnston, each making a hefty salary of $300 a week, were unaffected. The burden shifted to ink-and-paint department staffers considered lowest on the totem pole, who made only $18 a week. Accusations of favoritism followed, and Walt's messaging to his staff didn't help. Other animation shops around town, including those of the Fleischer brothers and Looney Tunes creator Leon Schlesinger, had unionized under the Screen Cartoonist's Guild. Many Disney staffers felt they should too. On May 28, Disney fired two-dozen staffers he considered agitators, possibly Communists. He did not want a union shop, no

matter what. The next day, more than two hundred, out of the over six hundred, employees of the studio went on strike. Tempers ran high, as animators from other studios joined the picket line that Disney had to drive through in order to access the lot. Looney Tunes animator Chuck Jones went shirtless with a black executioner's mask and brought a life-size guillotine to the protest, with a fully functional, if blunted, blade. The victim inside it was a dummy made to look like Gunther Lessing, Disney's lawyer.

The strike lasted most of the summer of 1941. On one occasion animator Art Babbitt, considered to be the leader of the strike, caught sight of Disney in his car, jumped on top of a flatbed truck, and yelled, "There he is, the Great Man! He wants brotherhood for all except himself! Shame on you, Walt Disney!" Disney was so furious he jumped out of his car,

The picket line of the Screen Cartoonist's Guild outside the Disney studio on May 28, 1941.

threw off his jacket, and appeared ready to charge at Babbitt before cooler heads separated them.

When the South America trip presented itself as an opportunity, Disney seized it. The US government planned to underwrite the entire journey and even guarantee whatever films he produced from it. He couldn't have hoped for a better deal. Getting to Rio, the first leg of their trip, was much more complicated in 1941 than it is today—passenger aircraft barely traveled over 200 mph. With the strike still raging, Disney and his group of eighteen flew out of Burbank to Nashville and then to Miami Beach. While in Florida, animator Frank Thomas had an unnerving encounter. He wrote his wife Jeanette to say, "Some people came in today from Peru and said everyone was laughing up their sleeves because everything [there] is pro-Nazi, and they point out the ridiculous side of the US attempts to win the people over. Accordingly, we're cautioned increasingly to keep still about the half million the government is sinking into this adventure." On August 15, they left Miami Beach en route to San Juan, then flew to Belem in the far north of Brazil. Three days after they departed Miami Beach, the Disney group landed in Rio.

The colors and sounds of Rio proved intoxicating. Thomas and the other artists produced drawings and watercolors of what they saw: the wavelike black-and-white sidewalks of Copacabana beach, the cable cars ascending to Corcovado, glittering lights around the rim of Guanabara Bay, dances at the Urca, icy caipirinhas that quench one's thirst and quicken the pulse. This city was a jewel and the perfect inspiration for the artists to open their paint boxes—when they weren't busy at diplomatic functions, of course. They had at least one outreach event organized by the OCIAA each day. Gathered in the lobby of the Hotel Gloria, they'd wait for the bellhop to announce "El Grupo!" referring to their group, and they'd then be whisked away to whatever event Nelson Rockefeller's office had arranged. Somehow the animators found time to create a new character from the Brazilian parrots that animal handlers presented to them: José Carioca, a green feathered friend to Donald Duck based on and voiced by actual musical star José Oliveira, who went by the stage name Zé Carioca ("Zé" being the nickname form of "José" in Brazil), who'd performed alongside Carmen Miranda when she came to America.

The one-two punch of Carmen Miranda's Hollywood success and Walt Disney's visit, along with some hefty economic incentives, paid dividends for America's relationship with Brazil immediately. In January, President Getúlio Vargas, who had based his government program for Brazil on Mussolini's for Italy, broke off diplomatic relations with the Axis. Brazil had previously banned Hollywood films with anti-Nazi themes. In April 1942, Vargas allowed *The Mortal Storm* to screen in the nation's movie theaters, where it broke box-office attendance records.

On September 8, 1941, El Grupo checked in at the Alvear Palace Hotel in Buenos Aires, Argentina. Disney had wanted to make a film with a gaucho theme, so a trip to the Pampas was arranged for the demonstration of Argentine roping techniques and for a folk dance. But Marcelo Niño, curator of Buenos Aires's Museum of Caricature, says that the rumor that spread rapidly throughout the city was that Disney was a spy. That suspicion is not surprising: the Argentine military was led by Fascist sympathizers and the country never did break off relations with the Axis. (As a special envoy to South America at roughly the same time, Douglas Fairbanks Jr. actually did gather military intelligence, so one could say he was indeed a spy.) Three days after he arrived, Disney made a quick side trip by ship to Montevideo, Uruguay, to attend that country's premiere of *Fantasia*. More than a thousand children greeted him at the port town of Colonia upon his arrival—a school holiday had been declared in honor of Mickey Mouse and Donald Duck. And the local newspaper *El País* reported that the very next day Uruguay dismissed the German ambassador. It was after that triumph that Disney received some terrible news: he learned via telegram that his father, Elias, had died. They had had a fractious relationship: despite Elias never having achieved business success himself, he didn't believe Walt's work as an artist constituted a real career. He had also been a leftist, an ardent follower of five-time Socialist Party presidential candidate

ABOVE: Walt Disney let actor Robert Benchley take audiences on a tour of the sprawling new Burbank studio campus in the compilation film The Reluctant Dragon (1941). **BELOW:** José Carioca was the green parrot Disney's animators dreamed up while on their stay in Brazil. Where Donald is loud and brash, Joe is suave and smooth. Panchito, the red rooster who represents Mexico the way Carioca stood in for Brazil, rounded out the title trio for The Three Caballeros (1944), the second film made from the South American trip after Saludos Amigos (1942).

Eugene V. Debs, while his son was a conservative. The reporters who followed Disney in Uruguay consoled him. But there was never any question about him abandoning his South American trip to attend his father's funeral.

———

The Disney expedition returned to Burbank at the end of October. While they had been away, the strike was resolved: to save money, an equal number of strikers and nonstrikers were to be laid off—about half the staff—and those who remained were allowed to unionize with the Screen Cartoonist's Guild. Disney lost some talented artists in the process: among them, Tyrus Wong, who would become a fixture in the Warner Bros. live-action art department, helping design the look of films such as *Rebel Without a Cause* (1955), *Rio Bravo* (1959), and *The Wild Bunch* (1969); Frank Tashlin, who would become a live-action director; and Bill Melendez,

Walt Disney strums a guitar in Quilicura, Chile.

best known for directing *A Charlie Brown Christmas* (1965). The strike had deeply rattled Disney, and he was now beholden to his creditor, Bank of America, in a profound way: the bank put a moratorium on Disney making any new features beyond *Dumbo* (1941) and *Bambi* (1942) until the studio was more solvent and placed one of its members on Disney's executive board. But the South American trip had given him a new purpose—to be an ambassador of America to the world, and a communicator of American values. It was a role he'd play in various other forms for the rest of his life, until he'd finally become an embodiment of the nation. In the near term, he came back from South America with ideas for four cartoon shorts that would symbolize the bonds of friendship he'd created on his trip.

HOLLYWOOD ON DEFENSE

The two most important years for Hollywood during the war may actually have been the two years directly before the start of America's participation: 1940 and the first eleven months of 1941. Not only did the images onscreen pivot away from the population's widely felt isolationism—and the artists who created them now toggled between cultural warfare and cultural diplomacy—some in Hollywood joined the fight against Fascism in more direct ways.

King Kong co-director Merian C. Cooper had left Hollywood behind following executive stints at RKO, Selznick International, and a few turns as an independent producer for films that ended up at MGM and Paramount. In March 1940, he joined Claire Lee Chennault, formerly a captain in the US Army Air Corps and now an adviser in the Republic of China Air Force. He had gone to China after their air power had crumbled almost completely in the early stages of the war with Japan. Having completed an assessment of how they could rebuild it, he felt that bringing American pilots to China to serve in the Chinese air force could be the fastest way to regroup. Plus, they could train Chinese would-be flyers to follow in their wake. In this endeavor, Chennault reported in to Madame Chiang

The story of the American volunteers who became the de facto Chinese air force came to the big screen via Republic Pictures with <u>Flying Tigers</u> (1942), starring John Wayne, with Anna Lee and John Carroll. It borrows more than a little from Howard Hawks's masterpiece <u>Only Angels Have Wings</u> (1939).

Kai-shek herself, Soong Mei-ling. Cooper met up with Chennault when the old flyer had returned to America to look for recruits. In December, a full year before America entered the fight outright, President Roosevelt authorized the transfer of one hundred Curtiss P-40 fighter planes and one hundred pilots—sixty from the navy and Marine Corps and forty from the Army Air Corps—to the Chinese government under Chennault's command, plus an additional two hundred support personnel.

Cooper, forty-six years old when he left the movie business, had always made films about daring adventures. He himself had been a World War I flyer and then an American volunteer with the Polish air force during Poland's war with the Soviet Union in 1920 (Cooper spent nine months as a Soviet prisoner of war). When the flyers he helped assemble finally took to the skies against Japan from their base in Kunming, it was December 20, 1941, thirteen days after Pearl Harbor and the US entry into war with Japan. But the critical effort that made this group of flyers—nicknamed the Flying Tigers, and analogous in the China campaign to the Americans who had joined the Royal Air Force during the Battle of Britain—able to fly so quickly was all the work that was done in the two years before Pearl Harbor. Actions like this in 1940 and 1941 made America's transition into a state of war that much easier. John Ford said he was "green with envy" at how Cooper had left Hollywood behind to join the fight.

Ford's time would come, but first he had to see his frequent producer Darryl F. Zanuck get in uniform. In January 1941 the 20th Century Fox boss, who had produced four of Ford's last six movies, accepted a commission as a lieutenant colonel in the Army Signal Corps reserve. The War Department took a particular interest in Zanuck because he had not only shown an interest in fighting Fascism but, as the chairman of the Academy of Motion Picture Arts and Sciences' Research Council, was in a position to help mobilize Hollywood resources for military propaganda and training purposes. To start, they wanted him to commission four training films to help standardize induction protocols. The draft was up and running, after all. Zanuck immediately recruited Ford for an assignment, a twenty-six-minute short called *Sex Hygiene* (1942), for which Ford took two or three days to shoot dramatic situations that conveyed how venereal disease might be transmitted. Those scenes were then placed around preexisting medical footage: gruesome close-ups of genitals riddled with welts from STDs. "I think it made its point and helped a lot of young kids," Ford said. "I looked at it and threw up."

Ford had been in the Naval Reserve since 1934, when he bought a 106-foot ketch he named the *Araner*, in honor of his mother, who had been born in Ireland's Aran Islands. In early 1940, after wrapping *The Grapes of Wrath* for Zanuck, he went on a voyage around Baja California and conducted a little bit of spying for navy intelligence. He suspected the Japanese shrimp trawlers that made their way to the Mexican coast might include some of their own military personnel. He wrote to the head of intelligence at the navy base in San Diego of some Japanese sailors who gave him pause: "All carry themselves with military carriage . . . I am positive they are Naval men . . . They constitute a real menace." It was around that time in 1940 Ford started making his proposal for a navy photographic unit that would recruit Hollywood talent and use professional filmmaking techniques for the accumulation of intelligence and dissemination of propaganda. By April, the 11th District Naval Command in San Diego approved the idea and put Ford in charge of Naval Reserve photography; his unit was called Field Photo and it was up to him and his *Grapes of Wrath* cinematographer Gregg Toland, just three months away from serving as Orson Welles's director of photography on

Citizen Kane's shoot, to recruit up to two hundred Hollywood experts.

In September 1941, members of Field Photo were called up to active duty, including Ford, who outright volunteered for enlistment and was granted the rank of lieutenant commander. Just three weeks before, Ford had finished *How Green Was My Valley* (1941), which would win him his third Best Director Oscar, as well as Best Picture. Now he'd work closely with William "Wild Bill" Donovan, the chief of information in a new interbranch intelligence unit President Roosevelt had commissioned. Often one branch of the US Armed Forces had no idea what the other was doing. Donovan's role evolved into him being the head of the new Office of Strategic Services and finally being considered the "founding father of the CIA." And in Ford's work he took a particular interest.

———

Even after taking up his Army Reserve role, Zanuck's films still fell under extraordinary scrutiny by Joseph Breen and, increasingly, alarmed Washington politicians who felt that his commission indicated collusion between Hollywood and the Roosevelt administration to force America into war. Debuting on June 13, 1941—just nine days before Nazi Germany launched its surprise invasion of the Soviet Union—Fritz Lang's *Man Hunt*, about a British hunter who once had Adolf Hitler in his rifle sights and is chased around London by Nazi

agents thinking he was an assassin, was excoriated by Breen as a "hate film" for its refusal to have any "good German" characters. It is indeed a stirring indictment of Nazi cruelty and a call for armed intervention, with Walter Pidgeon's lead character indicting Hitler: "He's guilty . . . guilty against me and against humanity! Against every decent, peaceful person in the world! He's guilty of hatred, intolerance, and murder! Yes, I intended to kill! I intended to avenge the crimes of this monstrous tyrant!" The movie ends with Pidgeon parachuting into Germany on a mission of revenge, accompanied by stirring narration: "And from now on, somewhere within Germany, is a man with a precision rifle, and the high degree of intelligence and training that is required to use it. It may be days, months, or even years, but this time he clearly knows his purpose and, unflinching, faces his destiny." Then "God Save the King" swells—to Americans, the same tune as "My Country, 'Tis of Thee." If you were watching *Man Hunt* for the first time, you'd be forgiven for thinking it was made after the United States and Germany were at war, not before.

On August 1, Republican senator Gerald P. Nye from North Dakota made a speech to the isolationist America First Committee ranting against the "foreigners," all with "non-Nordic" last names, who controlled Hollywood and "in at least . . . 20 pictures

John Ford is most often associated with the dusty expanse of Monument Valley, but it's arguable his first love was the sea. His Eugene O'Neill adaptation The Long Voyage Home (1940), about a merchant marine ship in the early days of World War II's Battle of the Atlantic, captured the briny obsession that made him want to enlist in the navy.

Darryl F. Zanuck, left, attended the premiere of <u>How Green Was My Valley</u> in October 1941, right around the time he passionately defended the American movie industry at the Nye Committee.

produced within the last year" set about "inoculating [the audience] with the virus of war." He summed up: "Go to Hollywood. It is a raging volcano of war fever. The place swarms with refugees. Are you ready to send your boys to bleed and die in Europe to make the world safe for Barney Balaban and Adolph Zukor and Joseph Schenk?" Nye and Democratic senator Bennett Clark of Missouri set a Senate hearing for September 9, 1941, in which the movie industry was forced to defend itself. The industry lobbying body, the Motion Picture Producers and Distributors of America, hired their single greatest advocate, the pro-intervention former Republican presidential candidate Wendell Willkie, who lost the 1940 election when Roosevelt won his third term. Willkie felt the United States should be providing more aid to Britain and China and that outright war was inevitable. And he didn't feel the moguls should

shy away from the anti-Nazi statements they had made in movies like *Confessions of a Nazi Spy*, *The Mortal Storm*, *The Man I Married*, and *Man Hunt*. They should embrace their anti-Nazi stances. So finally, Hollywood would stand up for itself. The crowning moment of the Nye Committee hearings was when Zanuck, whose commission in the Army Signal Corps reserve had led the isolationist senators to suggest that Hollywood was taking marching orders from Roosevelt in the first place, gave his testimony: "I look back and recall picture after picture, pictures so strong and powerful that they sold the American way of life not only to America but to the entire world. They sold it so strongly that when dictators took over Italy and Germany, what did Hitler and his flunky Mussolini do? The first thing they did was to ban our pictures, they wanted no part of the American way of life."

JIMMY STEWART GETS HIS WINGS

It's hard not to think the notion that Hollywood was a projection of American ideals was part of what attracted Jimmy Stewart to the motion picture business in the first place after a stint on Broadway in the 1930s; it was certainly an impulse to strive for American ideals that made him the first movie star to volunteer for military service. Actor Robert Montgomery, already under contract with MGM for over a decade, had driven ambulances in France for the American Field Service leading up to the evacuation at Dunkirk but didn't officially enlist in a branch of the US Armed Forces—in his case, the navy—until the day after Pearl Harbor. Stewart knew exactly what he wanted to do. He wanted to fly. In fact, he had wanted to be a flyer since he was a kid growing up in Indiana, Pennsylvania, but he never pursued it due to a childhood of ill health. In fact, a battle with scarlet fever contributed to Stewart not being able to graduate high school until he was twenty. Much like how Ford had bought his yacht in the dream of possibly joining the navy, Stewart finally did learn to fly, buying a Stinson 105 two-seater, logging three hundred hours in it, and earning his commercial pilot's license. That was after he had already scored his initial Hollywood success with the three hit films of his breakout year, 1936: *Rose Marie*, *Born to Dance*, and *After the Thin Man*. He tried to join the Army Air Corps in November 1940, a full month before *The Philadelphia Story* came out. Stewart saw the writing on the wall: America was going to end up in this war whether its citizens liked it or not. Better to be ready than caught unprepared. And military readiness was in his family: both his grandfathers had fought in the Civil War and his father, Alex Stewart, had fought

in the Spanish-American War and World War I. Yet in that initial attempt at enlistment in November, he was underweight by ten pounds and thus rejected for service. He'd have to wait a few months before he could try again.

Why did Stewart want to enlist so badly? Partly due to his family's military history, partly due to his awareness of the threat of Fascism, and partly because he was unsatisfied with the roles he'd been getting in Hollywood since arguably his greatest triumph: 1939's *Mr. Smith Goes to Washington*. The final three films of his that would be released in 1941—*Come Live with Me*, *Pot o' Gold*, and *Ziegfeld Girl*—he thought were lightweight and disposable. Even the film from the previous year for which he was getting Oscar buzz, *The Philadelphia Story*, didn't give him one of his favorite roles. "I never thought much of my performance in *The Philadelphia Story*," Stewart said. "But I guess it was entertaining and slick and smooth and all that. But *Mr. Smith* had more guts. Many people have suggested that I won [the Oscar] as a kind of deferred payment for my work on *Mr. Smith*. I think there's some truth in that because the Academy seems to have a way of paying its past debts. But it should have gone to Hank that year." Meaning Henry Fonda for *The Grapes of Wrath*. In fact, Stewart felt so strongly about it, he voted for Fonda, his friend from when they roomed together on the then rough-and-tumble Upper West Side of Manhattan as aspiring Broadway actors in the early 1930s. Stewart won nonetheless. Twenty-three days after he collected his Oscar, he took the oath of service at Fort MacArthur in San Pedro as a newly minted army private. It was March 22, 1941, and he was two months away from turning thirty-three.

The cutoff for induction into the Army Air Corps was twenty-six, but due to his education—Stewart was a Princeton graduate—and his commercial pilot's license, he was put on the Air Corps track.

Stewart had realized what all of Hollywood soon would: celebrity only mattered at all if it could be leveraged in the fight for freedom. Otherwise, it was best to not get caught up in it. Now, there could be no more inaction. The fight was here.

OPPOSITE: While other actors who'd later join up wanted to use their celebrity to encourage enlistment, Stewart rarely sought publicity while in uniform—in fact, other than for a few fundraising events, Stewart practically ran from reporters for the four and a half years he served. He feared some might think his war service was a PR stunt. **ABOVE:** Despite his seeming desire to walk away from Hollywood completely, Stewart did attend the 1942 Oscars to present the Best Actor award to Gary Cooper for <u>Sergeant York</u> (1941).

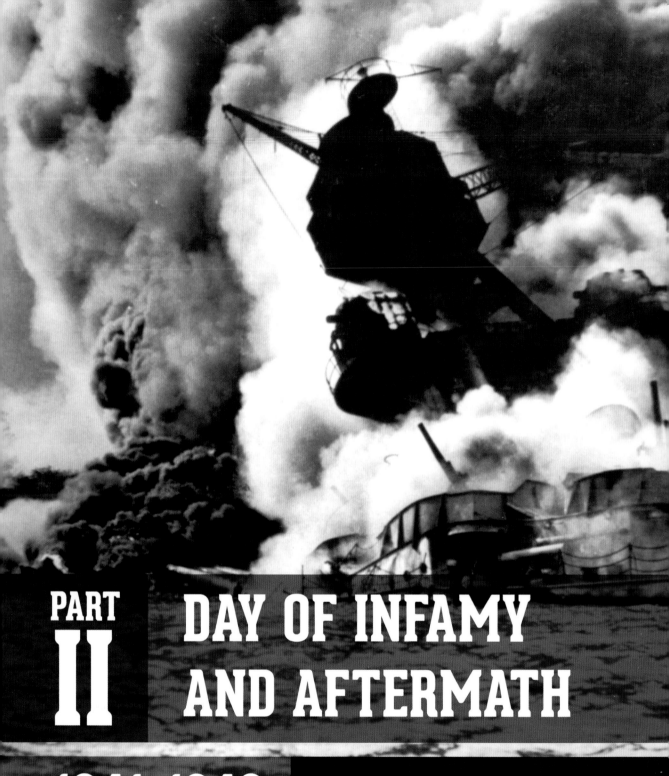

PART II

DAY OF INFAMY AND AFTERMATH

1941-1942

The USS Arizona burns before sinking to the bottom of Pearl Harbor on December 7, 1941.

A SUNDAY IN DECEMBER

"The sun is shining, the grass is green / the orange and palm trees sway" goes the opening of Irving Berlin's oft-discarded verse to "White Christmas." It could have described the quiet Sunday morning Hollywood experienced at the start of December 7, 1941. Berlin intended to take a day off of work on *Holiday Inn*, the movie based on his own idea that was set to feature his new song. Just a few days before, Bing Crosby recorded the version of "White Christmas" he'd lip-synch to in the movie in a rapid-fire studio session on the Paramount lot. Berlin considered "White Christmas" to be his baby, and he hid in a corner of the studio behind some soundproofing partitions to make sure it sounded exactly the way he heard it in his head. Now here was a pleasant Beverly Hills Sunday when he could let that stress melt away.

In fact, music was on the minds of many in Hollywood that December 7 morning. The New York Philharmonic's Sunday performances on CBS Radio were always among the most popular broadcasts each week. That morning, listeners heard conductor Artur Rodzinski lead Shostakovich's Symphony No. 1 and Arthur Rubinstein playing Brahms's Piano Concerto No. 2. At 11:25 a.m. Pacific Time, newsman John Charles Daly cut in to the broadcast and announced, emotion straining his voice, that Pearl Harbor had been attacked by Imperial Japan. Just an hour and seven minutes earlier, the first wave of 182 torpedo bombers and Mitsubishi Zero

fighters had begun unleashing their payloads on American battleships and cruisers in Pearl Harbor as well as airfields around Oahu. The second wave of 171 Japanese aircraft was still attacking at the very moment of Daly's broadcast. The result was traumatic: 2,403 Americans had been killed with 1,178 injured, and six of the eight US battleships present were damaged—four of them sunk outright. It had proved what the Warner brothers, Litvak, Zanuck, Ford, Stewart, and so many others had known: America's entry into the war was inescapable. Was America prepared or had it been caught unaware? To many, it appeared like the latter. But that feeling that we should have seen this attack coming quickly turned into a resolve to never let it happen again. Putting it another way: the Japanese attack on Pearl Harbor was a tactical psychological victory for Hirohito and his empire, but a strategic psychological defeat. The terror inspired by those 353 planes traversing the length of Oahu from its northern

Bing Crosby recorded the version of "White Christmas" that appears in <u>Holiday Inn</u> (1942) in the week leading up to the Pearl Harbor attack.

Attacks from Japanese aircraft occurred all over Oahu, including at the Hickam Field air base, not just at the harbor proper.

coast to rain fire on that south-shore naval base quickly turned to determination. And strategically, Japan achieved almost none of its objectives: all of the battleships they'd sunk would be raised, save for the *Arizona*, and returned to service and to the fight. Plus, none of the Pacific Fleet's three carriers had been present.

Japan could possibly have struck a more crippling blow if they had proceeded to launch a third wave from the six carriers they had parked north of Oahu, one that could have destroyed the military infrastructure on the island itself. But that would have required extending the attack beyond the ninety minutes that it had taken—to the point where any third-wave planes could have only returned to their carriers at night. Admiral Chūichi Nagumo, who had masterminded the attack, decided a third wave wasn't worth the risk: most of the twenty-nine Japanese planes the US forces did manage to shoot down during the attack itself came during the second wave. With a third wave, the Americans were sure to be even more prepared. A smarter tactic, and one that the Imperial Japanese Navy considered, was an invasion of Oahu outright. That might have required only ten thousand to fifteen thousand soldiers, but the Imperial Army, even more disconnected from the Imperial Navy than the US Army was from the US Navy, would never have allocated the resources. Japan wanted to cripple American naval power so that they could begin their lightning conquests of the Philippines, Malaya, and the Dutch East Indies (Indonesia) with less opposition from the only other major Pacific power. But it's hard to see what they accomplished at Pearl Harbor other than a senseless loss of life and a near instantaneous dispelling of American isolationism, previously so intractable. The 20th Century Fox film *Tora! Tora! Tora!* (1970) depicted the Japanese navy's commander in chief Admiral Isoroku Yamamoto (played by Sô Yamamura) saying, "I fear all we have done is to awaken a sleeping giant." That line is almost certainly the invention of that film and not a historical quote, as has been widely thought. But it feels so right because it's essentially what Japan had done.

Daly's news of the attack at 11:25 a.m. shook Hollywood like a thunderclap. Imagine the disruption to the film productions that were shooting that morning. Ginger Rogers was on the set of Fox's *Roxie Hart* (1942) when the word came down. "The sound stages were filled with radios giving out fresh information," she later said. "The sound booth had to block out the squeaking from midget radios in the middle of a take, and much film was wasted during the time because we were so eager to hear the news."

Alfred Hitchcock at work on preproduction notes for <u>Saboteur</u> (1942), about Nazi agents living in America, with his wife, Alma Reville, right around the time of the Pearl Harbor attack. Hitchcock and his art director Robert Boyle were working on the film at Selznick's Culver City studio when someone threw open a door and shouted to them that Pearl Harbor had been attacked. "And we went right on working," Boyle said. "It was just too much to take in, and there wasn't anything we could do about it anyway."

Orson Welles, the boy wonder turned instant pariah after *Citizen Kane* (1941) rankled Tinseltown's many William Randolph Hearst acolytes that summer, spent much of his December 7 rewriting the opening to radio essayist Norman Corwin's "Between Americans," which Welles was hosting that night on CBS's *Gulf Screen Guild Theater*. Noting the day's events, he concluded, "This is a time for energetic and unashamed patriotism on the part of all of us. I know we all agree to that because I know that none of us will be satisfied with anything but complete victory."

Among the less productive that morning, Frank Sinatra, already a superstar since scoring the first-ever Billboard number one hit with "I'll Never Smile Again" sixteen months earlier, was still asleep at Lana Turner's house after an all-night party. Clutching his hungover head, he bristled as Turner's mother stormed in to share that America was now at war.

Alcohol also accompanied the news for John Ford. He and his wife, Mary, were having a leisurely luncheon at Rear Admiral Andrew Pickens's home

in Alexandria, Virginia, when the War Department suddenly called. Jimmy Stewart learned of the attack from Moffett Field, near San Jose, where he had recently been promoted to corporal. William Wyler and John Huston were playing tennis when Wyler's wife, Talli, came running out and interrupted their game. The direction of the films the two men were working on at the moment—*Mrs. Miniver* (1942) and *Across the Pacific* (1942), respectively—would change in the months ahead due to America's sudden involvement in the war.

As that next line of Berlin's verse goes, there'd "never been such a day, in Beverly Hills, L.A."

───────

Walt Disney, who'd just scored a hit with *Dumbo*—his only major hit of the 1940s, in fact, and enough of a success that it helped relieve the financial burden on his studio—was at home listening to the New York Philharmonic, like so many others, when he heard Daly's announcement. Disney thought his rocky 1941 might have a quiet ending; instead the year went out with a bang. The next day, Disney's studio manager called him early in the morning. "Walt, the army is moving in on us," he said. "They came up and said they wanted to move in. I said I'd have to call you and they said, 'Call him, but we're moving in anyway.'" The US Army stationed five hundred troops at Disney's Burbank campus for the next eight months—it was the only Hollywood studio ordered to accommodate a garrison during the war. The expansive facilities were the perfect place to quarter troops. It was near Los Angeles, but not too close to incite a panic. This force would be stationed there just in case a Japanese invasion of the West Coast was imminent; it was not a coincidence these soldiers were from the 121st Anti-Aircraft Artillery Gun Battalion. They used a soundstage to repair equipment and were poised to defend any of the nearby aircraft factories that might come under attack. Disney also accepted a $90,000 contract to make twenty films for the navy.

In a very different engagement on December 8, the local police, at the order of the federal government, raided the Silver Legion's compound near Pacific Palisades and arrested the fifty supporters of the Fascist movement there who were maintaining its facilities. Its leader, William Dudley Pelley, was ultimately sentenced to two to three years in prison for violating an earlier probation by creating a secret military organization.

Also on December 8, producer Hal Wallis at Warner Bros. made a fateful decision. A play that had come across his desk called *Everybody Comes to Rick's* suddenly had new relevance. Written by Murray Burnett and Joan Alison, it seemed like the perfect metaphor for America's recent history. It just needed a new title.

Three days later, on December 11, Germany declared war on the United States, in what historians think was a decision made by Hitler himself, without consulting his advisers. German foreign minister Joachim von Ribbentrop summoned the American chargé d'affaires, Leland B. Morris, to his office and handed him the declaration. To the words printed on the page severing diplomatic ties, Ribbentrop added an extra verbal dagger aloud.

"Your president has wanted this war! Now he has it."

WHY WE FIGHT

In the months ahead, more than six thousand studio employees left for active military duty. On December 9, Frank Capra accepted a commission as a major in the Army Signal Corps to make propaganda films. His anti-Nazi activism had grown to where he'd made a pointed rebuke of how populism could curdle into Fascism in *Meet John Doe* (1941) earlier in the year. Given how viciously that film suggested Americans could fall under the sway of a Hitler figure, it's surprising that it actually made money. He was following it up by making an adaptation of the hit Broadway play *Arsenic and Old Lace*. Beyond that, he had no idea what he'd do. An attempt at finding a permanent new studio home following his years of service to Harry Cohn's Columbia had been frustrating, especially his negotiations with Charlie Chaplin to join United Artists (Capra called Chaplin "an absolute shit"). And he had been shaken when he learned from journalist William L. Shirer's book *Berlin Diary* that *It Happened One Night* (1934) was one of Adolf Hitler's favorite films. "That was the first bad thing I'd heard about *It Happened One Night*," Capra had said that year. "I was shocked and started to analyze it, but I gave it up. But I resent it like the devil."

Having also been a Sicilian immigrant, Capra clung to his adopted American identity even more fiercely than many of his American-born peers. Showing that he was as American as anyone seemed to be a perpetually urgent matter for him. Which is why decades later in his autobiography, *The Name Above the Title*, he still wrote of his new army commission with such obvious pride: "Two Signal Corps officers [one was screenwriter and future *Cape Fear* producer Sy Bartlett, now an army captain] came to

the studio stage to swear me in. I was in the Army. I asked for, and was granted, six weeks' leave of absence to finish, edit, and preview *Arsenic*. Nights, a tailor fitted me for uniforms. A little frightened by it all, I entered an Army-Navy store to try on caps and buy some major's leaves and Signal Corps crossed-flags insignia. I had no idea how to put them on, and neither did the tailor." Joining the army meant Capra resigning his presidency of the Directors Guild of America. He'd made a $125,000 salary from Warner Bros. for *Arsenic and Old Lace*, which he was hoping to use as leverage to lock in a long-term $250,000-per-picture salary. In the army, he'd make just $4,000 a year. He'd finish up *Arsenic and*

Much like how creative frustrations played a role in Jimmy Stewart seeking purpose outside of Hollywood by joining the Army Air Corps, Frank Capra was at a crossroads in his directing career. No one was being paid more to direct films, which may ultimately have led to fewer offers.

Old Lace (1944) by mid-January 1942, then wait for nearly three years until it could be released after the triggering of a clause in the adaptation rights that said the film could only open once the play closed. It's doubtful he was thinking much about that, though, because as soon as the shooting wrapped, this time it was Mr. Capra who went to Washington.

Capra could veer between swagger and insecurity with startling suddenness. At a meeting with General Frederick Osborn—head of the Morale Branch, dedicated to the creation of training and propaganda films—and Zanuck, who as a lieutenant colonel also outranked him, Capra bellowed, "In any discussion of film, where I sit is the head of the table." Maybe it's because he had experienced a blocker in his first immediate supervisor, Lieutenant Colonel Richard T. Schlosberg, who had been in charge of producing films for the Signal Corps since 1929—and was resolutely committed to avoiding Hollywood storytelling techniques. "You Hollywood big shots are all alike, a pain in the ass," Schlosberg told Capra. "If you can't get what you want, you cry. One Darryl Zanuck around here is enough."

Zanuck was on the move, though. After a quick return to Los Angeles to pick up the Best Picture Oscar his film *How Green Was My Valley* (1941) had won (its director, Ford, was in Hawaii working on the documentary *December 7th: The Movie* [1943]), Zanuck successfully petitioned General George Marshall, the army chief of staff, to serve as an advisory filmmaker in London, closer to the action. This satisfied Zanuck's taste for adventure. From his suite at Claridge's, London's most elegant hotel, he'd host viewing parties to watch the antiaircraft barrages during the still-ongoing Blitz. On one occasion he even accompanied Lord Louis Mountbatten as a US observer on a *coup de main* raid the new British Combined Operations head was launching on Saint-Valery, a coastal town in occupied France directly across the English Channel.

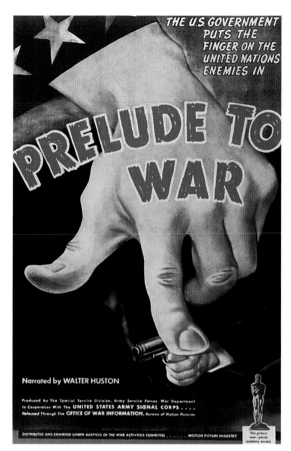

Prelude to War (1942) is what would have happened if you just took the voiceover-led essay-film parts of Confessions of a Nazi Spy and expanded them into an entire documentary. Originally intended just to motivate soldiers, Capra was so taken by his work that he campaigned to open it in theaters and win an Oscar for it—Hollywood ambitions he neglected to run by General Osborn of the Morale Branch.

Capra would have no such thrills. He'd spend the war shuttling back and forth between Washington and Hollywood. Having a direct line to General Osborn after his distasteful experience with Schlosberg, Capra received his first orders from the Morale Branch head: make a series of films about why the United States was fighting Germany and Japan. So Capra called the series simply *Why We Fight*. Anatole Litvak, the director of *Confessions of a Nazi Spy*, served under Capra, and it's hard not to detect the influence of the film that had set off such a firestorm in 1939 in all the *Why We Fight* films (1942–1945) that followed. In fact, Litvak co-directed five of them. These documentaries would be passionate appeals to emotion, mixing propagandistic narration (much like the emphatic voiceover in *Confessions*) with chilling newsreel footage of Nazis on the march, Axis propaganda films, and arresting animation, supplied by the Walt Disney Studios. Certain key moments Disney contributed in the first *Why We Fight* film, *Prelude to War*, first shown to troops later in 1942 and then to general moviegoers, are unforgettable: narrator Walter Huston talks about "the Nazi whale" swallowing up Europe, at which time the European territories under Nazi control, shaded black as was common on maps for the rest of the war years, morph into a whale with jaws that surround and then clamp down on Britain. The Japanese home islands become a scaly dragon.

To think that less than a year before audiences were watching a very different kind of Disney animation in *Dumbo*. Historian Steven Watts said that, even beyond the five hundred soldiers the studio was garrisoning, "within a few weeks of the Pearl Harbor attack the Disney fantasy factory had transformed itself into a wartime industrial plant." Disney's animators, sleeping on cots brought to the studio so they could work eighteen-hour days, created a short for the Treasury Department that they needed to deliver in weeks called *The New Spirit* (1942). Donald Duck, eager to take up arms against the enemy, learns, to his chagrin, that the single most important thing he could do to help the new war effort is pay his income tax: "Taxes to beat the Axis!" And by the time the studio finished

their contribution to *Prelude to War*, government contracts accounted for 93 percent of Disney's production. The studio was producing shorts on every conceivable subject, from how to spot enemy aircraft to how to use a tank-busting heavy rifle.

Prelude to War is about as persuasive as propaganda filmmaking can get. For all its appeals to emotion, animated Nazi whales and all, it also lays out the case against Fascism with surgical precision. It's ultimately the anti–*Triumph of the Will*. It doesn't supplant Hitler and Mussolini with a cult of personality around Roosevelt or Churchill; it speaks to higher ideals about what it means to be free. Walter Huston's narration compares two different ways of modern life: "This is the free world," he begins in his exploration of the Allies. "And this is the slave world," he continues, turning his attention to the Axis. Broad and simplistic, perhaps, but Capra fills in the details like a showy trial lawyer making a devastating closing argument. What's amazing is that the director was able to pull this off after nearly being willing to surrender himself when he first saw *Triumph of the Will*.

"The first time I saw that picture," Capra said of Leni Riefenstahl's film, "I said, 'We're dead. We're gone. We can't win this war.'" That was at a screening at New York's Museum of Modern Art in March 1942. Somehow within a few months he mustered an eloquent cinematic response. Indeed, of all the *Why We Fight* films, the one that feels most like Capra is *Prelude to War*, with its unique blend of the simplistic and the profound that had defined his biggest hits. It was the only one on which he was sole director, although he'd never take a credit on any of these films, preferring instead to champion the collective filmmaking effort. The other films bore the styles of others: he even lured away *Arsenic and Old Lace* screenwriters Julius and Philip Epstein, deep into the writing and development of Warner Bros.'s adaptation of *Everybody Comes to Rick's*, now titled

German schoolchildren taking their loyalty oath to Hitler, as seen in <u>Prelude to War</u>.

Casablanca (1942), to put that project aside for a bit and come to Washington, where desks at a makeshift office at the Library of Congress awaited them. Each being paid $20 a day, they'd end up contributing to all six of the remaining documentaries, though Capra's paranoia began to set in. Always fearful that, being a Sicilian immigrant, he wouldn't be thought of as American enough, he pored over the scripts (five other Hollywood writers had joined the Epsteins at the Library of Congress) to see if there were any coded Communist messages. "Frank thought everything was full of Communist propaganda," Leonard Spigelgass (screenwriter on 1942's *All Through the Night* and 1943's *The Youngest Profession*), one of the other *Why We Fight* writers, said. "If you said 'Hello' to Frank, you were a Communist."

Maybe there was a legitimate reason for Capra to feel so insecure. Of the $50 million the Armed Forces would spend on filmmaking during the war, Capra received only $400,000 to make all seven *Why We Fight* films. Ford, with the navy's Field Photo, had requested several million dollars a year for his budget, with 150 personnel and world travel. $400,000 was a fifth of what *Mr. Smith Goes to Washington* (1939) had cost. Capra's frustrations grew. He'd say that he "felt like a fool who'd turned his back on Camelot" by leaving Hollywood for the army. And he grew disenchanted with working with other Hollywood talents such as the Epsteins, ultimately preferring to make these movies with Morale Branch lifers who wouldn't question his orders. "We had to go back to *Casablanca*," Julius Epstein said. "And when we told him we were leaving he didn't raise any objections."

MOBILIZING STAR POWER

On December 10, 1941, the day after Capra joined the Signal Corps, some of Hollywood's biggest stars met at the Roosevelt Hotel to form the Hollywood Victory Committee. This group leveraged their celebrity in the most important way they could, by monetizing it; they'd embark on multipronged campaigns to raise money for the war effort. And money indeed needed to be raised.

The United States had just about put the Great Depression firmly in the past by the time of Pearl Harbor. But the country still wasn't financially prepared to conduct a world war on multiple continents and across the Pacific. Rationing was encouraged for a number of commodities deemed crucial to the war effort. Three million cars had been manufactured in the United States during 1941. After Pearl Harbor, only 139 more were made until after VJ Day. You had to keep your pre-1942 car in good shape during the war years. You weren't going to get another one new.

The sheer volume of money the government needed was unprecedented. Over the next four years, sixteen million men and women joined the Armed Forces, with an average service stint of thirty-three months. They needed to be paid, clothed, fed, and equipped. The median per capita income for a man in 1941 was $956 a year, while an enlisted man made only $855.96. Soldiers and sailors didn't just have to

Alan Mowbray and Henry Fonda visit troops at a base in the Mojave Desert on behalf of the Hollywood Victory Committee in 1942.

give up their careers for who knew how long, they also had to tighten their belts. That's a big part of why the men who served in the American military during World War II were primarily conscripts, not volunteers: 38.8 percent signed up voluntarily, while 61.2 percent were drafted.

The size of the American Armed Forces would also grow beyond any size previously imaginable. In 1939 there were 334,000 Armed Forces personnel, 50,000 of which were cavalry, with horses still expected to pull artillery. By 1941, with the introduction of the draft the previous year, that number had risen to 1.8 million. In 1942, it climbed to 3.9

ABOVE: FDR called for an unprecedented expansion of production capacity to produce weapons of war, such as the sturdy, reliable B-17 Flying Fortress, which was the backbone of the US bomber fleet. **OPPOSITE:** As this image from Connie Field's documentary <u>The Life and Times of Rosie the Riveter</u> (1980) attests, millions of women took war industry jobs to help ramp up the nation's production of the armaments needed to win.

million, then 9.2 million in 1943. By 1944, it was 11.6 million, and in the last year of the war 12.2 million—exponential growth from just six years earlier. FDR called for 60,000 war aircraft to be produced by the end of 1942, then 125,000 the next year. One hundred twenty thousand tanks were expected to be produced during the same period, along with 55,000 antiaircraft guns. At least this meant higher-paying government-subsidized jobs in war industries. Twenty-four million Americans took up these factory jobs, sometimes moving long distances to do so. Many of these migrating workers looking for better pay in war industries were women, now given the opportunity to make more money than many had ever dreamed of, in government contract jobs.

Much of 1942 was a "gearing up" year for the American forces. The production of personal automobiles had ceased, but General Motors made airplane engines, guns, trucks, and tanks. Rolls-Royce engines for Royal Air Force warplanes came off the Packard assembly lines. Chrysler made airplane fuselages. The skill and sophistication that American workers brought to these aircraft only grew over time: by the middle of 1944, it only took sixty-three minutes for Henry Ford's Willow Run plant near Detroit to produce, from start to finish, a B-24 Liberator bomber with more than 450,000 parts held together by 360,000 rivets.

The production capacity of the United States during this time is hard to overstate. Consider this: in the year 1944 alone, more planes were built in the United States than the Japanese had produced during the entire period from 1939 to 1945. American shipyards were so productive that by the fall of 1943 all of the Allied ships that had been sunk since 1939 had been replaced. Looking at the American war effort as an enormously vast ledger sheet, it's obvious: the Axis didn't stand a chance. But of course none of this production capacity would have mattered at all if the United States couldn't answer one question: How were they going to pay for it?

That's where Hollywood came in. Stars could leverage their celebrity to sell war bonds, government-guaranteed loans ordinary citizens made to the Treasury Department, with the promise of having that money repaid with nominal interest at a fixed time in the future. Essentially it went like this: you've paid all your taxes to the government, now you want to give extra money to the government as a loan, which eventually you'll get back with interest. As such, it was the Internal Revenue Service itself that issued war bonds. (To raise more money, the IRS had also reduced deductions taxpayers could claim.) FDR had inaugurated the voluntary Series E US Savings Bond back in April 1941 by buying the very first one; it was another move by his administration to lay the groundwork for fighting a war that was unavoidable. The idea the Hollywood Victory Committee came up with at that December 10, 1941, meeting at the Roosevelt Hotel was simple: stars would meet and mingle with ordinary people in tours all around the country and convince their fans to part with their money. And if a moviegoer couldn't attend one of these events, the IRS had set it up that they could buy war bonds along with their ticket and concessions at most movie theaters in the country.

The stars who gathered there, still all decked out in their most glittering ensembles, put politics to the side, even if their own embrace of wartime austerity took longer to arrive. The fight against Germany and Japan was an existential struggle that required unity and real leadership to set an example.

CAROLE LOMBARD: A STAR LOST

The chairman of the actors branch of the Hollywood Victory Committee was Clark Gable, flanked by his wife, Carole Lombard, at that Roosevelt Hotel meeting. They had been married for more than two years, since they tied the knot during a production break on *Gone with the Wind* (1939). It was his third marriage, and her second. They were both Midwesterners, she from Fort Wayne, Indiana, he from Cadiz, Ohio. Their nicknames for each other? "Ma" and "Pappy." In fact, they could hardly have been a more perfect match for each other: they shared the same rough-and-tumble sense of humor that seemed at odds with the gentility Hollywood usually tried to project. Suspicious of the possibility that Gable might stray before leaving on her own war bonds tour, Lombard left a naked, blonde mannequin in his bed to keep him company.

Gable and Lombard threw themselves enthusiastically into the war effort. They lent horses from their Encino ranch to a group of mounted air-raid wardens who patrolled the San Fernando Valley. On December 22, fifteen days after Pearl Harbor, Gable convened a meeting of the actors branch of the Victory Committee at the Beverly Wilshire Hotel, where he'd once lived. This event was considered one of the last all-out displays of Tinseltown glamour before more frugal days ahead. In attendance were Myrna Loy, Claudette Colbert, Charles Boyer, Bob Hope, Rosalind Russell, John Garfield, Bette Davis, Tyrone Power, Gary Cooper, Ginger Rogers, Ronald Colman, Irene Dunne, Jack Benny, and Cary

Grant—who had donated $100,000 of his $160,000 *Arsenic and Old Lace* salary to wartime charities. The women were dripping in jewels and furs. But all agreed that, in addition to the fundraising efforts they'd embark upon, they'd spend time visiting with and entertaining ordinary soldiers and sailors, particularly those who'd ended up in military hospitals. To start, those on the committee who were MGM stars hosted a Christmas Day party on the studio lot for enlisted men. Gable served as master of ceremonies for a nearly impromptu revue featuring Red Skelton, Eleanor Powell, Judy Garland, and Mickey Rooney. Wallace Beery played Santa Claus. Across

Lombard in her final film, <u>To Be or Not to Be</u> (1942).

town, Jimmy Stewart, on leave from Moffett Field for the holidays, played Santa Claus as well—at Henry Fonda's house for the amusement of Hank's four-year-old daughter, Jane.

The night before, on Christmas Eve, the public had heard "White Christmas" for the first time when Bing Crosby sang it on his NBC radio show *Kraft Music Hall*; this debut didn't make a big impression with the audience. Overall, it was a quiet Christmas in Hollywood: both a reprieve from the trauma of the previous eighteen days and a kind of collective deep breath in which everyone could brace themselves for the struggles to come. There was anxiety too about the possibility that the Japanese could next launch an air raid on Los Angeles. Or even attempt an invasion.

On Christmas Eve, Lombard had wrapped *To Be or Not to Be*. What she really wanted for Christmas was her husband in uniform. But it had to be real service, "not one of those phony commissions," she wrote. Gable wanted to sign up too, but he had one last film to make for Louis B. Mayer: a drama called *Somewhere I'll Find You* (1942), about innocents caught up in the Japanese conquest. It's believed Lombard even personally lobbied FDR to make sure her husband would be able to see action. First, though, she had a mission of her own.

Lombard embarked on a multicity tour to sell war bonds during the second week of January 1942. The Victory Committee was now working directly with the Treasury Department and Internal Revenue Service. With her husband starting to shoot *Somewhere I'll Find You*, she set out for Salt Lake City and then Chicago. She was filled with patriotic zeal at the enthusiasm of the crowds in these cities, telegraphing her husband, "Hey Pappy, you better get into this man's army." Finally she made it to Indianapolis so fans could cheer their fellow Hoosier who'd risen to Hollywood stardom. For her home state, Lombard had a fundraising target of $500,000 from the Treasury Department. Instead, in one day she raised $2 million.

Maybe Lombard thought that such a huge success meant she'd done her part. Or maybe rumors had reached her that Gable was allegedly having

Lombard and Gable inaugurated their marriage in 1939 with a slightly tongue-in-cheek domestic photo shoot, including images of the couple carving a turkey, tending a fireplace, using an air pump to blow up a raft, and playing with their dogs. The two of them seemed to share everything—including a boisterous sense of humor.

an affair with his costar Lana Turner. Either way, she canceled the rest of her trip, including the return journey to L.A. by train. She'd rush back to her husband by air. The tickets for herself and her mother were for TWA Flight 3, the next flight out of Indianapolis, at 4:00 a.m. on January 16. Nonstop cross-country travel was impossible in those days, so Flight 3 needed to make stops in St. Louis, Albuquerque, and Las Vegas. That model of aircraft, a Douglas DC-3-382 propliner, had a cruising speed of just 207 mph. So by the time it took off from Las Vegas at 7:05 p.m. Pacific Time for the final leg to Burbank, complete darkness had already fallen. At Albuquerque, fifteen of the nineteen passengers had been replaced by a contingent of Army Air Corps personnel and a new three-person crew. Since the flight overbooked, the Air Corps asked if Lombard and her mother could stay there overnight and catch the next plane. But Lombard argued that her fundraising efforts made her just as essential to be on that plane as any of the servicemen. Fifteen minutes after takeoff from Las Vegas, Flight 3 crashed into Potosi Mountain, hitting a vertical cliff face head-on about eighty feet from its top. The plane had strayed seven miles from its intended course.

When word of the crash reached MGM that night, Louis B. Mayer's crisis manager and "fixer" Eddie Mannix immediately arranged for him and Gable to travel to Las Vegas, booking them both bungalows at the El Rancho Vegas Hotel while search parties scoured the scene. Gable held out hope that his wife might still be alive. Wracked with worry, he stayed behind at the bungalow while Mannix went to the crash site. Gable thought a soft glow in the distance was flames from the wreckage. When Mannix got there, a grisly scene awaited. Blood and personal effects were sprinkled on the waist-high snow around the mangled fuselage; the bodies, compressed into a ten-foot space, unidentifiable at first glance. A little while later, Mannix sent

him a telegram: "No survivors. All killed instantly." All Mannix could find was a strand of blonde hair Gable would always believe had come from his late wife. Though he wanted to enlist in the Armed Forces, as his wife had wanted him to do, he still had to finish *Somewhere I'll Find You* for MGM—a film newly poignant even from its title alone.

Gable was never the same again. Though he had initially refused alcohol in the days after he received that fateful telegram in Las Vegas, saying he was "already numb," he'd start regularly drinking a quart of scotch a day, a habit he'd keep for the rest of his life. The "King of Hollywood" began to withdraw into himself.

Each day on set he took his meals alone in his trailer, never sitting in his usual chair at the end of a large table at the MGM commissary, where he had been known to hold court. It was almost like his throne, his seat of power where he lorded over the eight-thousand-square-foot dining room—as much a fixture for everyone who worked on the lot as Leo the Lion himself.

When Gable finally did enlist in the Army Air Forces in August 1942, some onlookers said they thought he had a death wish. He didn't. In fact, his work during the war, including his filming of a documentary, deserved more praise than it's ever properly received. But this was a heartbreak he'd never get over.

February 19, 1942, saw the premiere of Lombard's final film: *To Be or Not to Be*. In so many ways, the Jack Benny comedy from Ernst Lubitsch was as daring as *The Great Dictator*. And critics hailed it as a triumph for Lombard, if not in many other respects. In the sixteen months since Chaplin's film, the mood of the country had changed dramatically. No one wanted to laugh at Nazis now. Few took their ideology seriously, sure, but they were too great a threat to disarm with chuckles alone. Benny's own father walked out of the movie after seeing his son in a Nazi uniform. Lubitsch, Jewish like Benny, even had to defend to *The Philadelphia Inquirer* that he was not "a Berlin-born director who finds fun in the bombing of Warsaw." In the years after the war, people finally came to consider *To Be or Not to Be* one of Lubitsch's best films. Benny's own father, after furious explanations from his son, went to see it again. Giving it another chance, he loved it so much he ended up seeing it forty-six times.

Lombard had an incandescent final statement on film. It was not enough to allay Gable's grief. "Why did Ma have to go?" Gable kept asking his friends. "Did you ever see anyone more beautiful? There was never a person in the world who was as generous, who was so full of fun. God damn it, why Ma?"

It hadn't even been six weeks since Pearl Harbor when Lombard died on January 16, 1942. She was widely considered to be Hollywood's first casualty of the war. But she would not be the last.

Gable, in the Army Air Forces in December 1942, with MGM vice president Eddie Mannix, who gave him the terrible news about Lombard.

THE WAR OUGHTA BE IN PICTURES

"A world-shaking tragedy comes into our lives," said Mary Astor of the attack on Pearl Harbor. "And characteristically all anybody was thinking of was, 'How will it affect the picture?'" America's sudden entry into the war caused several filmmakers to shift gears on films they then had in production. *Holiday Inn* (1942), Mark Sandrich's film built around Irving Berlin songs, including "White Christmas," got an expanded Fourth of July sequence. In addition to a spectacular firecracker dance by Fred Astaire, Bing Crosby now sang "Song of Freedom," accompanied by newsreel images of American military might, culminating in a loving close-up of FDR.

James Cagney became associated with the George M. Cohan biopic *Yankee Doodle Dandy* (1942) after *The New York Times* had listed him as part of a group of suspected Hollywood Communists on its front page. Martin Dies's House Un-American Activities Committee had even cleared Cagney of the association, but the actor still told his producer brother William, "We're going to have to make the goddamndest patriotic picture that's ever been made. I think it's the Cohan story." The composer had written "You're a Grand Old Flag" and "The Yankee Doodle Boy," after all. In the wake of Pearl

Harbor, director Michael Curtiz added the coda in which "Over There" is reprised and Cagney's Cohan marches alongside a group of soldiers singing the song he wrote. Plus, the lyrics Cagney sings while his Cohan plays FDR on Broadway in the musical *I'd Rather Be Right*, something restaged for the movie, were altered. Larry Hart's original lyrics to "Off the Record" now became "I can't forget how Lafayette helped give us our first chance / To win our fight for liberty, and now they've taken France / We'll take it back from Hitler and put ants in his Japants / And that's *for* the record!"

Among the films to make a creative pivot after Pearl Harbor was Astor's follow-up to *The Maltese Falcon* (1941) called *Across the Pacific* (1942), also directed by John Huston. *Across the Pacific* was originally going to feature Humphrey Bogart journeying on a ship alongside a pretty fellow passenger (Astor) and several Japanese agents. Their destination? Honolulu, where the agents planned to blow up

Joe Totsuiko (played by Victor Sen Yung) comes across as an all-American guy. He was born in America. He loves baseball. He has no accent at all. In fact, he uses American slang and wears a straw hat. But he's completely loyal to Imperial Japan and is at the center of their plot to blow up the Panama Canal in <u>Across the Pacific</u>.

US Navy ships at Pearl Harbor. Remarkably, author Robert Carson had predicted the real-life attack in his *Saturday Evening Post* serial published the previous July on which *Across the Pacific* was based. As soon as the actual attack had occurred, Warner Bros. knew that, out of good taste, they had to change the story. Instead Bogart would thwart an attempt by Japanese agents, and their ally played by Sydney Greenstreet, to blow up the Panama Canal. The film halted production for three months to retool the script, but by that point, according to Astor, some of the Japanese characters had to be recast by Chinese actors.

The actual Japanese-American actors were no longer available; they had been interned in government camps. After President Roosevelt signed Executive Order 9066 on February 19, 1942, regional military commanders were allowed to expel anyone they felt was a threat to military security, or place them in government-run camps. About 112,000 Japanese-Americans were living on the West Coast, around 80,000 of whom were nisei ("second-generation" Japanese-Americans, born and raised in the United States, with full citizenship) or sansei (third generation). Military commanders did in fact order Japanese-Americans out of Alaska and out of major population centers in California, Oregon, and Washington. A few thousand left the region entirely, but most of these West Coast Japanese-Americans ended up in camps. (By contrast, the vast majority of the 150,000 Japanese-Americans living in Hawaii were not ordered to leave the islands or enter camps, perhaps just due to the logistical difficulty of carrying out such an order.) Astor said several nisei were employed on *Across the Pacific* initially.

Chinese-American actors, generally speaking, were more than willing to play Japanese parts in a negative way, given the massive suffering of China at the hands of the Japanese military. That's why San Francisco–born Chinese-American actor Victor Sen Yung stepped into the role of Joe Totsuiko, who seems calibrated as a walking justification for internment. The idea that Japanese-Americans were more loyal to Japan than to America is one based in racist assumptions and magnified by an unfortunate occurrence after the attack on Pearl Harbor. One of the Japanese Zero pilots who participated in the raid, his plane shot up by antiaircraft fire, couldn't make it back to the six Japanese aircraft carriers north of Oahu that had launched the attack. Instead, he made an emergency landing on the westernmost populated Hawaiian island, Ni'ihau. Once on the ground, three civilians of Japanese heritage gave him aid, until he was killed by five indigenous Ni'ihauans in pursuit. The fact that the Japanese-Americans in the Ni'ihau incident rushed to the aid of an Imperial Japanese fighter pilot set off a wave of paranoia, on top of reflexive racism, by US military commanders responsible for homeland security.

There can be no justification for the internment of Japanese-Americans during World War II. Forty-six years later, President Reagan, who in 1942 was prepping to shoot one of the first movies about American flyers in action after Pearl Harbor, *Desperate Journey* (1942), signed into law the Civil Liberties Act of 1988, which admitted the internment was based on "race prejudice, war hysteria, and a failure of political leadership." Every Japanese-American who had been interned, or their heir, then received $20,000 in reparations from the government.

War hysteria was very real on the West Coast in the first couple of months after Pearl Harbor. And that paranoia exploded into sheer panic a couple days before the 1942 Academy Awards.

WOULD AMERICA BE INVADED?

"The Battle of Los Angeles."

It wasn't really a battle, though you'd have been hard-pressed to convince Angelenos of that as it was happening. It was more a window into the fear that people had that American naval and air power had been so crippled at Pearl Harbor that a Japanese or German invasion of the United States couldn't be repelled. Fears centered largely on the Japanese: they had aircraft carriers—which the Germans never did, as Hitler preferred land-based bombers—so the Japanese could extend their air superiority much farther. The Japanese also had experience in amphibious landings dating back to their capture of Guangzhou in 1938. Germany had none, which was part of the reason Hitler ultimately called off an invasion attempt of Britain even as the Blitz was still raging.

Life magazine published elaborate multipage maps suggesting six possible invasion routes the Axis could carry out against the United States. Combining their forces completely with Japan (something that never actually happened), the Germans could attempt an invasion at New Orleans, by going up the St. Lawrence River, or, after invading Bermuda to use as a base for their long-range bombers, launching a frontal assault at Norfolk, Virginia. If the Japanese took the lead on the invasion themselves, without more than German naval assistance, they could hopscotch up the Aleutians and down the Pacific Northwest coast (probably the most likely scenario); or launch an all-out attack to control the Panama Canal, then march invasion forces up from Ecuador; or invade Hawaii and then attack San Francisco. It's hard to see how *Life's* illustrated maps contributed much that was useful

to its civilian readership, but they do convey the near panic that was gripping the country. Central to all six of these possible invasion scenarios would be "fifth columnists" living in the United States who'd spring into action to help Japan and Germany at the first sign of invasion: the message was that your Japanese and German neighbors could not be trusted.

On February 23, 1942, Japanese submarine I-17 opened fire with its surface cannon for twenty minutes on Santa Barbara starting at 7:15 p.m. Their target was the Ellwood oil field, and they destroyed one pump. In fact, since Pearl Harbor there had been seven Japanese submarines that patrolled the West Coast of the United States, attacking multiple merchant ships. This submarine shelling began during one of FDR's fireside chats, which were broadcast on the radio. Never had there seemed to be more of a disconnect between the president's reassurances and the threat that appeared to be bearing down. Especially given the terrorizing effect of Japan's lightning conquests throughout Southeast Asia immediately following Pearl Harbor: their invasion of the Philippines, which had been under US control since 1898, as well as Malaya and the Dutch East Indies. Not to mention that Japan had invaded Wake Island, capturing or killing the entire five-hundred-strong US Marine Corps garrison.

Then, late in the evening of February 24, and stretching into the wee hours of February 25, a rumor spread across Los Angeles County that a fleet of Japanese planes was en route for an aerial attack. At 2:25 a.m., air-raid sirens began sounding across the whole county and the authorities ordered a total blackout. For the next hour and forty-nine minutes, the antiaircraft artillery divisions based in the area,

The acting winners at the Academy Awards on February 26, 1942: Gary Cooper, Joan Fontaine, Mary Astor, and Donald Crisp, already in uniform with the United States Army Reserve, for which he'd rise to the rank of colonel during the war years. London-born, he had served in UK army intelligence during World War I. Until the ceremony two years later, the Supporting Actor and Actress winners received plaques instead of full-size statuettes —which had been the case since the supporting categories were introduced in 1937.

such as the group headquartered at the Disney studio, fired more than 1,400 shells into the air at what were suspected to be Japanese fighter planes. However, there were none at all. Secretary of the Navy Frank Knox said the next day it was "war nerves" that led to the panic. Maybe it was a stray weather balloon spotted in the night sky where it wasn't expected to be. People in L.A. were sure they'd seen something, but after the war the US government confirmed in the records of the Japanese military that they had never at any point flown planes over Los Angeles. Five American civilians were killed on the ground indirectly due to the antiaircraft fire, though. And the next day was the Academy Awards.

After Pearl Harbor and then the crushing blow to Hollywood that was the death of Carole Lombard, the Academy of Motion Picture Arts and Sciences governors had considered calling off the ceremony altogether. New AMPAS president Bette Davis suggested a scaled-back ceremony. To this point, the Oscars had been much like what the Golden Globes ceremony is today: a lavish banquet at which A-listers ringed large dinner tables, and then spent the announcement of the awards eating and, especially, drinking. Davis wanted to have the Oscars held in an auditorium instead, with the public allowed to attend as well via the purchase of tickets to benefit the Red Cross. The governors vetoed that plan, prompting Davis to resign her presidency just three weeks after she'd assumed it. The Academy Awards on February 26 would remain a dinner at the Biltmore Hotel, with the only real acknowledgment of the war being that formalwear was discouraged and there were no searchlights outside the hotel—hardly the thing after the Battle of Los Angeles, which newspapers around the country were suggesting had involved a government cover-up of a real attack.

Bob Hope hosted this fourteenth Academy Awards ceremony, his third year in a row. Wendell Willkie, just five months after he served as the industry's collective advocate before the Nye Committee, gave a speech praising Hollywood's films of the past year for "laying bare the vicious character of Nazi plotting and violence." Best Picture of 1941 went to *How Green Was My Valley*, accepted by Darryl F. Zanuck shortly before his relocation to London. Some of the evening's biggest names weren't there: *Valley*'s Best Director winner John Ford was in Honolulu working to save *December 7th: The Movie* (1943), which his *Grapes of Wrath* cinematographer Gregg Toland had turned into a bloated feature-length invective against Japanese-Americans that even internment-minded government officials found too racist. The only major event of awards season that Ford did attend was the New York Film Critics Circle dinner in early January, where he picked up that body's Best Director prize, having just returned from a photographic survey of Iceland to consider its potential as a US military staging area for General William "Wild Bill" Donovan's intelligence office. He'd then head to a similar assessment of the Panama Canal. Orson Welles was also absent, as he was in Brazil filming Carnaval for his documentary *It's All True*. He'd win Best Original Screenplay alongside his cowriter Herman J. Mankiewicz for *Citizen Kane*. When Welles's name rang out as the winner, hisses and boos were heard all around the ballroom from the pro-Hearst crowd. But other than Gary Cooper winning Best Actor for the decidedly prowar *Sergeant York*, the newly created Best Documentary category being stacked with war-related nominees, and the winner of Best Original Song being *Lady Be Good*'s "The Last Time I Saw Paris" (presumably a sympathy vote, given nearly two years of Nazi occupation at that point), you'd barely know a war was on.

ITCHY TRIGGER FINGERS

he hysteria that prompted the Battle of Los Angeles wasn't completely unfounded. The Japanese actually did launch a seaplane attack over Oregon later in 1942, as part of an attempt at creating a massive forest fire. They'd attack Oregon again in 1945 with a Fu-Go balloon bomb, a slow-moving method of aerial attack, that killed a pregnant woman and five children who were part of her pastor husband's Sunday school. They launched hundreds of such balloon bombs, some reaching as far as the outskirts of Detroit, but that one in Oregon was the only one to actually succeed in bringing death to the unsuspecting American public.

Producer Hal Wallis of Warner Bros. and director Howard Hawks planned for *Air Force* (1943) to be the first A-movie production to capture

John Garfield on the defensive in <u>Air Force</u>, which had to shoot scenes set in Hawaii and the Philippines in Tampa, Florida, due to the worry of inciting panic on the West Coast if the production flew aircraft painted in Japanese colors overhead. The movie captures those frantic early days of America's entry into the war, when victory was by no means guaranteed.

Stewart gives a broadcast on NBC in support of war relief alongside Major Tommy Power at Moffett Field in 1942.

the experience of Pearl Harbor and its aftermath, including the fighting in the Philippines. In part, it told the story of a flight of B-17 bombers that arrived at Oahu from the continental United States during the middle of the Pearl Harbor attack—an incident that actually happened. This meant repainting several American military aircraft in Japanese colors. But Wallis ultimately decided that the West Coast was simply too jittery to consider flying planes with Japanese markings overhead. He moved the filming of scenes that required the planes to Drew Army Airfield in Tampa, Florida—a tropical-enough setting to stand in for Hawaii and the Philippines. But even in Florida, war anxiety had a powerful effect. When the repainted aircraft flew over the Gulf of Mexico, a US Coast Guard ship still fired at them. It missed, thankfully.

Military action also affected the production of *Across the Pacific* by pulling its director, John Huston, midway through filming. He was on a career high, having directed *The Maltese Falcon* the previous year and earned two Oscar nominations (Adapted Screenplay for *Falcon*, and Original Screenplay for *Sergeant York*). But this was also the second film in a row he'd suddenly abandon. After *Falcon*, he directed *In This Our Life* (1942), an attempt at a "prestige" picture based on a Pulitzer-winning novel, which Huston thought signaled he'd arrived. It was also a chance for him to woo Olivia de Havilland, with whom he'd have an intense affair over the next few months. But as soon as Pearl Harbor happened he entered the Army Signal Corps as a lieutenant—he had accrued desirable military experience serving with the Mexican cavalry during the 1920s—and Raoul Walsh had to finish the picture. Huston was granted leave to make *Across the Pacific*. It was finally rushed into production in March, after having its script retooled away from its Pearl Harbor–centric plot and several of its Japanese-American actors being interned. Where *Falcon* had used wit and wordplay to give Bogart's Sam Spade his edge, here Bogie became a proto–Bruce Willis figure, forced to take on the Japanese all by himself as a one-man army. The film's climax actually takes place on December 6, 1941, complete with an awkward zoom-in to the date on a newspaper, so you're sure to understand precisely the significance of the moment.

But another problem presented itself: Huston had to report for active duty on April 22, and production on *Across the Pacific* was to continue until May 2. He'd have to abandon this film too. So he left the script deliberately unfinished for his successor, Vincent Sherman, to figure out. The final scene he'd written had Bogie tied up and held at gunpoint by the bad guys. "Bogie will know how to get out," Huston said. And with that, he was done with *Across the Pacific*. When they reunited after the war Bogart said, "John, you sonafabitch! Leaving me tied to a chair!"

Huston's first project for the Army Signal Corps was to help finish an eighteen-minute recruitment short called *Winning Your Wings* (1942), starring Second Lieutenant James Stewart. It begins with an airborne BT Trainer coming in for a landing. Once it stops, out climbs Stewart, wearing a flight suit and aviator sunglasses. Having been in the army for fourteen months and passed the Air Corps' officer school training, he was now using this kind of plane to teach other airmen how to become pilots. Stewart does a double take to the camera: "Well, hello. Gee, it looks like I'm back in the movies again, doesn't it?" What follows was as effective as any recruitment film of the war. He talks about the necessity for "the greatest mobilization in the history of the world," and that "this war we're fighting today, tomorrow, and the next day until we win is a war of the air." Stewart lays out what the Army Air Forces (the new name as of March for what had been the Army Air Corps) needed: two million men, among them fifteen thousand captains, forty thousand lieutenants, and thirty-five thousand flying sergeants. He then goes about interviewing different people, obviously actors, who think they might not be the best fit to become airmen: a guy who has a year left in college, a college athlete worried about his grades, a twenty-six-year-old gas station attendant and family man (twenty-six then being the usual cutoff for air forces enlistment), even a high school kid. He allays all their fears and makes what's unquestionably a hard sell, touting "the effect those shiny little wings will have on a gal." *Winning Your Wings* hit theaters on May 28, a little over a month after Huston abandoned *Across the Pacific* for good, and it's believed to have resulted in 150,000 new recruits. Talk about tangible results. Who needs Uncle Sam and "I Want You!" when you could have Jimmy Stewart? But the film is compromised in one critical respect: only possible recruits who were white were featured. It was felt that depicting Black flyers would cause some white men to decide not to sign up. The Armed Forces were segregated at this point, but units of all-Black airmen were already being trained, especially those currently in flight school at Alabama's Tuskegee Institute. It's an omission in *Winning Your Wings* that speaks to the stark, virulent racism that pervaded the country.

FIGHTING FOR FREEDOM ABROAD WITH NONE AT HOME

I n May 1942, William Wyler, who'd just finished directing *Mrs. Miniver*, would try to give Black recruits their due. He had accepted an assignment from Capra to make a film called *The Negro Soldier* (1944). They'd attempt to celebrate Black excellence and show why Black men should enlist in the Armed Forces, despite the systemic racism that touched almost every aspect of their lives. Wyler embarked on a trip across the American South to conduct research for the project. He was so appalled by the racism he witnessed that he withdrew from the project, concluding that he couldn't understand why Black men would want to risk their lives for a country that barely recognized them as human beings.

This fundamental question—why fight to bring democracy to others while being barely allowed to participate in democracy themselves?—is something that the white gatekeepers of Hollywood tried to reckon with for the Black audience. As early as February 1942, Lowell Mellett, the newspaperman

FDR appointed to be a liaison between the government and the motion picture business at large, told Hollywood's moguls that they needed to increase Black representation in their films. Black actors needed to have better roles, not just stereotypical portrayals that reaffirmed long-standing cultural biases. There needed to be studio-made productions with all-Black casts to specifically target the Black audience. And even when just presenting crowd scenes or any other kind of moment in which extras might be used, Black people should be present. Mellett felt this was important culturalization for the white audience: if they got used to seeing Black Americans onscreen more often, they might be more accepting of them in day-to-day situations in real life too, including when they encountered them in the Armed Forces or in military-adjacent jobs. The hope was that it would also make African-Americans feel like they were fully a part of the fabric of America, and have enough of a stake in the country that they'd be willing to fight for it.

Members of the St. Louis chapter of the NAACP call for meaningful anti-lynching legislation on January 25, 1942, following a white mob pouring gasoline on Cleo Wright and burning him alive in Sikeston, Missouri, after a Black man had reportedly attacked two white women. Black residents of Sikeston had been forced to permanently flee the town. Injustices like this called into question why Black Americans should support the war effort at all.

Rex Ingram, right, along with Sabu and June Duprez, on the set of The Thief of Bagdad. Ingram played the genie, part of a career of distinctive, memorable roles.

Early concepts for *The Negro Soldier* included a pointed debunking of the idea that Japan's military successes should give hope to the "colored" races of the world, an idea sometimes seized upon by white racists to suggest that a Negro-Japanese alliance could be possible. Japan did attempt to reach African-Americans via shortwave radio propaganda throughout the war: they'd force Black POWs to go on air and make broadcasts about how well they had been treated by the Japanese in contrast to how they were treated back home. One Japanese broadcast specifically focused on lynching, then still a widespread horror throughout the United States (and not just in the South)—the broadcast concluded, "Notorious lynchings are a rare practice

even among the most savage specimens of the human race." These broadcasts struck a nerve; the NAACP even made note of them. Though few African-Americans at the time had shortwave radios, historians Sato Masaharu and Barak Kushner say the broadcasts "evoked a variety of responses within the Black community and the sum total of these reactions forced America's government to improve conditions for Blacks in the military and society."

One impact of the new sensitivity Hollywood gave the depiction of Black lives showed up right away: on August 20, 1942, George Stevens's *The Talk of the Town* premiered, and a Black character played by Rex Ingram was, though a personal valet to Ronald Colman's character, decidedly

Hattie McDaniel in charge of a group of entertainers about to perform at Minter Field, near Bakersfield, California.

nonstereotypical. Cultured, soft-spoken, and intentionally seeming like a Black doppelgänger of Colman, Ingram's Tilney is not a servant so much as an employee—and someone whom Colman turns to for advice, not because he's especially wise, but as a friend.

African-American actors contributed to the war effort directly, and with as much vigor as anyone. Hattie McDaniel was the head of the Negro Division of the Hollywood Victory Committee and threw herself into wartime activities throughout 1942. In April, she sang and danced for a group of airmen at the San Bernardino Army Air Field. In June she emceed a multi-act show at nearby Camp Hahn. And then three months before the start of the Hollywood Canteen, McDaniel organized an

event for servicemen on leave in Hollywood that involved a parade and bowling. With the exception of the Hollywood event, these were for all-Black crowds. But further up north, Paul Robeson led a rousing rendition of "The Star-Spangled Banner" at a morale-boosting event for an integrated crowd of Oakland Shipyard workers that September. He had made a landmark recording with "Chee Lai (Arise!)," a patriotic battle cry for China—now it was time to do the same for his own country's national anthem. Finally, in August 1942, McDaniel played her largest integrated audience yet at a massive victory rally to sell war bonds in Indianapolis, Carole Lombard's final stop seven months earlier. Speaking to the crowd of forty thousand, she made no mention of her race and spoke in terms of unity. "They are fine and clean and brave," she said of the soldiers she had encountered on her camp shows in previous months. "Their lives have been interrupted. They have put aside professions, college careers, love affairs, all the things that make up a rich, full life; the way of life that has always been called 'The American Way.' I have not found a grumbler in the bunch."

Meanwhile, McDaniel's *Gone with the Wind* costar Butterfly McQueen often appeared as a comedian on the Armed Forces Radio Service show *Jubilee*, a program geared to Black servicemen that began in 1942 and continued until 1953. The host was Ernie "Bubbles" Whitman. Here McQueen could be herself: still be funny, yes, but so that people laughed with her rather than at her, as had arguably been the case in *Gone with the Wind*, in which, because of her high-pitched voice—"I don't know nothin' 'bout birthin' babies!"—she's basically coded as stupid. "I didn't mind playing a maid the first time, because I thought that was how you got into the business," she said. "But after I did the same thing over and over, I resented it. I didn't mind being funny, but I didn't like being stupid." On *Jubilee*, she could be funny without being the punchline—and provide entertainment that respected the taste and intelligence of the show's Black servicemen audience. By the end of 1942, there were almost three hundred thousand African-American enlistees who'd volunteered for the Armed Forces.

Hattie McDaniel, appearing on an NBC broadcast in 1942. She threw herself into entertaining the troops as much as anyone in the first nine months after Pearl Harbor.

FIFTY MOVIE STARS BOARD A TRAIN . . .

"Entertainment is always a national asset," President Roosevelt said. "Invaluable in time of peace, it is indispensable in wartime." Carole Lombard had shown just how much money star power could raise to fill the government's coffers. Three months after her death, the US Treasury Department sponsored the Hollywood Victory Caravan, a fourteen-city train tour across the country, in which fifty stars staged multihour shows when they disembarked. Tickets cost $11, with the proceeds going directly to the government. Cary Grant, Laurel and Hardy, James Cagney, Humphrey Bogart, Barbara Stanwyck, and Desi Arnaz were on board when the train left Los Angeles on April 26, 1942. "They had no trouble getting stars," Bob Hope said. "Who in Hollywood had the guts to tell the IRS he was going to be out of town?" Four days later they reached the East Coast and their first major stop: Washington, DC. These luminaries joined Eleanor Roosevelt for tea at the White House and then staged an elaborate photo shoot on the front lawn, in which they were also accompanied by Joan Blondell, Charles Boyer, Risë Stevens, Merle Oberon, Eleanor Powell, Frances Langford, Claudette Colbert, Joan Bennett, and Groucho Marx—all proudly flanking the First Lady. Present as well were Bing Crosby and Bob Hope, who served as masters of ceremony for each

Dick Powell, Fred Astaire, Paul Henreid, Betty Hutton, Kay Kyser, Greer Garson, Judy Garland, Mickey Rooney, Harpo Marx, James Cagney, and Lucille Ball, photographed at one of the stops of the Hollywood Victory Caravan.

stop's whiz-bang show, and director Mark Sandrich, fresh off completing *Holiday Inn*, who directed each of the Caravan's numbers.

The Caravan couldn't have come at a better time: America faced its darkest hour of the war. On April 9, after holding out for four months, the US Army forces that had fought so valiantly to slow the Japanese invasion of the Philippines surrendered at Bataan, a peninsula that jutted out protectively in front of the mouth of Manila Bay. A total of sixty-four thousand Filipino soldiers and twelve thousand American soldiers became Japanese prisoners of war. Never before, not even during the Civil War, had such a large group of US military personnel been captured. The United States had controlled the Philippines for over forty years;

Lieutenant Colonel James Doolittle's assembled B-25B bombers on the deck of the USS <u>Hornet</u> on April 18, 1942, shortly before takeoff on the raid of Tokyo that gave the US public a much-needed morale lift after the year's devastating losses. It would be immortalized in <u>Thirty Seconds Over Tokyo</u> (1944).

Manila harbor was considered the finest deepwater port in all of East Asia, an astonishing prize for Japan to claim to defend its new holdings nearby in the East Indies and Malaya. It's hard to imagine anything more traumatic to US belief that it was possible to win this war, unless the Japanese had in fact invaded Hawaii. The US Army withheld the

most horrific news from the public for two years: after the Filipino and American forces surrendered, the Japanese forced them on a sixty- to seventy-mile march north to what would become their new POW camp, the former US Army base Camp O'Donnell. Thousands of Filipinos and at least six hundred American soldiers died during the movement, later known as the Bataan Death March.

After this catastrophe, America at least did score a psychological victory—if not in any way a tactical or strategic one—with the Doolittle Raid, in which sixteen B-25B bombers launched from the USS *Hornet* on a mission to bomb Tokyo itself. The goal was to scare the Japanese and show that even their capital wasn't safe—and even more importantly, to have a morale-boosting "win" to lift American spirits when

there was nothing else but losses to speak of. John Ford was on the *Hornet* to film the bombers taking off. The April 18 bombing of Tokyo accomplished nothing militarily. It even, by design, resulted in the pilots of all sixteen B-25s bailing out and crashing the planes in China afterward since they didn't have enough fuel for a return trip. But it showed how boosting morale could be so desperately important:

James Doolittle, the lieutenant colonel who planned the raid, was later promoted to command most of the air forces operations against the Axis in Europe. But less than three weeks after the psychological victory above Tokyo, the last Filipino-American stronghold, the island of Corregidor in Manila Bay, which served as a Gibraltar-type fortification looming over ships passing in and out, fell on May 6, and another eleven thousand became prisoners of the Japanese. By the end of May, about forty American POWs died each day in the appalling conditions of the Japanese camps.

America had been knocked off its feet. How refreshing then to have the celebration of American excellence that was the Hollywood Victory Caravan shows. Each show lasted about three and a half hours and much of it was restaged in 1945 for the nineteen-minute Paramount short simply titled *Hollywood Victory Caravan*, which gave moviegoers a sense of what the tour had been like if they had missed it in person. As Hope later put it, the show was a mix of "popular songs, dances, comedy sketches, dramatic scenes and readings, even operatic arias." It was all parts razzle-dazzle, from Betty Hutton singing "Plain Jane Doe (The Sweetheart of the USO)" while hoofing with a line of chorus girls in WAC uniforms, to Carmen Cavallaro leading his orchestra in Gershwin tunes, to Crosby and Hope trading quips, to finally a serious, from-the-heart appeal by Humphrey Bogart in his no-nonsense style about why it all mattered. One of the liveliest numbers came from New York–born Puerto Rican singing star Olga San Juan, whose act, Hope joked, was "from south of the border but north of the Hays office." When she slaps him after he attempts to steal a kiss, he says, "She just set back the Good Neighbor Policy eight years."

The Santa Fe railroad donated fourteen cars to the Caravan, including two that had portable dance floors and bolted-down pianos so the stars could rehearse their acts. "We all came in on a special train called the Victory Train," Hope said. "I don't know why they call it the Victory Train. I sat next to Merle Oberon for 3,000 miles and I'm still calling her Miss Oberon." After Washington, the tour went to Boston and Philadelphia, then swung through Cleveland, Detroit, and the Midwest before ultimately ending up in Houston, where the train journey concluded on May 12.

There had been one ray of hope just four days earlier: the US Navy engaged a Japanese fleet off the New Guinea coast in what became known as the Battle of the Coral Sea. The United States had arguably suffered a tactical loss, including the sinking of the aircraft carrier USS *Lexington*. But the action had been sufficient enough to prevent any Japanese advance on the New Guinea town of Port Moresby as well as a possible invasion of Australia. It also made it easier for General Douglas MacArthur—the US Army Forces in the Far East commander, now based in Australia himself after vowing "I shall return" upon fleeing the Philippines—to consider the first US counteroffensive of the war at Guadalcanal that August.

On May 19, the Victory Caravan, having left the train in Texas, played one final stop in San Francisco. The tour had raised over $800,000. This phenomenal success spurred other stars to consider different gimmicks for supporting the war effort. In June Clark Gable decided to follow in his late wife's footsteps and embark on his own war relief tour. Joining him was Lana Turner, his costar in *Somewhere I'll Find You*, to be released by MGM on August 27. Turner inaugurated a new idea: selling kisses to the highest bidder. To start, she sold two kisses to one man in Portland, Oregon, for a $5,000 bond. And they kept escalating. Soon thereafter she sold just one kiss to an elderly man for $50,000. Using this strategy, she'd raise $5.25 million in just ten days.

Navy men climb down ropes to escape the burning USS <u>Lexington</u> at the Battle of the Coral Sea on May 8, 1942. A Navy destroyer then fired upon the derelict aircraft carrier and sent it to the bottom of the sea to keep it out of Japanese hands.

PART
III

TURNING POINTS

1942-1943

Bob Hope, in a publicity shot for 1941's <u>Caught in the Draft</u>, became the ultimate wartime entertainer—and synonymous with the USO.

THANKS FOR THE MEMORIES

It was Lana Turner's fundraising strategy of selling kisses that Bob Hope went on to satirize in the 1945 *Hollywood Caravan* short. "I only sold one and Boris Karloff wants his money back," he joked. Watching that short, it's obvious that Hope was the perfect master of ceremonies for such a tour: as far from a heartthrob as any man in Hollywood, Hope was not someone the troops could find threatening for his sex appeal. He was not someone the boys had to worry about stealing their girl while they were off in uniform (the way many worried about just such a thing with Frank Sinatra). Hope was a conduit to Hollywood glamour, one who introduced starlets the soldiers lusted after, but always somehow apart from it. In part, this was due to his unique brand of self-deprecating humor—"I would have won the Academy Award if not for one thing . . . my pictures"—and the fact that, though he appeared in movies, no one really considered him an actor. Hope was a personality. One big enough to host both the Oscars as well as countless shows for soldiers, sailors, marines, and airmen all over the world. His USO shows became his signature, and in doing them he helped create the idea of the stand-up comedian.

However, Hope initially had to be cajoled into performing for the troops at all. He wasn't certain it was the best thing for his career or for the troops—why would they find him funny? But from his first performance for the USO on May 6,

1941, at March Field, he was sold. Ostensibly, he was there to promote his new movie *Caught in the Draft* (1941), which resonated with the draftees in attendance since FDR's conscription order of the previous year had caused a high level of resentment. Seven months before Pearl Harbor, the draftees, most of whom had been called up the previous October for a twelve-month stint, had one motto: "O.H.I.O."—"Over the Hill in October," when they'd finally be let out of the service. But the crowd in attendance loved him. "We soon discovered you had to be pretty lousy to flop in front of these guys," Hope said. "They yelled and screamed and whistled at everything."

Hope had found his favorite audience. "We

Paulette Goddard serves as caddy for Bob Hope at 1942's Victory Golf Tournament in Hollywood. Proceeds went to the Citizen's Committee for the Army and Navy.

LEFT: During an appearance to entertain the troops on the Armed Forces Radio Network show <u>Command Performance</u>, Bob Hope is smitten with his fellow entertainer's zoot suit. **ABOVE:** Bob Hope with African-American soldiers in Britain in 1943. **BELOW:** Bob Hope golfing for the troops.

Bob Hope putting on a USO show for American servicemen in Britain in 1943.

made a great point of researching the military lingo, favorite watering holes, and commanders' last names," Hope wrote near the end of his long life in 2003. "The stern military regime evoked laughs, as did the soldiers' resentments, hardships, and habits. They laughed at me, but most of all they laughed at themselves. This was the beginning of my love for the GI."

After the Hollywood Victory Caravan wrapped up on May 19, 1942, Hope set out on a sixty-five-show tour to perform for the troops at military bases and hospitals. Like his initial performance at March Field, these shows were organized under the auspices of the USO, or the United Service Organizations, which had been founded in February 1941 at the urging of FDR. The USO represented the coming together of six civilian organizations—the Salvation Army, the YMCA, the YWCA, National Catholic Community Service, the National Travelers Aid Association, and the National Jewish Welfare Board—that worked directly with the Department of War to, in the words of the president, "handle the on-leave recreation of the men in the Armed Forces." Frances Langford, Jerry Colonna, Tony Romano, and Patty Thomas joined Hope on his tour—each being paid just $10 a day, since it was figured celebrities could afford to donate their time—and in September they'd made their way to Alaska, with stops in Galena and Nome. They were just 1,051 miles away from the nearest Japanese forces, probably making them the US wartime entertainers who'd been closer to "the action" than any others thus far.

Over two days, on June 3 and 4, a couple dozen Nakajima B5N2 torpedo bombers rained fire on Dutch Harbor in the town of Unalaska, destroying an oil repository and a hospital. Two days later, five hundred Japanese soldiers invaded the island of Kiska, capturing the ten sailors stationed at the small US Navy base there. The next day they claimed Attu, the westernmost island in the Aleutians. It was the first time since the War of 1812 that American soil had been conquered by an enemy force. Kiska and Attu featured only a civilian population of the Indigenous Unangax̂ people, whom the Japanese later relocated to concentration camps in Hokkaido. By the time of Hope's Alaska trip, the United States had responded by occupying the island of Adak, exactly 246 miles east of Kiska. Based at Adak at that moment was the director John Huston, assigned with making a film about how the US Army Air Forces was turning the island into an air base. The Corps of Engineers used prefab materials to build a runway on Adak from scratch. From there, pilots flew B-24 Liberators to bomb Japanese targets on Kiska, presumably stopping the Japanese from building their own runways—the fear was

that they could then launch long-range bombers to target at least Seattle. During his four months on Adak, Huston tagged along on a B-24 for several of these bombing missions. One time when he was standing over a gunner's shoulder to take some film, the gunner fell before him, shot dead by enemy fire inches away from where Huston himself stood.

Huston's resulting film, *Report from the Aleutians* (1943), was a work of strange beauty, showing the remarkably inhospitable climate of these remote North Pacific islands—all mud, rocks, and moss— that army engineers had to overcome to complete an air base. It also showed just how sprawling the war effort really was: imagine any climate and the war was probably being fought there.

THE GOOD NEIGHBOR POLICY VS.
THE MAGNIFICENT AMBERSONS

J ust at the moment that Huston and Hope were leaving for the far north, Orson Welles was returning from way down south. Down South American way, specifically. He had spent over six months in Rio contributing to the Good Neighbor Policy, easily making him the most high-profile Hollywood talent to spend significant time in Brazil since Walt Disney. It's hard to over-state how critical diplomatic outreach to the "ABC"

countries—Argentina, Brazil, and Chile—was at that moment. The March 2 *Life* magazine spread that imagined six possible invasion scenarios for the Axis to attack the United States included South America: "Plan Four is the much-discussed invasion by way of Gibraltar-Dakar-Natal-Trinidad, which President Roosevelt's Good Neighbor Policy has tried to defend against." Natal, one of Brazil's east-ernmost cities, would have made an ideal rallying

Week-End in Havana, starring Alice Faye and Carmen Miranda, was Miranda's third Hollywood film and biggest hit to that point. The Hollywood Reporter at the time said that the Fox production spent a month in Havana for "atmosphere shots" and "process plates."

point for Axis land and long-range air forces to regroup after crossing the Atlantic. In fact, before she'd died, Carole Lombard had even been planning a speech praising the culture and character of the ABC countries to help the Good Neighbor Policy. A copy of the speech in her handbag had helped Eddie Mannix identify her body.

Carmen Miranda's career had only grown since her breakout Hollywood smash, *Down Argentine Way* (1940). Early in 1941 she was invited to be the first Latin American star to enshrine her handprints and footprints in a cement block outside Grauman's Chinese Theatre. Her next films for 20th Century Fox, *That Night in Rio* (1941) and *Week-End in Havana* (1941), built on *Argentine*'s success. As you can tell, each of these movies was set in a different country: Zanuck's idea for casting as wide of a net for the Good Neighbor Policy as possible. But box-office success aside, Miranda was still beholden to a deeply unfair original contract she'd signed with the Shuberts—the producers who first brought her to America to star on Broadway—which gave them half of her earnings. Don Ameche, costar in her first two films, helped her negotiate more equitable representation, and visibility. With Miranda now getting second billing, *Week-End in Havana* bowed just one week after *Citizen Kane* expanded nationwide and immediately dethroned it from the top of the box office. *Kane* was only ever number one in that first weekend.

Welles may have had other reasons to commit such a significant chunk of 1942 to his Brazil trip. As being dethroned so quickly from the top of the box office might suggest, *Citizen Kane* had lost $160,000 in its initial run. In October 1941 he'd begun work on *The Magnificent Ambersons* (1942), production of which stretched into January, but relations with his distributor, RKO, were becoming strained. Nelson Rockefeller—a major stakeholder in RKO, and now the head of the OCIAA in charge of Good Neighbor

Policy work—had John Hay Whitney reach out to Welles about becoming a goodwill ambassador. The night of Pearl Harbor, Welles said on the *Gulf Screen Guild Theater* radio show, "We've got a nerve calling ourselves Americans all the time, when we're really only United Staters. We're a little selfish about that. It's America down there in Chile too, all the way down the spine of the Andes. If any of you folks are hearing this down around Mexico, or Honduras, or Salvador, or Argentina . . . or even if you're an Eskimo in the Arctic, we hope you'll overlook our calling ourselves Americans as if we were the only ones in the hemisphere. We do that just because it's so much easier to say than anything else . . . and also because it sounds so good."

On December 22, Whitney telegrammed the director with an offer to make a documentary about Rio's Carnaval: "Personally believe you would make great contribution to hemisphere solidarity with this project." But before he could leave, Welles not only had to finish *Ambersons*, he had to act in Norman Foster's fellow Mercury Theatre film *Journey into Fear* (1943) in January 1942—and he had to give sufficient notice to CBS about winding down his weekly radio show. Welles was starting to take on so much work that it was inevitable he would take his eye off certain projects. Acting in *Journey into Fear* (plus, handling some uncredited directing work on it, and rewriting the script with Joseph Cotton), while finishing up directing *Ambersons*, and then departing for Rio to make his Carnaval documentary—trusting *Ambersons*' final cut to his editor Robert Wise and RKO—was highly unwise. The cast and crew on *Journey into Fear* worked for twenty-four hours straight to finish Welles's scenes before he departed. By that point Welles had decided that his Carnaval footage would comprise just one segment of an anthology film—kind of like live-action versions of the anthology films Disney was making from his Good Neighbor trip. He already had one segment

done and dusted: a short filmed in Mexico by Foster the previous year called *My Friend Bonito*, about a young boy's friendship with a bull destined to face a matador in the arena.

"*It's All True* was not going to make any cinematic history, nor was it intended to," Welles said after the war. "It was intended to be a perfectly honorable execution of my job as a goodwill ambassador, bringing entertainment to the Northern Hemisphere that showed them something about the Southern one." On a pit stop in Miami, he threw together a rough cut of *Ambersons* with Wise, and recorded the narration you hear in the film. "I went to the projection room at about four in the morning, did the whole thing," Welles said of his final work on *Ambersons*, which took place February 4. "And then got on the plane and off to Rio—and the end of civilization as we know it." He started shooting Carnaval four days later. In addition to his filming work, he'd make radio broadcasts both to the Brazilian people and aimed back at the United States with messages of goodwill from Brazil. One

Welles wasn't spending six months in Rio just to make a film. He was there for cultural outreach—the city was Brazil's capital at the time. But of course, there was always time for fun at a Carnaval club.

----

broadcast for NBC Blue on April 18 was simply titled "President Vargas's Birthday," a half-hour tribute to the strongman running the country. He'd give in-person lectures and talks to local audiences on subjects such as visual art and Shakespeare, much like Disney's "El Grupo" had. Disney's staffers on that trip were at least being paid. Welles, dedicated to the idea of this cultural outreach as pure service, neither received nor requested any payment. It was his pleasure to be a cultural ambassador. It's also possible he had a covert additional role: to gather intelligence for use in the war about what Vargas and his neighbors were really up to. This was all too much for any one person to handle and expect to keep their vision on their film projects intact. To use the kind of language Welles often employed on his

radio shows . . . little did he know that what followed next would result in total disaster.

Film historian Catherine L. Benamou puts it like this: "The ambassadorial appointment would be the first in a series of turning points leading—in 'zigs' and 'zags,' rather than in a straight line—to Welles's loss of complete directorial control over both *The Magnificent Ambersons* and *It's All True*, the cancellation of his contract at RKO Radio Studio, the expulsion of his company Mercury Productions from the RKO lot, and, ultimately, the total suspension of *It's All True*." After the Pan Berman / Samuel Briskin era at RKO, the studio fell into the hands of George Schaefer, the most supportive backer Welles ever had in Hollywood and would ever have. But after major financial losses in 1941 and 1942, Schaefer was out as studio president, and so was his ally on the board: Nelson Rockefeller, who had arranged for Welles to go to South America in

RKO took the footage Welles, seen here on a break from shooting in the northeastern Brazilian town of Fortaleza on June 26, 1942, had shot and dumped it into the sea. That is not a metaphor. Only small fragments of what would have been It's All True exist.

the first place. Charles Koerner took over in June 1942 and announced a new motto for the studio: "Showmanship in Place of Genius: A New Deal for RKO." Welles knew this was a swipe at him.

Without the director's input, RKO ordered Wise to cut forty-three minutes from the preview version of *Ambersons*, which had already been cut by seventeen minutes. Wise complied. He maintained throughout his life that he was proud of the eighty-eight-minute final cut, which had a shabby new "happy" ending (admittedly much like that of Booth

Tarkington's original novel). Composer Bernard Herrmann did not feel likewise. He ordered that his name be taken out of the credits. Welles said he never would have gone to South America if RKO had not given him assurances he would be allowed to finish editing the film there. "And they absolutely betrayed me and never gave me a shot at it," he said. "You know, all I could do was send wires . . . But I couldn't walk out on a job which had diplomatic overtones. I was representing America in Brazil, you see. I was a prisoner of the Good Neighbor Policy. That's what made it such a nightmare. I couldn't walk out on Mr. Roosevelt's Good Neighbor Policy with the biggest single thing that they'd done on the cultural level, and simply walk away. And I couldn't get my film in my hands."

RKO did in fact send Welles a full-length workprint of *Ambersons* for him to fiddle with while in Rio. That has enticed cinephiles ever since to think that it might still be sitting somewhere in Brazil, awaiting recovery and restoration, to this day. Otherwise, what is known to be true is that the studio took those excised portions of the film and destroyed them. Welles's theory was that since the studio was restructuring, it actually made better financial sense to Koerner to play up the expense of the film, the losses incurred—*Ambersons* lost $620,000 in release, compared to *Kane*'s $160,000—and use the failure as a tax write-off. That was actually more lucrative than if the film had been a hit.

Seeking to sever ties with Welles altogether, RKO, unconcerned about appearing unpatriotic by breaking off their commitment to the Good Neighbor Policy, then did the same thing to *It's All*

Some incomplete fragments of It's All True, such as this scene in color, were restored and made available to the public in 1993.

True. They canceled the film, rendering Welles's time in Rio, aside from his lectures, radio broadcasts, and in-person forms of cultural outreach, a waste. He had shot two hundred thousand feet of film at Carnaval. In the late sixties or seventies, RKO's new corporate overlords (it had long since ceased to be an actual studio) dumped that footage into the Pacific Ocean. "It was a tax write-off, so they lost nothing," Welles later said. "Otherwise they would have been struggling to get something out of it. However bad, they could have made a bad musical out of just the nightclub footage. They would have got a return on their money. But they didn't want a return on their money. It was better for them to drop it in the sea, which is what they did."

Welles's time in Rio had come to an end. "So I was fired from RKO," he later recalled. "And they made a great publicity point of the fact that I had gone to South America without a script and thrown all this money away. I never recovered from that attack." Welles's Hollywood fortunes would never be the same. All his more ephemeral, in-person cultural diplomacy may have helped tie Brazil that much closer to the United States, however. He had lost his creative battles, and he'd have to fight a virtual war to get every single one of his films made after this. But in his own way, he'd helped his country win the war.

As Welles was preparing to leave, Disney finally unveiled the fruits of its South America trip, the compilation film *Saludos Amigos*, on August 24, 1942, with a world premiere in—where else?—Rio de Janeiro. Intended not as a moneymaking endeavor but as goodwill outreach, the film actually surprised by grossing over $1 million in worldwide box-office rentals, meaning that the subsidy the government had promised Walt Disney wasn't needed at all. And just two days before that Rio premiere, Brazil declared war on the Axis powers.

Disney's and Welles's efforts can be summed up simply: mission accomplished. *Saludos Amigos* "did more to cement a community of interest between peoples of the Americas in a few months than the State Department had in fifty years," film historian Alfred Charles Richard Jr. said.

As Welles was about to board the plane back to the States, he found himself captivated by a woman on the cover of *Life* magazine: it was Rita Hayworth.

He told his companions that he was going to find this woman and marry her.

One sequence from <u>It's All True</u> that does survive in fragments is the story of the Jangadeiros, a re-creation of a real-life incident from just the previous year when four fishermen sailed a tiny raft (<u>jangada</u>) 1,600 miles from the northeastern town of Fortaleza all the way to Rio to appeal to President Vargas for greater workers' protections.

VICTORIES ONSCREEN AND AT SEA

The first Hollywood film to channel the post–Pearl Harbor emotions Americans were feeling about the war wasn't actually about America at all. It was *Mrs. Miniver* (1942), the tale of a middle-aged Surrey couple weathering the dark, early days of England's struggle against the Nazis. Greer Garson played the title role. She'd had a breakout success in *Goodbye, Mr. Chips* (1939) three years earlier. Her husband was Walter Pidgeon, the star of *Man Hunt* in 1941. Together, they embodied middle-class British values: fidelity, thrift, a passion for hard work and community engagement, and a good sense of humor—all the ingredients for that famous British stiff upper lip. And yet *Mrs. Miniver*, a movie about Britain, inaugurated one of the most popular wartime film genres for American viewers: the home front film. It was also MGM's biggest hit of the war years. Louis B. Mayer had gone from being the mogul most resistant to criticizing the Nazis to the producer of the film that was their most effective cinematic condemnation.

The Miniver family's life is perfectly calm and pastoral until that fateful day, September 3, 1939, when Britain declared war on Nazi Germany. The couple's older son, Vin (Richard Ney), volunteers for the RAF after falling in love with Carol (Teresa Wright), the granddaughter of the local aristocrat Lady Beldon (Dame May Whitty). Class barriers, previously so sturdy in Britain, come tumbling down as the old dowager allows her estate's vast cellars

to become an air-raid shelter. Mr. Miniver sails his boat out to sea to join the other "small boats" that famously helped the Royal Navy evacuate the trapped British troops off the beach at Dunkirk. Later, the family huddles together in a makeshift shelter they created in their backyard—just as so many British families did—to protect themselves from falling German bombs during the Battle of Britain. As explosives tumble out of the sky and nearly destroy their beautiful home, Mrs. Miniver reassures her children by reading them *Alice in Wonderland*.

One wonders if *Mrs. Miniver* would have resonated as much if America had not yet entered the war. The film opens with onscreen text calling the English "a happy, careless people who worked and played, reared their children and tended their gardens, in that happy, easy-going England that was so soon to be fighting desperately for her way of

Clem and Kay Miniver, like so many British subjects, built their own bomb shelter in their backyard.

life." The travails that follow become more and more difficult, and it's hard not to think that American viewers watching *Mrs. Miniver* would have thought, "If she can keep going and hold her family together, even with bombs dropping around her, so can I." MGM had actually plucked the character from the pages of *The Times* of London, where since 1937 she appeared in recurring, fictional stories that captured the very real mood of Britain. As *Times* editor Peter Fleming (older brother of James Bond creator Ian) put it, Mrs. Miniver was "an ordinary sort of woman who leads an ordinary sort of life—rather like yourself."

Director William Wyler started production on November 11, 1941, with the United States still in peacetime and neutral. "I jumped at it because it was an out-and-out propaganda film," said Wyler. And at that moment, "You were not supposed to make propaganda pictures." One of the film's most dramatic scenes is when a downed German flyer (Helmut Dantine), wounded from his crash and half-dazed, holds Mrs. Miniver at gunpoint, makes her prepare him food, and expounds on his Nazi philosophy. Mayer strongly objected to how the pilot was "self righteous" and "fiendish" in the initial version Wyler shot. "Rotterdam . . . Rotterdam we destroy in two hours!" the pilot says. Mrs. Miniver

protests that so many innocent lives were lost, and the Nazi interrupts, "They were not innocent! They stood against us!" Film critic David Thomson said on BBC Radio, "Wyler took it upon himself to toughen that character up in the scripting and the shooting—and in fact he really turns into a Nazi. The story goes that Louis B. Mayer . . . was alarmed when he saw this footage . . . Wyler is reputed to have said, 'Mr. Mayer, do you know what's going on—this man is a shadow of the nastiness that's going on there.'"

Mayer's perspective on the scene with the Nazi flyer was that America was sympathetic to Britain in its struggle but at peace with Germany. "It's very sympathetic to them—but it's not directed against the Germans," Mayer said. "We're not at war with anybody. We don't hate anybody." Wyler's response was blunt. "Mr. Mayer, if I had several Germans in this picture, I wouldn't mind having one who was a decent young fellow. But I've only got one German. And if I make this picture, this one German is going to be a typical Nazi son of a bitch. He's not going to be a friendly little pilot but one of Goering's monsters." The day after Pearl Harbor, Mayer immediately struck a different tone. "I've been thinking about that scene," he told his director. "You do it the way you

want." Now that America was in the war, Wyler even reshot it so that Mrs. Miniver slaps the flyer.

Wyler also needed a new ending. He had four credited screenwriters on *Mrs. Miniver*. But to close out the film, he sat down and worked with the actor Henry Wilcoxon, who was to deliver its final lines. Wilcoxon was playing the vicar, who gives a sermon from the bombed-out ruins of his church. Tragedy has struck the Miniver family. Young Vin married Lady Beldon's granddaughter Carol. The film makes you think it's Vin, the RAF flyer, who'll face death. Instead it's his wife of two weeks, Carol, who's killed by enemy aircraft fire while riding in a car with his mother. That's how close to home the war could hit. Originally, Wilcoxon was just to deliver the 91st Psalm to end the movie, which Wyler felt wasn't working. But on the night before that finale was to shoot, Wyler and Wilcoxon worked through the night to script a new speech for the ending. The actor had already joined the navy and intended to leave for service as soon as shooting wrapped. In fact, he had already requested two days' leave just so he and Wyler could arrive at the perfect ending. What they came up with put into words what the film now meant. This wasn't just a movie about sympathizing with the fight against Fascism and feeling bad about the suffering of innocents any longer. It was a film in which you saw their struggles as your very own fight. The reality of the Minivers was now your own. In fact, in real life, Wilcoxon's own brother Robert had been on a boat during the evacuation of Dunkirk and been killed by a falling German bomb.

"This is not only a war of soldiers in uniform," Wilcoxon's vicar says in his new sermon. "It is a war of the people—of all the people—and it must not only be fought on the battlefield, but in the cities, and in the villages, in the factories, and on the farms, in the home and in the heart of every man, woman, and child who loves freedom!" Then "Onward Christian Soldiers" swells as the camera tilts toward

the sky, RAF warcraft flying overhead. This wasn't just a war against Germany and Japan. It was a holy crusade for all that was right.

FDR loved this closing speech so much he ordered it translated into French and German and dropped over Axis-occupied Europe. When *Mrs. Miniver* opened on June 4, 1942, it quickly became the biggest hit MGM ever had to that point, save for *Gone with the Wind*. And it had all but created the idea of the home front film, soon to be replicated with an American setting over and over again. Even Joseph Goebbels was impressed. "*Mrs. Miniver* shows the destiny of a family during the current war, and its refined powerful propagandistic tendency has up to now only been dreamed of," the Nazi propaganda minister wrote. "There is not a single angry word spoken against Germany; nevertheless the anti-German tendency is perfectly accomplished." *Mrs. Miniver* had accomplished what the *Why We Fight* films (none of which had been seen by the general public at this point) set out to do. It showed why this tyranny was worth fighting, what it meant when innocents were targeted for no reason but hate and conquest. For that reason, it had to be Teresa Wright's Carol who died at the hands of the enemy. If you avoid the war, it will come to you.

It's a cosmic synchronicity that on the very day *Mrs. Miniver* landed in cinemas in the United States, America was about to achieve the turning point of the Pacific war. After months of defeats and endless retreating actions—even as the Japanese were conquering Kiska and Attu in the Aleutians—the decisive battle that stopped Imperial Japan was fought. One thousand miles northwest of Honolulu, at the westernmost part of the uninhabited Hawaiian Islands, Admiral Nagumo of the Imperial Japanese Navy began an attack on Midway atoll with four aircraft carriers. A small US Navy base was located at the atoll, which included an airstrip, barracks, commissary, and a hospital.

Mrs. Miniver greets her husband as he returns in the boat he sailed, with hundreds of others, to help evacuate the British soldiers trapped on the beach at Dunkirk.

Atop the facility's power station, filming a wave of one hundred Japanese Zeros as they came streaking in for the attack, was John Ford. He managed to get color footage of the striking planes and witnessed some horrific sights, such as a US flyer being shot by an enemy Zero as he slowly fell to earth hanging from a parachute. The power station itself was a target, certainly, and a bomb that destroyed part of the structure resulted in shrapnel causing a three-inch gash on Ford's left arm (which Louella Parsons later said, hyperbolically, had been "rendered almost useless").

The Japanese wanted to cripple the US support facilities on land before redirecting their attention to whatever naval power the Americans had amassed nearby. Japan's goal was to push the American presence in the Pacific back all the way to Pearl Harbor if they could, so that another attack on Japanese soil like the Doolittle Raid would be impossible. Instead, the four Japanese carriers—all of which had participated in the Pearl Harbor attack—were met, to their surprise, with three US carriers: the *Hornet*, the *Enterprise*, and the *Yorktown*. The dive-bombers and torpedo bombers launched from these three aircraft carriers succeeded in sinking all four Japanese warships. The only American carrier lost was the *Yorktown*, which had already suffered major damage at the Battle of the Coral Sea and was operational

Douglas SBD-3 Dauntless dive-bombers about to attack the Japanese cruiser <u>Mikuma</u> during the Battle of Midway, the decisive naval battle of the war that was actually won through air power.

at Midway only after a stunning seventy-two-hour push to make her battle-ready in a last-minute refit at Pearl Harbor days before the battle.

How did the United States win so resounding a victory? In part, it was because naval intelligence had broken the Japanese codes, so Admirals Chester Nimitz, Frank Fletcher, and Raymond Spruance knew all of the enemy's battle plans in advance.

Japan would never recover from this. They only had two fleet carriers left, one badly damaged at the Battle of the Coral Sea, the other having lost much of its crew in that engagement. A new carrier couldn't be launched until 1944, during which time the United States would have produced literally dozens more. And Japan had lost so many experienced crew, particularly aircraft maintenance support, at Midway. Their military academies couldn't possibly produce replacement officers and technicians quickly enough. Midway represented the last Pacific offensive by Japan during the war. From here on out it would be a war of attrition, with the Japanese digging in to try to slow the relentless island-hopping of the Americans. What no one knew was just how long that would take.

FLEEING NAZIS, ONLY TO PLAY NAZIS

The next year, both *Mrs. Miniver* and the documentary John Ford had made out of his Midway footage, simply titled *The Battle of Midway* (1942), won Oscars. Ford's short won the Oscar for Best Documentary in a four-way tie, which also included *Prelude to War*. Collecting six statuettes overall, *Mrs. Miniver* took home the most prestigious prize: Best Picture. Both Greer Garson and Teresa Wright picked up acting Oscars, but it was an undeniable fact that one of the most striking performances in the film had been that of Helmut Dantine, who played the downed Nazi pilot who holds Mrs. Miniver at gunpoint. Dantine exemplified a trend, however. He was an exile of the Nazis himself, and like so many refugees from their tyranny, the roles he found himself being offered in Hollywood were those in which he'd play the very villains who had oppressed him.

Four years before he boasted of the Nazis destroying Rotterdam in *Mrs. Miniver*, Dantine actually had been imprisoned by the Nazis. The actor's father had been the head of Austria's railway system, and as a teenager Helmut was active in Vienna's anti-Nazi movement. When he was nineteen, the Anschluss occurred and he was interned for three months in a concentration camp outside Vienna. Using his powerful connections, Dantine's father pulled strings and sent him to California to study at UCLA. Dantine did not return.

Fleeing Nazis to play Nazis was common. Conrad Veidt, the trim, lanky actor with clipped, patrician elocution, best known to viewers today as the villain Major Strasser in *Casablanca*, had already played several Nazis before that. He had even tangled with Humphrey Bogart once before, in the Warner Bros. caper *All Through the Night*, which debuted on January 10, 1942. Bogie is a Runyon-esque tough guy who gets caught up with the Nazis when he investigates who's been shaking down his favorite local baker. Turns out, the pastry chef—Ludwig Stössel, who played the would-be immigrant to America in *Casablanca* determined to speak only English despite saying things like "What watch?" instead of "What time is it?"—is being blackmailed by agents of the Third Reich, including a mastermind played by Veidt. Where Veidt is menacing in *Casablanca*, he's comical in *All Through the Night*. He's such a Teutonic buffoon that he even carries a dachshund with him named Hansel. "I'm sorry I've been neglecting you, Hansel," he tells his dog at one point. This is the kind of film where, when someone

Conrad Veidt, staunchly anti-Nazi in real life, loved playing Nazis so as to expose their malice for all to see. In <u>Nazi Agent</u>, he plays twin brothers: one an agent of the Third Reich, the other strongly opposed to it.

says, "It's about time someone knocks the Axis on its heels," Bogie replies, "It's about time somebody knocked those heels back on their axis."

Eleven days later, Veidt had another film open, and this time he was playing the lead: in fact, in MGM's *Nazi Agent* (1942), he plays twin brothers, one who's a suave, preening Nazi, the other a bookish stamp dealer living in New York. The good brother, who hates the Nazis, actually kills his twin and assumes his identity so as to foil the plans he'd set in motion. It becomes a kind of *Tale of Two Cities* story about the expanding reach of Nazism, with an emotionally overwhelming ending. It's hard not to see how *Nazi Agent* might have struck such a chord with Veidt. He had all but put German cinema on the map, playing one of the lead characters in *The Cabinet of Dr. Caligari* in 1920, a smash hit and arguably the first horror film. But as the Nazi influence over Germany grew, Veidt became a prominent dissident. In 1933, after Hitler had assumed power, the new government decreed that the German film industry be purged of Jews and anti-Nazi activists. Instead of swearing fealty to the new regime, Veidt married his love, Ilona Prager, a Jewish woman, and fled to Britain. Before leaving, he filled out the "racial questionnaire" that Joseph Goebbels was making everyone in the German film industry sign. Veidt wrote that he was Jewish, as a sign of solidarity with his wife, even though he had not been born Jewish himself. It's likely that the Nazi propaganda minister had given him an ultimatum: if he had renounced Prager, he could have stayed and worked in German film. Some took Goebbels up on that offer: Thea von Harbou, the wife of Fritz Lang, had done just that after her husband left Germany. When Veidt and Prager fled the country, Goebbels declared the actor would never work in Germany again.

Lean years followed for Veidt and Prager in Britain, but he had brought his fortune from Germany with him. Before leaving for Hollywood in 1940, he donated most of his wealth to the British government to help in the war effort. Upon arriving in Los Angeles, he signaled that he was open to playing Nazi characters—so long as they never be portrayed as anything less than foul, snarling villains. He insisted that stipulation be written into his contracts. (Even before *All Through the Night* and *Nazi Agent*, he had played just such a goosestepping thug in Mervyn LeRoy's 1940 film *Escape*.)

Peter Lorre, though Jewish himself (he was born László Löwenstein) and an emigre from Axis-aligned Hungary, played one of Veidt's Nazi henchmen in *All Through the Night*. Regrettably, he also played a Japanese villain, Baron Ikito, in *Invisible Agent* (1942) the same year. In the years to come, Lorre made shortwave radio broadcasts in Hungarian to rally the resistance forces there and undermine the morale of Hungary's Nazi-allied government. When the broadcasts came to the attention of the local authorities, however, they made Lorre's family suffer. In the words of Lorre's brother Francis, their aunt was "dragged off to Auschwitz, but got sick on the long march to the Austrian border, and fell by the wayside and was too ill to continue. So that probably saved her life, for the time being, anyway. And my grandmother, who was very, very upset by the whole thing, tried to commit suicide, unsuccessfully, but at least having landed in the hospital at that stage we prevented her from being dragged in front of the Gestapo."

Of course, Francis Lederer, the fanatical Nazi of *Confessions of a Nazi Spy* and *The Man I Married*, was Jewish in real life and became an American citizen the year *Confessions* was released. But perhaps the most amusing onscreen Nazi popped up in Fox's *The Pied Piper* (1942). That film stars Monty Woolley as an Englishman summering in France when the blitzkrieg begins. Trapped in Nazi-occupied territory, he takes several children under his wing as their protector. But a Nazi commandant

Arguably, Otto Preminger's greatest acting successes—the kind that paid the bills until he was in regular rotation for plum directing gigs—were as playing Nazis.

thinks it odd that this Englishman should have been right in the path of their panzers—surely he must be a spy. The commandant? Played by none other than Otto Preminger, working in Hollywood at Darryl F. Zanuck's behest since 1935, and destined to direct such legendary films as *Laura* (1944), *Angel Face* (1953), and *Advise & Consent* (1962). With his shiny bald pate, Preminger stares down Woolley in a clash of "big personalities" for the ages. This Nazi thinks Woolley was somehow involved in a plot to kill Hitler when the Führer came to gloat over the conquest of France. "I say . . . Did they get him?" Woolley asks. "Get whom?" "Hitler." "Of course not!" "That's too bad!"

Preminger, an Austrian Jew who'd been in Hollywood since before the Anschluss, tore into his Nazi roles with relish. He directed himself as the Nazi consul living in New York in *Margin for Error*, Fox's 1943 adaptation of the 1939 Claire Booth Luce play, in which Preminger had played the same character for 264 performances on Broadway. He followed that up with a role as a German spy in *They Got Me Covered* (1943), a zany Bob Hope–Dorothy Lamour comedy. Before his smash success directing *Laura* in 1944, playing Nazis was a lucrative business for Preminger. He, like all of these other actors, knew the unique power of the movies: what better way to undermine the idea of the Nazis in people's minds than portraying them negatively on the big screen? Attack the image and the ideas behind it lose power.

HOW CHINESE- AND KOREAN-AMERICAN ACTORS FOUGHT JAPAN

Many Chinese-American actors followed the playbook of Dantine, Veidt, Lorre, and Preminger, but in their own way: they wanted to portray Japanese characters onscreen as negatively as possible whenever they could. Victor Sen Yung had even delivered a Japanese-American character who was a walking call for internment in *Across the Pacific*. He was joined in that film by Spencer Chan, who played Mitsuko, the Japanese chief engineer. Chan also played a Japanese army captain in *Wake Island* (1942). Maui-born Chinese-American actor Richard Loo played especially vicious Japanese characters in *The Purple Heart* (1944) and *God Is My Co-Pilot* (1945).

Chinese-Americans felt intense antipathy for the way Japan had terrorized their ancestral homeland ever since annexing Manchuria in 1931. The atrocities Imperial Japan committed against China were as brutal and being carried out on as massive a scale as those being carried out by Nazi Germany in Europe. The Nazis may have boasted of leveling Rotterdam in two hours. Imperial Japan boasted of destroying the then Chinese capital, Nanjing. In a six-week period after the Imperial forces captured the city on December 13, 1937, soldiers systematically murdered disarmed soldiers

and civilians—often by beheading. The exact figures are impossible to determine, but it's believed that over two hundred thousand Chinese were murdered, with the Japanese also extensively using rape as a weapon of war. This is an atrocity that should make the entire world shudder—but then as now, the Nanjing Massacre, and other atrocities the Japanese committed in their occupied territories in China, were widely underreported in US media.

That the horrors Japan inflicted on China were rarely reported in the United States may explain the willingness of Chinese-American actors to portray Japanese in such a starkly negative light—even contributing to an atmosphere that supported Japanese-Americans' internment. Richard Loo's daughter, Beverly Jane Loo, spoke of the pride her father felt in exposing Japanese war crimes. "He was

The ideological underpinnings of Victor Sen Yung's character Joe Totsuiko are dangerous: through him, it feels like the movie is saying that any Japanese-American could be a traitor.

always either stabbing himself or committing hara-kiri or kamikaze," she told *The New York Times*. "He always played the big honcho who was really going to make life tough for the Americans, the really nasty Japanese general or colonel who ended up killing himself as a point of honor because he never got the best of the Americans . . . He felt very patriotic about being in those movies." Even an actor such as the Chinese-American Keye Luke, who'd later appear with Loo in the TV series *Kung Fu* (1972–1975) and generally avoided playing Japanese characters during the war years, could find himself dragged in—though he was uncredited for the two wartime Japanese characters he played. Luke didn't need them: he had his own burgeoning franchise at his fingertips as Dr. Lee Wong Howe in MGM's *Dr. Gillespie* movies—a way of getting viewers used to celebrating accomplished characters of Chinese heritage—who even popped up in a crossover in *Andy Hardy's Blonde Trouble* (1944). Benson Fong followed very much the same approach: whenever he played a vicious Japanese character, he went uncredited.

The Korean-American actor Philip Ahn, yet another future costar of *Kung Fu* along with Loo, Luke, and Fong, enthusiastically played Japanese villains during World War II and did get credits for that work. So many, in fact, that white audiences assumed Ahn was actually Japanese—he received death threats as a result. Among those roles, he had played a Japanese informer in *Across the Pacific*, a Shinto priest in the longer Gregg Toland cut of *December 7th: The Movie* (which suggested the Japanese worshipped their emperor as a god), 1945's *Betrayal from the East* (also with Richard Loo and

Victor Sen Yung), *Blood on the Sun*, and *Back to Bataan*. Ahn's selection of roles was motivated by his activist spirit: his father had been a leader of the Korean independence movement ever since Japan annexed the Korean peninsula in 1910. He had played a Chinese character too, in 1939's *King of Chinatown*, arguably the first Hollywood film to call for armed US intervention in World War II. In that film, he had been the husband of Anna May Wong.

Wong herself never portrayed villainous Japanese characters. She wanted only to embody the nobility of China. To show what was being fought for, not just against. In 1942 she appeared as the lead in two extremely interesting films, in which she was an armed Chinese insurgent fighting against Japan. The first of these, *Bombs Over Burma*, premiered on June 5, 1942. It begins in Chungking (today more commonly spelled as Chongqing), the Chinese Nationalist government's wartime capital, where Wong is a schoolteacher. A Japanese bombing raid causes chaos across the city; one particularly

Philip Ahn, left, plays Colonel Coroki in **Back to Bataan**. The Korean-American actor played Japanese villains so often he received death threats because the audience assumed he was Japanese too.

agonizing sequence has a young child, riddled with panic, unable to get out of the schoolhouse while a Japanese dive-bomber comes ever closer. The poor little kid perishes. Wong then goes on a secret mission for the Chinese government to Burma to secure supplies for Chungking. She's on a bus with several white American characters and a phony British aristocrat. One of the white American characters says, "Now China will help keep us alive with that wonderful stubborn purpose of theirs," to which his female companion says, "Yes, I can see it in that Chinese woman's face." This illustrates Wong's mission in these movies: to embody the strength of Chinese resistance and show that the success of China meant success for America. It's a starkly propagandistic film: Wong delivers slogans throughout such as "China will never be conquered." But in the hands of its director, Joseph H. Lewis, a compelling one. To make this movie, Wong had left behind the major studios altogether—she hadn't been in movies for almost three years to focus on war-related outreach efforts—instead making *Bombs Over Burma* through the "poverty row" Producers Releasing Corporation. But she knew: the smaller the studio, the smaller the budget, the more control she could have. (MGM's *Dragon Seed*, on the other hand, released two years later in 1944, told the story of China's fight against Japan with Chinese characters played entirely by white actors.) Around the same time, she wrote the preface to one of the first English-language Chinese cookbooks, *New China Recipes*, and donated the proceeds to United China Relief.

Wong's second film of 1942, *Lady from Chungking*, is even better. She plays Kwan Mei, a Nationalist army official sent to organize the peasants of a small village. The Japanese are approaching, but luckily the farmers of this town are now equipped with guns as well as scythes. Two American airmen with the Flying Tigers—the group of civilian mercenary flyers Claire Lee Chennault had organized to help defend China, which had virtually no air force of its own—parachute to safety in the village. Kwan Mei decides that hiding the pilots is so important her group will, temporarily at least, allow the Japanese to occupy the town without any resistance. Keeping the Americans safe is more important than fighting back.

Of course, one of the flyers gets captured, so the movie becomes about springing him while nursing the other back to health—so that they can get back to their base, get back in the cockpit, and bomb the hell out of the Japanese forces occupying the place. To buy them time, Kwan Mei seduces the Japanese general. In *Lady from Chungking*, the Chinese heroes are played by Chinese-Americans, but the Japanese are played by white actors—a conscious choice, and one wonders if it might be a commentary on how the European powers had engaged in exploitative, colonialist practices in China that softened the country up for Japanese invasion. At the end, after the Flying Tigers have escaped, and Kwan Mei's gambit is uncovered, the general has her taken out and shot. Before the bullets fly, she gives a speech about the birth of a "new China"—and then after she's shot and her body falls, Wong remains onscreen in a ghostly double-exposure to continue her speech even after death.

Lady from Chungking was the last movie Wong made during the war, and her last overall for seven years. But she remained extremely busy in the war effort, nonetheless. The latest project she immersed herself in? The Hollywood Canteen.

THE HOLLYWOOD CANTEEN

Los Angeles had quickly become the main point of departure for servicemen being shipped out to staging grounds in the Pacific. In August 1942, the Allies launched their first major offensive against Japan, in the Guadalcanal campaign. The enlisted men in L.A. typically had just a couple of days to relax and have fun before possibly heading to active battle zones. Their superiors encouraged them to live it up. Warner Bros. star John Garfield, 4-F himself due to a heart condition, came up with the idea of a place where he and some of Hollywood's brightest lights could give them the time of their lives. Bette Davis would help make it a reality.

Davis had been burned by the Academy Board of Governors' refusal of her suggestions for the 1942 Oscars. But her choice to resign as Academy president three weeks after assuming the role only freed her up to focus that much more on wartime fundraising efforts. When Jack Warner criticized her choice to bully crowds into submission to buy war bonds, she told him it was her "bitch" roles that audiences had always connected with the most. At one point, she sold more than $2 million worth of bonds in two days, including a signed photo of herself in *Jezebel* (1938) that she sold for $250,000. There never would be any doubt about Davis and Garfield's political priorities: they had starred together, though didn't share any scenes, in Warner Bros.' anti-Fascist film *Juarez* (1939).

Garfield told Davis about his idea for a Hollywood version of the Stage Door Canteen, which Broadway stars had quickly set up on Forty-Fourth Street in Manhattan between Seventh and Eighth Avenues. Actors served food to servicemen, allowed them to dance with female stars, and put on performances. Now it just needed to be transplanted to the West Coast. But "one step below an eyesore" is what Davis called the Cahuenga Boulevard barn she bought to become the Hollywood version of this. Some major renovations were needed to turn it into a dining and performance space, and she called in favors from studio production staff to whip it into shape. Her agent, Jules Stein, cofounder of mega-agency MCA, set about publicizing it, while Davis worked the phones to make sure that on opening night there really would be more stars at the Hollywood Canteen than in the heavens.

Rita Hayworth, working as a coat-check girl, at the Hollywood Canteen.

Joan Leslie dancing with a soldier in 1943. The film <u>Hollywood Canteen</u> (1944) presented Leslie as the crush of a soldier—but before she became that film's love interest, she worked the Canteen in real life too.

Davis's plan for opening night was that each star would pay $50 for bleacher seats, where they'd applaud the servicemen walking the red carpet—stars gawking at fans, a complete role-reversal. This would be in addition to the stars already set to work as cooks, waiters, busboys, and floor scrubbers—as well as actual entertainers putting on live acts. (All the stars had to undergo a thorough FBI background check beforehand.) Servicewomen were allowed in too, of course—though, as in the Armed Forces at the time writ large, there was an obvious gender imbalance. The key was that the servicepeople in attendance were enlisted personnel—officers were forbidden.

Davis and Garfield also intended for the Hollywood Canteen to be racially integrated from the start. As a statement, Davis attended a pre-opening fundraising party for the Canteen at Ciro's with the Black actor and supporting player in *The Talk of the Town* (1942), Rex Ingram, as her date. In the Warner Bros. film *Hollywood Canteen* that debuted two years later, the third act presented is the Golden Gate Quartet, a Black proto-doo-wop singing group—they had performed at President Roosevelt's third inauguration. And throughout that whole film you see Black, white, and Asian soldiers mingling. As for who the soldiers could dance with, it would be a mix of established stars and young pretty women of all races, maybe under contract to a studio or maybe just hoping to "make it." Davis and Garfield did not establish any rules prohibiting these girls from asking soldiers of another race to dance. Anyone could dance with Anna May Wong, who was among those hitting the dance floor. But John Ford's wife, Mary, who helped out at the Canteen throughout the war, kept reporting to the LAPD whenever she saw interracial dancing. Instead of acting on her tips, the police notified her husband John, then staying at Claridge's in London and getting ready to fly to Morocco to help photograph

The Hollywood Canteen at night.

the Allied invasion, about his wife's incessant worry over this—which, interracial dancing not being a crime, could have been considered filing false police reports. Ford told the LAPD his wife "was inclined to become agitated and excited about racial matters," and said the officers "should take Mrs. Ford out of the Canteen" if they wished.

In general, the rules here were few: this was a dry establishment, no alcohol ever being served, though there was free coffee, sodas, sandwiches, and cigarettes. The most important stipulation was that no Canteen hostess was ever to meet an enlisted man off-site. That also meant exchanging contact information was forbidden—in fact, the hostesses kept little cards in their pockets with their studio's address on it to give to soldiers as a suggestion for where they could write them. Otherwise, even second dances were prohibited.

The Hollywood Canteen officially opened on October 3, 1942. If lovers of Old Hollywood could travel back in time and be a fly on the wall at any Tinseltown happening, they'd be hard-pressed to choose any venue other than this converted barn at 1451 Cahuenga, just south of Sunset Boulevard. Bette Davis was there as mistress of ceremonies almost every night for the next three years. When you first entered, Rita Hayworth might be the coat-check girl to take your jacket. In one famous photo, Hayworth was caught wearing a bathing suit and high heels in the kitchen while slicing an apple pie. Claudette Colbert might be playing gin rummy with a group of soldiers; maybe Mary Pickford, recovered from her flirtation in the thirties with Fascism, could then join in, bringing some doughnuts with her. Frank Sinatra might croon a few songs. Maybe Eddie Cantor and Nora Martin would perform "We're Having a Baby (My Baby and Me)." After which you'd take a spin around the dance floor with Marsha Hunt (who said she must have danced with thousands of servicemen in her years at the Canteen). Spencer Tracy could be carving a turkey. Davis then comes and fixes the ties on his apron. Also in aprons and serving food? Vice President Henry Wallace alongside Bob Hope. In the kitchen, Gary Cooper could be helping to cook the food, while Jack Benny is washing the dishes. Then Benny could be relieved by Marlene Dietrich and Hedy Lamarr at the sink. "Get those two krauts out of the kitchen!" Davis jokes. Why keep Dietrich

Master of ceremonies Bette Davis addresses the crowd.

and Lamarr hidden away? Dietrich then might be cutting a giant cake for your dessert. Need something to wash it down? Here's Linda Darnell with a glass of milk.

Talk about the stuff dreams are made of.

How much the stars and servicemembers actually did interact outside the Hollywood Canteen is unclear. One dancer hoping to make it in Hollywood, Meg Nesbit, couldn't resist: she married a soldier she met at the Canteen in April 1943. He was killed in battle shortly thereafter. Davis herself even had an affair with Corporal Lewis A. Riley, and went to visit him at his army base in Georgia. In 1959, Riley ended up marrying Dolores del Rio.

Speaking of Del Rio, the Mexican actress had been in a relationship with Orson Welles since 1940, but she and the director broke up upon his return to America in 1942. Having seen that *Life* magazine cover photo of Rita Hayworth and vowing to marry her, he sought her out. Hayworth had worked in the Canteen, serving customers in her best glamour wear—the idea was to present a star like her as both a fantasy and, with her doing ordinary domestic tasks, as attainable as well: the fantasy that could be yours. Finally, Joseph Cotton arranged an introduction: he threw a dinner party and invited both Welles and Hayworth. She didn't know what to make of him. Constantly underestimating her appeal, she thought he wasn't serious. But within a few weeks of his persistent courting, she was won over.

Welles also rebounded from his disastrous divorce with RKO by throwing himself into patriotic radio broadcasts. His next project? A rival to the Hollywood Canteen located just a short way down Cahuenga. His feeling was that the Canteen

shouldn't have a complete monopoly on entertaining the troops—after all, the Canteen hadn't been motivated entirely out of altruism. It was stellar publicity to show how united and patriotic the movie industry was, after years of being accused of immorality. Welles wanted some of that goodwill for himself. Especially since Hearst reporters had questioned his patriotism ever since *Citizen Kane*: Why hadn't Welles been drafted? The answer was simple: with his eating habits, Welles was not in good health. "I felt guilty about the war," Welles later said. "I was guilt-ridden about my civilian status." Thus *The Mercury Wonder Show* was born. And he hoped it could be a showcase for the woman he loved.

Davis was a Warner Bros. star, but she's surrounded by so many sailors at the Canteen she might as well be in an MGM musical.

HOLLYWOOD'S ROSIES

"I remember sitting up in a bare attic with my mother," recalled Anthony Loder of his mom, Hedy Lamarr. "She said, 'Look, I got a patent.' 'You got a patent, mom?' 'Yeah.' 'You invented something?' 'Yeah! I invented a secret communication system."

The women of Hollywood had stepped up to support the war effort in extraordinary fashion. Lamarr was putting in hours at the Hollywood Canteen with the best of them. Two months before the Canteen opened, she had achieved something singular: she had registered a patent for a frequency-skipping technology that could have made a major impact in the war. Lamarr had starred in MGM's *Boom Town* two years earlier, the biggest box-office success of 1940. Not many stars with that level of clout pursued a side passion with Lamarr's level of diligence, but tinkering with mechanics had been an interest of hers ever since she took apart a music box as a child in Austria and found a way to put it back together without anyone being the wiser. Howard Hughes knew she had the mind of an inventor, and so he gave Lamarr a set of equipment that could fit in her trailer on the MGM lot. She could then pursue her inventions in between takes. Upset at the losses the British were suffering on account of German U-boats, she came up with a radio-controlled torpedo that allowed the launcher to alter its course after it had been fired. If it was controlled by just one frequency, the Germans could identify it and jam it. So Lamarr invented the idea of frequency hopping, in which the radio signal that controlled the torpedo constantly jumped around on the spectrum.

Hedy Lamarr tends her Victory Garden in 1943. The Department of Agriculture encouraged the planting of Victory Gardens during the war, which could supplement households' ration allotments and give a sense of satisfaction at having tended and grown something. Vegetables, needed for people in uniform, were in short supply for civilians.

Lamarr and her co-inventor, composer George Antheil, donated the idea to the National Inventors Council as a contribution to the war effort. But the US Navy rejected it. They didn't see how it could be built quickly enough to have any practical effect on their war strategy. But the navy also labeled this patent top secret, so that Lamarr and Antheil couldn't even receive credit for it, and they removed Lamarr's ownership over it entirely. Hailing from Austria, she was an "enemy alien," after all. "And today we have Wi-Fi and Bluetooth," Loder said, "that's my mother's technology." The navy told her she would better serve the war effort by selling war bonds: which she did, to the tune of $25 million.

Lamarr's experience was that of countless women across America during World War II: they would make essential contributions, but more often than not didn't get the credit they deserved. And there was no question about it—without women, the war couldn't be won. As men left their jobs to serve in the Armed Forces, women needed to take their place. In 1940 there were twelve million women employed in the United States. By 1944, twenty million were, of which over five million worked in the defense industries. US war production would almost be as impressive as its actual military actions: in the factories where many of these women found employment, out came three hundred thousand military aircraft, eighty-nine thousand tanks, sixty-five thousand jeeps, three million machine guns, and seven million rifles, and they'd supply more than half the armaments used by Britain, Russia, and the Free French.

Popular culture offered encouragement for women to take factory jobs too: bandleader Kay Kyser recorded a song by Redd Evans and John Jacob Loeb called "Rosie the Riveter" in 1942, and an icon was born. There are at least three competing candidates for the real-life Rosie: Rosina Bonavita, who worked at the Corvair factory in San Diego and assembled an entire wing of a torpedo bomber in one shift, having assembled 3,345 rivets; Rosalind P. Walter, the most likely inspiration for the song itself, an heiress who worked in a factory and would later be a ubiquitous name before PBS programming as a sponsor, and died in 2020 at age ninety-five; and Rose Will Monroe, who worked at the Willow Run aircraft factory in Ypsilanti, Michigan, and was featured in a propaganda short with actor Walter Pidgeon to encourage women to work defense jobs. But many women with names other than some variation of Rosie considered themselves to be Rosies too: the longest to be employed was Elinor Otto,

LEFT: Rosies at work. **OPPOSITE:** Westinghouse Electric's "We Can Do It!" poster is the single most iconic wartime image of Rosie the Riveter.

who began her career during World War II, but was still assembling rivets in an aircraft factory until the age of ninety-five. Otto turned one hundred in 2019. One of the long-since-retired Rosies, Mae Krier, helped assemble B-17 and B-29 bombers at a Seattle factory. At the age of ninety-four, in 2020, she turned her skills toward fighting the coronavirus pandemic by making face masks in the style of the red bandanna with white polka dots a Rosie wears on Westinghouse Electric's iconic, bicep-flexing "We Can Do It!" poster, designed by J. Howard Miller in 1943.

That bandanna in the "We Can Do It!" poster was important. Women with long hair needed to make sure it didn't get caught in factory machinery, something that California historian Kevin Starr has said actually did happen to hundreds of women. Keeping it tucked under a bandanna was one solution. Either way, long, luscious locks were not something to celebrate at the moment, and Hollywood met this challenge too. Veronica Lake, two weeks before Pearl Harbor, was celebrated in *Life* magazine for her cascade of golden hair. It said she had 150,000 follicles and her hair stretched eight inches below her shoulders. It was known as the peekaboo, because it would often fall so that it covered one eye. Not good for factory work. So in 1943 Lake participated in a short called *Hair Styles for Safety*, in which she showed off a new updo, the "victory roll," so named because it had a V-shape when viewed from the back. She wore this style in her film *So Proudly We Hail!*, which opened on June 22, 1943.

Somehow Lake's adoption of the victory roll updo became known as her "cutting her hair." She

had merely put it up, but Lake herself perpetuated this misconception twenty-four years later in an interview: "I almost caused a national crisis . . . years ago. When I wore what was known as the peekaboo hairdo, many women copied it. Women who worked in factories kept catching their hair in the machinery—causing accidents. Then I cut off my hair and the accident rates fell 22 percent." Alas, "cutting her hair" may have harmed Lake's career. She never seemed to have the same level of stardom after ditching her signature look.

Women on the big screen generally did adopt shorter curls for the rest of the war years. After *The Palm Beach Story* (1942), Claudette Colbert put her hair up. Betty Grable didn't hesitate either in her series of escapist musicals. After *Casablanca*, Ingrid Bergman cut her hair down to a short crop for *For Whom the Bell Tolls* (1943). Jane Wyman ended up with a short updo for much of her career. All of these women also played characters active in the war effort in some way, but a few portrayed characters who actually ended up in combat: Ann Sheridan wields a machine gun as a Norwegian resistance fighter in *Edge of Darkness* (1943); Maria Palmer plays a Russian sharpshooter in *Days of Glory* (1944); and in *A Guy Named Joe* (1943), Irene Dunne, realizing that her beloved Van Johnson is given a dangerous one-man aerial mission to take out a Japanese island outpost, steals his plane before he has a chance to take to the air himself and completes his mission on her own.

———

Female stars needed to model behavior to the women who were going to work. Women in movies started wearing more professional attire; unless a movie was an outright escapist fantasy, women wore less elaborate evening wear. *Mrs. Miniver* had helped set the tone: Teresa Wright and Greer Garson always wear two-piece skirt suits. A moment early in the film when Garson buys a florid hat is presented in context as something relegated to the prewar past, not something anyone should be thinking about during the conflict. Function would rule the day in fashion, especially in the new genre of home front movies.

And if you doubt that movies had such an immediate effect on women's style choices, keep this in mind: movie theaters started staying open around the clock to accommodate female workers leaving factory shifts at all hours of the day. Some theaters made it a regular practice to have an entire show, with shorts, a newsreel, and a feature, starting at 2:30 a.m. A movie was the most accessible and immediate form of escape you could plunge yourself into after a long, repetitive workday at a factory. And it was showing on studio ledger sheets: box-office rental grosses were higher than ever before. What better moment for the greatest movie ever produced by the assembly line studio system to arrive?

Lake in <u>So Proudly We Hail!</u> (1943), sporting the victory roll. Now this is an appropriate hairdo for the war effort!

REAL-LIFE REFUGEES GIVE
CASABLANCA ITS POWER

Only three of the credited actors in *Casablanca* (1942) were American-born: Humphrey Bogart, Dooley Wilson, and Joy Page, who plays the Bulgarian woman considering an affair with Claude Rains's Captain Renault to win passage to Lisbon for herself and her husband (Helmut Dantine). This is a movie that was created on the Warner Bros. lot, with nothing about the production design looking anything like the real Moroccan city—with even the Van Nuys airport standing in for the final scene. But if the surface details don't speak much to reality, the faces do. Most of the cast, even the smallest parts with just one or two lines, were actual refugees of the Nazis. Their experiences lent an emotional authenticity to *Casablanca* that's helped it remain so vital.

Though Austrian actor Paul Henreid played the idealistic freedom fighter Victor Laszlo in <u>Casablanca,</u> he had previously played Nazis: in the British film by Carol Reed <u>Night Train to Munich</u> (1940) and on Broadway, which brought him to the attention of Warner Bros.

Michael Curtiz's film is about higher truths: in Paul Henreid's Victor Laszlo, the convictions of a man willing to risk his life and lose his wife to serve the cause of humanity; and in Bogart's Rick Blaine, a journey from cynicism to idealism, from "I don't stick my neck out for nobody" to being willing to bet it all. Wasn't Rick every isolationist American who suddenly found themselves inspired to join the fight on the side of good? Name another Hollywood movie labeled a love story that's so all-embracing in its outlook it ultimately puts a love of humanity above a romance between two people.

And then there's "La Marseillaise." The emotions in that scene, a kind of sonic duel between the French national anthem, led by Henreid's freedom fighter Laszlo, and "Die Wacht am Rhein," the German march led by Conrad Veidt's vile Major Strasser, are so very real. Intense, but never manipulative. Because the actors whose eyes were welling up, their voices cracking from the emotion, weren't just playing this scene: they had lived it.

Henreid was born in Austria-Hungary to Karl Hernried, a wealthy banker and close adviser of Emperor Franz Joseph. If he has such a cool, aristocratic bearing onscreen, it's because he had grown up in the uppermost echelons of Viennese society. Early success on the Vienna stage brought him to the attention of scouts from Berlin's leading film studio, UFA. They offered him a contract that "practically guaranteed him instant stardom and a remarkable salary," his daughter Monika Henreid says. "But once he had signed, they gave him another piece of paper, which was the National Socialist German Actors' Guild contract, and he said, 'I'm not signing that. I'm not.'" They tossed away their offer, blacklisted him from Austrian as well as German films, and then did some digging into his family tree.

The actor's father, Karl Hernried, had been born Carl Hirsch, and he and his family stretching far back were Jewish. The patriarch had long since converted to Lutheranism. Neither he nor his actor son was ever churchgoing, though Paul did receive a Catholic school education at the behest of his staunchly Roman Catholic mother—but it's likely the leaders of the German film industry uncovered that the young actor was of Jewish heritage nonetheless. When he and his wife moved to Britain, he changed his name from Paul von Hernried to the slightly less Germanic Paul Henreid.

Part of the reason for that name change was that Henreid and his wife, Lisl, were met with suspicion in Britain. Could they be Nazis? Conrad Veidt, who leads "Die Wacht am Rhein" while Henreid leads "La Marseillaise" in *Casablanca*, helped vouch for him to the powers that be in the UK. "My father did need help in establishing himself as a safe, anti-Nazi Austrian who deserved recognition within England," Monika Henreid says. When being met with suspicion in a foreign land, "you want to surround yourself with people who've been there and done that, or people who have influence, and Connie was both. The story of them being great friends got blown a little out of proportion, but that's Hollywood." Veidt had been staunchly anti-Nazi himself ever since Joseph Goebbels asked him to leave his Jewish wife. Once the war started, Henreid and Veidt were considered "enemy aliens first class" in Britain, so migrating to the United States was the next step. Henreid was well aware of the dislocation the characters in *Casablanca* felt.

That feeling of being out of place was shared by much of the refugee cast. Those extras at the very beginning who look up and see the plane to Lisbon taking off, wishing they were aboard? Actual

---

OPPOSITE: Nineteen-year-old Madeleine Lebeau, who played Rick's ex, Yvonne, was married to Marcel Dalio, who played Emil, the croupier. They divorced shortly into the production of <u>Casablanca</u>.

émigrés who fled Nazi persecution. Nineteen-year-old Madeleine Lebeau, who played Rick's former lover Yvonne and gets so teary-eyed during "La Marseillaise": she and her husband Marcel Dalio, who plays Emil the croupier (and appeared in Jean Renoir's masterpieces *La Grande Illusion* [1937] and *The Rules of the Game* [1939] during a distinguished career in France), fled Paris as the city fell to the Wehrmacht in June 1940 and, just like the characters in *Casablanca*, made their way to Lisbon. They waited there for two months until they could get visas to travel to Chile. But halfway to their destination, they had to disembark in Mexico when it became apparent their Chilean visas were forgeries. At last, they received temporary Canadian passports to get them into the United States. Lebeau spent

S. Z. Sakall, nicknamed "Cuddles," giving himself higher billing at the dressing room near the <u>Casablanca</u> set.

the seven weeks she was aboard ship learning to speak English. Back home in France, the Nazis were putting Dalio's face on posters to show their sympathizers how to spot "a typical Jew," and all the other members of the actor's family died in concentration camps.

Hans Heinrich von Twardowski plays the German officer who is Yvonne's new boyfriend, introduced right before "La Marseillaise." He had fled the Nazis in 1933 because he was gay, even though he had been in German films since *The Cabinet of Dr. Caligari* (1920). As for Lebeau, she was the last surviving cast member of *Casablanca* when she died on May 1, 2016.

Remember the guy clutching a drink and breathlessly saying "waiting, waiting, waiting . . . I'll never get out of here . . . I'll die in Casablanca"? That's Louis V. Arco, who fled Germany when the Nazis took power in 1933 and fled them again in 1938 after the Anschluss. Trude Berliner asks Carl, the waiter, "Will you ask Rick if he will have a drink with us?" Being Jewish in real life, she had fled the Nazis too, though she'd had a successful film career in Germany opposite S. Z. Sakall, who played Carl.

Sakall himself, with his lovable, squeezable cheeks, was fifty-nine when he made *Casablanca*. He fled Germany after 1933 and returned to his native Hungary, then fled Hungary in 1939 when that nation joined the Axis. Sakall had initially hated the part of Carl and turned it down. Producer Hal Wallis kept insisting and Sakall was able to negotiate the size of his part up so significantly that he ended up having a bigger role than either Sydney Greenstreet or Peter Lorre. Most of Sakall's family was murdered in the Holocaust. He shares a few lines in German with Ilka Grüning and Ludwig Stössel, the elderly couple who are trying to speak only in English but finding their new language difficult. The Nazis imprisoned Stössel several times in Vienna before he could escape for Paris, and he and Grüning had been something of an onscreen couple in several previous Warner Bros. movies.

Wolfgang Zilzer plays the man with the expired papers who is shot near the film's start. He had been acting in films since 1915 and would keep acting until 1986, making for one of the longest careers in film history. He left Germany and used a pseudonym whenever acting in anti-Nazi films in the United States to protect his father, who still lived in Berlin. Zilzer's wife, fellow refugee Lotte Palfi, is the woman desperately trying to sell her diamonds to get a visa. She'd later chase Laurence Olivier down a street in *Marathon Man* (1976) as the concentration camp survivor who recognized the "white angel of death" who tormented her and so many others.

One career that was actually longer than Zilzer's was that of Curt Bois, the pickpocket who warns visitors of "vultures . . . vultures everywhere." Before fleeing the Nazis in 1934, he had spent his whole life in the German movie business and was one of the first child actors in film history, dating back to the movie *Bauernhaus und Grafenschloß* in 1907, when he was six years old. Bois continued acting until 1987, capping off his career with Wim Wenders's *Wings of Desire*.

"It must have been a . . . heartbreaking reunion for the people who worked in the movie," Billy Wilder later said. "Like meeting on the Alexanderplatz old pals, friends who were in the theater with you for years." If you ever wonder what people mean when they say "representation matters," look back at *Casablanca*: this cast is the very illustration of that point. Even if you never knew that so many of these actors were refugees, you are touched by the emotional power of their performances—even if those performances lasted but mere moments—because they were informed by real, lived experience. And life in Hollywood wasn't necessarily easy for all of these refugee actors: those who hailed from the Axis countries were designated "enemy aliens" by the War Department and subject to an 8:00 p.m. curfew. "There was little safe haven for them in Hollywood," Monika Henreid says. "It was ridiculous."

As sensitive as *Casablanca* is to the experiences of individuals, though, it's not a movie that privileges the individual's needs above humanity as a whole. This is a film about collective effort, and it's fitting, then, that it has never been regarded as the creation of a singular auteur: Michael Curtiz, for all his extraordinary gifts, has never been in the pantheon of singular visionaries, like Hawks, Ford, Chaplin, Hitchcock, or Welles, in part because you can identify other contributors who deserve as much authorial credit. In the case of *Casablanca*, that has to be the four individuals who wrote the script: Julius and Philip Epstein wrote its glistening dialogue; Howard Koch developed the sacrificial nature of the story; Casey Robinson structured the love story and insisted the female lead be a European actress. Then there's composer Max Steiner, whose contribution to the storytelling in leitmotifs powers the story along—notice how right up until the moment the Germans first speak upon arriving in any scene, Steiner teases a bit of "Deutschlandlied" (the famous German anthem with the line "Deutschland über Alles") on the score. And none of this would have jelled without producer Hal Wallis—whose idea it was to cast Ingrid Bergman—shepherding the whole production with as much vision and brio as David O. Selznick had on *Gone with the Wind*. How perfect, though, that the ultimate World War II movie, the film that best speaks to the hopes and fears and anxieties of the wartime years, would be a triumph of collective effort rather than singular vision. You could say it was an artistic metaphor for the collective effort needed to fight the war itself. And just like no one knew how the war would end, no one knew how *Casablanca* would end. Would Ingrid Bergman get on that plane with Henreid or stay with Bogart?

The story and script were still being written right up until the last moment of shooting on the dramatic finale. Hal Wallis himself stepped in to script some of the climactic lines, while Bogart sulked in his trailer, uncertain if he or Henreid would end up with Bergman. "During the day the company had several delays caused by arguments with Curtiz the director, and Bogart the actor," *Casablanca*'s unit production manager Al Alleborn wrote. "I had to go and get Wallis and bring him over to the set to straighten out the situation. At one time they sat around for a long time and argued, finally deciding on how to do the scene." Of course the ending they ultimately settled on became legendary. *Casablanca* was just one of forty-nine films Warner Bros. had in production at that time. No one realized the special destiny that awaited it in film history.

Some things just happen to be out of actors' and filmmakers' hands, though. One of those in this case was that this story set in Morocco suddenly received ripped-from-the-headlines relevance. On November 8, General Dwight D. Eisenhower launched Operation Torch, a series of three simultaneous landings at Algiers, Oran, and yes, Casablanca. The goal was to trap Germany's Afrika Korps, already on the run from Egypt and pursued by the forces of British General Bernard Montgomery after the Second Battle of El Alamein. That battle caused the Nazis to lose their offensive momentum—there was no more chance of the Axis capturing the Suez Canal—and retreat back to Tunisia. Thanks to the American landings, the Afrika Korps was trapped. Once they evacuated, the Allies controlled North Africa. And from a staging ground in Tunisia they could launch an invasion of Sicily and then Italy, opening up a second front to relieve the beleaguered Russians, who had finally stalled the German army.

Given this new relevance, Warner Bros. rushed *Casablanca* into release, opening at New York's 1,500-seat Hollywood Theater just eighteen days after the launch of Operation Torch. They didn't plan on giving it an Oscar-qualifying run at a Los Angeles theater until 1943, however. The Best Picture winner for 1942 was obviously going to be *Mrs. Miniver*. Better to let *Casablanca* compete the following year. (For that year, 1943, *Casablanca* did win Best Picture.) That following January, the film would get another boost anyway when FDR and Churchill met in Morocco to discuss war strategy at the Casablanca Conference. It was worth the wait. This film was special. As *New York Times* film critic Bosley Crowther put it, "The Warners . . . have a picture which makes the spine tingle and the heart take a leap."

And Operation Torch had been one final way, after so many, in which the art of *Casablanca* reflected real life.

Warner Bros. touted Conrad Veidt's Major Strasser as the villain of <u>Casablanca</u> in this publicity still—no noose appears in the actual film. Veidt, who had been such a prominent anti-Nazi voice, died eleven months before <u>Casablanca</u> won Best Picture at the Oscars. On April 3, 1943, he suffered a massive heart attack on the eighth hole of the Riviera Country Club golf course in Los Angeles. Aware of a congenital heart condition, Veidt was golfing with his personal physician, who pronounced him dead on the spot. He was fifty years old.

AND MAY ALL YOUR
CHRISTMASES BE WHITE

Casablanca was a wartime pinnacle for Hollywood artistry. It was a vision of America looking outward at the rest of the world. Arguably the only wartime work that has matched its extraordinary enduring popularity, even surpassing it, is not a film but a song. And a song that does just the opposite of *Casablanca*: it looks back home. "White Christmas" had been introduced on Bing Crosby's *Kraft Music Hall* show the Christmas before, but it was only in August 1942 that it really started to make an impact. That's when the Paramount film for which Irving Berlin had written it, *Holiday Inn*, opened; proceeds from its premiere benefited Navy Relief. (Strangely, all throughout the 1940s, films with a Christmas theme often opened during the summer.) "White Christmas" wasn't an instant hit after *Holiday Inn* opened, though—*Variety* didn't even mention the song in the trade's review of the film. It was more of a slow burn, steadily reaching listeners on the radio via a supple, strangely melancholy recording Crosby had made a few months before during an eighteen-minute studio session for his label, Decca.

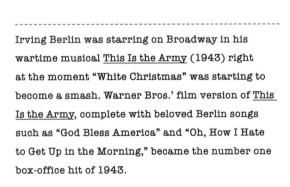

Irving Berlin was starring on Broadway in his wartime musical <u>This Is the Army</u> (1943) right at the moment "White Christmas" was starting to become a smash. Warner Bros.' film version of <u>This Is the Army</u>, complete with beloved Berlin songs such as "God Bless America" and "Oh, How I Hate to Get Up in the Morning," became the number one box-office hit of 1943.

By October 31 it was number one on Billboard. And it stayed there until Tommy Dorsey's "There Are Such Things" dethroned it on January 16, though it would top the charts again over the holidays in following years. On November 16 it also topped the

CBS radio show *Your Hit Parade*'s weekly chart of the nation's most popular songs and would remain at number one for an unprecedented ten weeks. Not a carol exactly, certainly not a religious song, "White Christmas" brought nostalgia into mainstream culture like nothing else ever quite had. It was inevitable then that it became the biggest single of all time—fifty million recordings sold of both the 1942 version and Crosby's 1947 rerecording, which was necessary because the master cylinder of the original was nearly worn down, it had been copied so much. It's still the highest-selling record of all time, and there's nothing to indicate that anything will ever dethrone it.

Somehow, like Babe Ruth pointing his bat at the outfield to mark where he intended to hit a home run, Berlin had called it. When he walked into his office at 799 Broadway in New York City on Monday, January 8, 1940, he told his arranger Helmy Kresa, "I want you to take down a song I wrote over the weekend. Not only is it the best song I ever wrote, it's the best song anybody ever wrote." The market for Christmas songs wasn't even especially massive at the moment; popular interest in Christmas carols had been revived by Bing Crosby only in 1935, with his smash-hit recordings of "Silent Night" and "Adeste Fideles." Very quickly, Berlin, then fifty-one and riding almost three decades of extraordinary success as America's favorite songwriter, settled on Crosby as the man to sing his new creation.

In the weeks leading up to Christmas 1942 its popularity exploded as a kind of sonic encapsulation of everyone's desire for a return to home and the simple pleasures of normal life. For the troops, it became an anthem. As cultural historian Jody Rosen writes, "It aired on Armed Forces Radio request programs. It was played on jukeboxes in USO halls and PX stores. It arrived in the recreation kits that the military had developed in recognition of the importance of music in boosting troop morale . . . Above all the song appealed to servicemen in the warmest climes—posted on Guadalcanal in the Pacific, heading into combat in North Africa." There had been a flurry of other wartime songs. To take the top spot on *Your Hit Parade*'s chart, "White Christmas" dethroned the Merry Macs' "Praise the Lord and Pass the Ammunition." But "White Christmas" succeeded precisely because, unlike all those other wartime songs, it wasn't about getting hopped up to fight but about the dreams that keep us going, the Gatsby-esque hope that we could re-create cherished memories of the past in whatever present reality we faced—even if you were in Algiers or New Guinea. Rosen writes, "'White Christmas' was no 'Over There.' It was an 'over here' . . . inciting patriotism in its most primal form: homesickness." This was the sonic equivalent of that new type of wartime movie, the home front film.

How remarkable that the most beloved Christmas song ever was an American pop tune written by a Jewish immigrant from Russia? Berlin was born Israel Baline in the town of Tyumen, located 1,300 miles east of Moscow in a remote part of Siberia. His earliest memory was at age four, when his Christian neighbors went on a pogrom against local Jews and set Berlin's home ablaze—these pogroms often happened on Christian holidays. It may well have been Christmas. Flash-forward to December 25, 1928, over thirty years after Berlin immigrated to America, and the songwriter's twenty-four-day-old son died suddenly. Given such a history, it would have made sense if Berlin tried to avoid Christmas altogether. Instead he turned his pain into a melancholy Yuletide masterpiece: a mission statement not about fighting what we hate but saving what we love.

If that isn't an American Dream worth cherishing, what is?

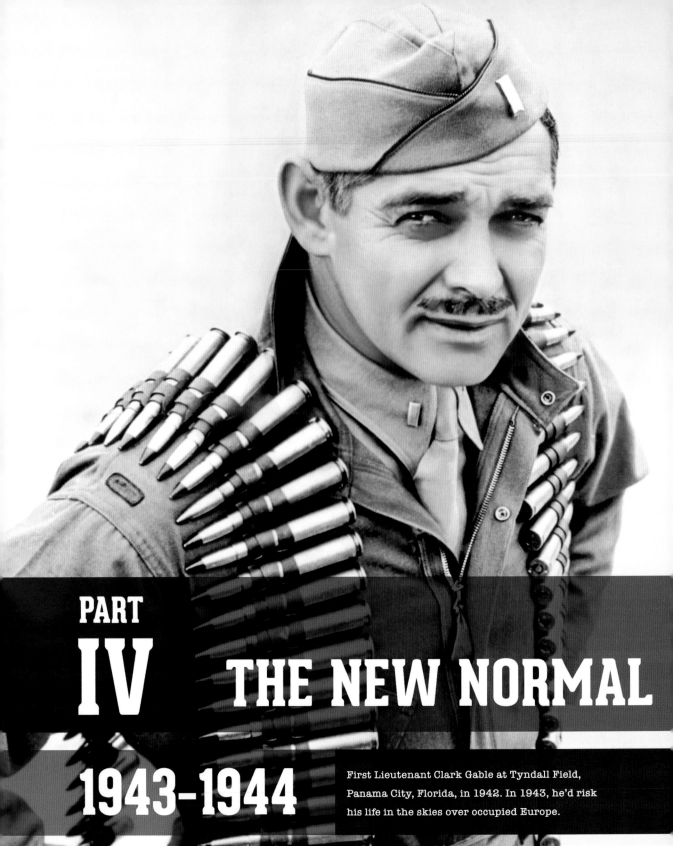

PART IV
THE NEW NORMAL

1943-1944

First Lieutenant Clark Gable at Tyndall Field, Panama City, Florida, in 1942. In 1943, he'd risk his life in the skies over occupied Europe.

STARS IN UNIFORM

The Hollywood actors who left their careers behind to join the Armed Forces found their military life dominated by one thing: like the opening narration of *Casablanca* says, they had to "wait . . . and wait . . . and wait . . ." before they'd see anything even resembling action.

The first two and a half years of Jimmy Stewart's service in the Army Air Forces took place entirely Stateside. Though he didn't see combat during this time, it was hardly uneventful: he spent most of 1942 teaching new pilots in the kind of training aircraft he'd brought to a clean landing at the start of the *Winning Your Wings* short. His combat readiness designation was classified as "static," meaning that unless strings were pulled at the highest levels it was uncertain the Army Air Forces would risk putting Stewart in harm's way. What would it mean if he were shot down? What if he were captured? Would he be paraded by the enemy before snarling crowds as a spoil of war? What a propaganda coup that would be.

Stewart wanted to see combat. He didn't just want to make war documentaries; he wanted to be like everyone else, risk what millions of others were risking. Already promoted to first lieutenant, Stewart was transferred to Gower Field, near Boise, Idaho, for six months. This was a pivotal time in showing he was command material—especially when tragedy struck. Stewart's bunkmate Tom Homer, a fellow Pennsylvanian, was killed on May

4, 1943, when a B-17 crashed about fifty miles southeast of the airfield. While mourning his friend, the actor turned military officer took charge of operations at the crash site, cataloging the wreckage, recovering what was recoverable, and submitting a report on what went wrong. No wonder his commander, Colonel "Pop" Arnold, recommended the removal of that "static" designation on Stewart's commission and urged him for appointment to the 445th Bomb Group with the new rank of captain. It meant Stewart was to command his own squadron. "I felt that if he wanted combat duty, to fight the war, that badly, I'd help him," Arnold said. That Colonel Arnold was twenty-eight while Stewart was thirty-five showed what an oddity the actor was

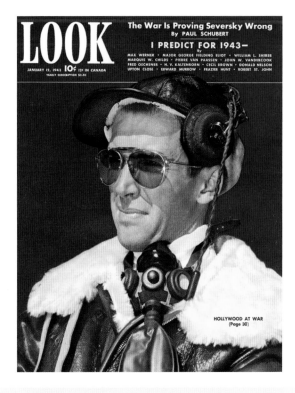

First Lieutenant James Stewart on the cover of <u>Look</u> magazine in 1943 in a special about "Hollywood at War."

in the decidedly young-skewing Army Air Forces. But he was one step closer to the action.

There was just one hitch: Stewart had to learn how to fly an entirely different bomber. The 445th was made up of B-24 Liberators. So for three months he'd have to be stationed in Sioux City, Iowa, to get the miles on this plane under his belt. It was more waiting. First, he'd make a pit stop back in Hollywood to attend Dorothy McGuire's wedding and appear in MGM's twentieth-anniversary class photograph. Could this be his last hurrah in Tinseltown? No one knew how long the war would last. Would there even be a career waiting for him when the fighting stopped?

Nothing came easily in the Army Air Forces. But finally, Stewart would see combat. He now commanded fifteen flight crews of ten men each, as well as the two hundred ground crew who kept the B-24s in flight-ready condition. Their destination: Fortress Europe.

Around the same time, Stewart's dear friend and one-time roommate Henry Fonda was being given a greater degree of responsibility in the navy. He had joined up in November 1942 as a seaman third class, after finishing one last movie for 20th Century Fox: *Immortal Sergeant* (1943), a film Fonda hated. It's probably not a coincidence that Stewart and Fonda had just come off making films they really despised when they joined up. Fonda's meticulous mindset lent itself to inventory work; starting in May 1943 he spent a sixteen-week rotation as a trainee quartermaster on the USS *Satterlee*. Comparing extant supplies with allocation was tedious work, a process of endless corrections, but Fonda seemed suited for it.

Right as Stewart was leaving for Sioux City in August 1943, Fonda was promoted to lieutenant junior grade. Like Stewart, he had no interest in making war documentaries. Fonda immediately swore off a suggestion he be transferred to Ford's

Henry Fonda in his sailor's uniform in 1943, giving a performance of <u>They Were Expendable</u> for the navy radio program <u>Anchors Aweigh</u>, alongside Tyrone Power, Gloria Holden, and Rear Admiral Francis W. Rockwell.

Field Photo or otherwise help make training films. He applied for air combat intelligence work instead and received a post on the USS *Curtiss*, a seaplane tender—a kind of carrier for planes capable of taking off and landing on water—assigned to the Pacific and with a crew of over 1,100. This ship had been damaged by a Japanese dive-bomber during the attack on Pearl Harbor, with nineteen of its crew killed. But like so many of those ships targeted on the Day of Infamy, it was refitted and sent back into service. In March 1944, he assumed his post aboard *Curtiss*, at harbor in Kwajalein in the Marshall Islands, shortly after US Marines had captured this atoll from the Japanese.

Fonda came armed with new skills in the art of reading reconnaissance photography and training in antisubmarine warfare—something communications officer Kirk Douglas specialized in at the same time aboard USS *PC-1139*, before his discharge in 1944 after being injured by a prematurely exploding depth charge. Fonda also brought fourteen bottles of Old Taylor to toast his new commission. Unfortunately, upon arrival, several of the bottles smashed, lending the distinct scent of spirits to his backup uniforms. "Mister, we can't have the ship smelling of Kentucky bourbon," his commanding officer said. "It's not only against Navy regulations, it'll make the damn crew thirsty as hell. Understand?"

On the other hand, Burgess Meredith had no qualms whatsoever about spending much of his service making training films. "Buzz," as his friends Jimmy and Hank knew him, told them both the night before the 1942 Oscars he was joining the Army Air Forces. By 1943, he'd pivot to the Office of War Information, helping to make films such as *The Rear Gunner* (1943) and *A Welcome to Britain* (1943), the latter designed to help American servicemen culturally acclimate to extended stays in the United Kingdom.

While Stewart was training pilots in the Army Air Forces, thirty-one-year-old Robert Taylor was doing much the same as a Navy flyer. Where the air force was primarily concerned with land-based fighters and bombers, Navy airmen included most of the pilots of planes, often shorter range, that would take off from aircraft carriers. In addition to training carrier-based pilots, Taylor narrated his own documentary, *The Fighting Lady*, which debuted in December 1944, about the operation of a then unnamed carrier (the USS *Yorktown*, the more advanced ship that launched in April 1943 to replace the carrier that had been sunk during the Battle of Midway). And he did all this after starring in one of the best films about the early days of America's involvement in the war, MGM's *Bataan*, which opened in June 1943. It was fitting he should have a starring role in that since he had been one of the most prominent Hollywood voices in 1940 and '41 urging US entry into the war. It is striking, though:

Lieutenant (Junior Grade) Robert Taylor during the swearing-in ceremony for his navy service in 1943.

three years younger than Stewart, Taylor was already considered too old to be placed into combat. It's a testament to Stewart's patience and stubbornness that he actually was allowed to fly missions when almost no one else at thirty-five would have been.

While these others had to wait for combat, Douglas Fairbanks Jr. had already made a fighting mark in his own military service. Two days shy of thirty-two when the attack on Pearl Harbor happened, Fairbanks had been part of the Naval Reserve since the decade before. During the war, he spent time learning the art of military deception in the company of Lord Mountbatten's commandos—Fairbanks Jr. was closely acquainted with the British monarchy, with King George VI even giving him an honorary knighthood for "furthering Anglo-American relations." And perhaps drawing on the tools of deception inherent in acting, he petitioned for the creation of a stealth strike squad. It would become the Beach Jumpers, a group of navy commandos who'd carry out diversionary amphibious landings to confuse the enemy about where any real invasion force was actually landing. The Beach Jumpers were

Navy Lieutenant Douglas Fairbanks Jr., with a Coast Guard ensign, watches a practice beach landing in April 1943.

----

critical to the Allies' first major amphibious landing in Europe: Operation Husky, the invasion of Sicily that commenced on July 10, 1943.

After all the prep throughout the previous year, events were now moving swiftly. The Allies had retaken Guadalcanal, one of the Solomon Islands that the Japanese intended to use as a major air base against New Guinea and Australia—actor Robert Montgomery served on a PT boat during the campaign. That opened the door to the US island-hopping strategy that would last until Japan's surrender. Meanwhile, on the other side of the world, the Red Army had stopped the Nazi advance once and for all with their capture of the German Sixth Army in Stalingrad in February 1943. All ninety thousand surviving soldiers of that Wehrmacht army surrendered to the Soviet forces, to be shipped to prison camps in Siberia (only five thousand survived to the end of the war).

And just fifteen days after the Allies' invasion of Sicily, which Fairbanks's Beach Jumpers had helped make possible, Italy's King Victor Emmanuel III removed Il Duce himself, Benito Mussolini, from power. The provisional government imprisoned the dictator in Hotel Campo Imperatore, high in the Apennine Mountains, while they carefully negotiated an armistice with the Allies. They hoped if they ended Italy's war in secret, the Allies would be able to land before Germany itself could invade Italy and restore Fascist control. Already, Hitler had transferred a massive number of troops to the border of Italy for just such a thing: 20 percent of his whole army, in fact, most of whom were diverted from the Eastern Front, allowing the Russians to take the advantage in the Battle of Kursk, the largest tank battle in history. Italy's king wanted to avoid, at all cost, Germany and the Allies simply dividing his country between them in an armed stalemate. That was an outcome worthy of fear, because it was an outcome so very inevitable.

GABLE FINDS PURPOSE, HOWARD BECOMES A MARTYR

While Italy's fate hung in the balance, and before most of his acting peers save for Douglas Fairbanks Jr. actually saw action, Clark Gable was flying daring missions over Europe. Despite Louis B. Mayer's best efforts to dissuade the draft board from recruiting MGM's stars, Gable volunteered in August 1942, after *Somewhere I'll Find You* made its debut. During his service, he'd be given only half pay from the studio: $3,750 a week. Unlike Stewart and Fonda, Gable was fine with making a war documentary—not that it meant he was any less in harm's way.

His assignment was to make a film advocating for the importance of aerial gunners, a position for which there had been difficulty recruiting. To make that film he'd need to be trained as a gunner himself, while MGM arranged for several studio employees to join him in creating an Army Air Forces filmmaking unit: cameramen Andrew J. McIntyre, Mario Toti, and Robert Boles, sound recorder Howard Voss, and screenwriter John Lee Mahin.

The expectation was that Gable, then forty-one years old, would enter the service as an officer, as many other celebrities would. But, like Stewart and Fonda, he accepted no favors and enrolled in Officer Candidate School instead, where it was far from guaranteed he would make the final cut—especially

as he dropped out of high school in the tenth grade. There were seven or eight hours of classroom work a day in the training program he enrolled in with McIntyre in Miami Beach. But even after "lights out" he'd lock himself in a toilet stall and study for hours. Out of a class of 2,600 he graduated at the end of October 1942 around 700th, and was given the rank of second lieutenant. Having ingratiated himself with his fellow officers—he was known to pull out his top row of fake teeth and gummily joke, "Look at me! I'm the King of Hollywood!"— Gable was chosen by his graduating class to be their commencement speaker. After completing a photography course in Spokane, Washington, he was promoted to first lieutenant and shipped out with his unit of filmmakers to Polebrook, England, where an RAF base had been built on a Rothschild estate several years earlier. Here he would join the 351st Bomb Group and take to the air in B-17 Flying Fortresses.

Time magazine's newsreel series, "The March of Time," dedicated a whole episode to "Show Business at War," featuring Gable.

On five missions over continental Europe, Gable squeezed in behind a gunner in a turret to photograph his actions on 16 mm color film. On his very first mission, on May 4, 1943, flying on a bombing mission to destroy the Nazi-commandeered Ford and General Motors factories in Antwerp, Belgium, he had to pinch hit and fire a .50 caliber machine gun himself when the gunner was injured. In an unpressurized cabin at thirty thousand feet, supplemental oxygen was required, as well as the proper insulating gloves. It could get down to forty-five degrees below zero inside the cabin at those altitudes. When Gable wore leather gloves instead, he ended up with a mild case of frostbite.

But that was far from the greatest peril he faced in the air. On his fourth aerial mission, and his only bombing raid on Germany itself, an unexploded 20mm shell ripped through the fuselage, tore the heel off Gable's boot, and exited the aircraft only a foot from his head. "I didn't know it had happened," Gable told reporters afterward. "I didn't know anything about it until we had dropped eleven thousand feet, and could get off oxygen and look around. Only then did I see the hole in the turret." His B-17, named *Ain't It Gruesome*, dropped its payload over Bochum, Germany, but of the 330 bombers in the group, 25 were shot down. After his fifth and final mission, on September 23, to bomb the port

Clark Gable with the crew of the B-17 bomber <u>Eight Ball</u>, with whom he flew over Antwerp on May 4, 1943—his very first mission.

Leslie Howard greets two US Army Air Forces
officers at London's Curzon Theatre in 1942.

of Nantes, France, Gable and his filmmaking unit
had shot fifty thousand feet of film. The time to
edit the documentary had arrived, and with it, the
end of his time in combat zones. Unfortunately, the
commanding general of the Army Air Forces, "Hap"
Arnold, had no more use for the footage. "Oh, we've
licked that," General Arnold said, about the earlier
problem of recruiting aerial gunners. It didn't matter. Maybe *Combat America* (1945) wouldn't have a
clear recruiting purpose any longer. It was still an
indispensable look at the war—shot in color, no
less. And the danger he had experienced was very
real: Gable's own commanding officer, Lieutenant
Colonel William Hatcher, would soon after be shot
down himself, captured by Nazi forces and forced to
spend the rest of the war in prisoner of war camps.
Only after the war did anyone on the Allied side
realize that when Gable was in the air Adolf Hitler
actually issued an order making the actor's capture
a priority.

After all, Gable was the Führer's favorite movie
star.

It's one of the bizarre coincidences of the war
that Gable not only lost his wife in a tragic airplane
crash, but that his *Gone with the Wind* costar Leslie
Howard met the same fate. While Lombard's death
had been a terrible accident, Howard actually was
shot down by the Nazis. Not that Gable and the
British actor were especially close: they weren't
just rivals for Scarlett O'Hara's affections, they
were completely different kinds of stars—Gable as
much a symbol of hard-charging American alpha-
maleness as anyone, Howard embodying a kind of
aloof, Old World sensitivity. Howard "had the kind
of distraught air that would make people want to
mother him," his friend David Niven said. "Actually,
he was about as naïve as General Motors. Busy little
brain, always going."

One thing Gable and Howard shared was an
urgent desire to serve their countries during the

war. Britain, fighting for its life for almost two years before America's entry into the conflict, summoned an intense patriotism in Howard. He had served during World War I, but was quickly drummed out of His Majesty's army due to ill health. Afterward, it seemed he wished to abandon Britain, moving to the United States for work on Broadway and eventually in Hollywood movies. *Gone with the Wind* was his last hurrah in America, however. Months before its December 1939 premiere, Howard had returned to Britain to help the war effort. The UK government prevented its subjects from holding foreign assets during wartime, so Howard had to relinquish more than £20,000 he had made in Hollywood upon his return. The patriotic zeal Howard channeled over the next few years might have to do with his background. Whereas immigrants, such as Frank Capra, or children of immigrants, such as John Ford, felt compelled to prove that they were as American as anyone, Howard might have felt the same in the UK. He was born in London but spoke German in his household as a child: he had Jewish ancestry from both his father, who originally hailed from Hungary, and his maternal grandfather, who had been a Jewish merchant in East Prussia. The actor's birth name was Leslie Howard Steiner.

Upon his return to Britain, he immediately dedicated himself to movies that celebrated the nation's fight against Fascism. The most important of his wartime propaganda efforts had to be *"Pimpernel" Smith* (1941), in which Howard revived his most beloved character: the title role in 1934's *The Scarlet Pimpernel*, a masked avenger who saved innocents from the guillotine during the French Revolution. *"Pimpernel" Smith*, which Howard directed as well, updated the story to the present, with Howard as an archaeologist apparently leading a historic dig in Nazi Germany, but actually in the country to rescue inmates at concentration camps. Howard said he couldn't care less if these films were

called propaganda. He believed in them. The actor next appeared in Michael Powell's anti-Nazi *49th Parallel* (1941) and in *The First of the Few* (1942) as R. J. Mitchell, the inventor of the Spitfire. The actor directed that one himself.

In May 1943, Howard embarked on a goodwill mission to Spain and Portugal. Both had Fascist leaders: Germany had sent the Luftwaffe to help Francisco Franco take power in the Spanish Civil War, but Franco kept Spain neutral during World War II itself. Howard's tour was to do in Spain and Portugal for Britain what the Good Neighbor Policy had done for the United States: these nations needed to remain neutral.

On June 1 in Lisbon, Howard boarded BOAC Flight 777, a Douglas DC-3 airliner set to fly to Bristol, England. He was one of thirteen passengers and four crew from Dutch airline KLM, which was operating the flight. He hadn't actually had a ticket aboard this particular flight. The plan was for him to return to England the next day. But a sudden urgency overcame him. He had the airline ask two other passengers, including then eight-year-old future actor Derek Partridge, to stay behind for a flight the next day so that he and a friend could travel now. BOAC agreed, but Howard then caused a slight delay by picking out some stockings—nylon being unavailable in the countries at war—in a Lisbon shop for his girlfriend back in the UK. It was a little after 7:30 a.m. when Flight 777 took off. At about 10:54 a.m., over the Bay of Biscay just off the northern Spanish coast, the Dutch pilot radioed, "I am being followed by strange aircraft. Putting on best speed . . . we are being attacked. Cannon shells and tracers are going through the fuselage. Wave-hopping and doing my best." The airliner, painted in camouflage, had actually been attacked by German fighters twice before, on the previous November 15 and April 19, but its pilot had been able to escape through evasive maneuvers each time. This time, Flight 777's luck ran out. A swarm of eight Luftwaffe Junkers Ju 88 C-6 maritime fighters succeeded in shooting the commercial airliner down. Its final resting place was directly north of the Spanish town of Cedeira. All lives aboard were lost.

After the war, the commander of the attacking Luftwaffe squadron, First Oberleutnant Herbert Hintze, said that if he had known it was a commercial airliner he would have escorted it into a landing in occupied France and taken its passengers captive instead. Conspiracy theories have swirled ever since

about Flight 777. Was Howard, as one of Britain's most effective cinematic propagandists, deliberately targeted? In his memoir of the war years, Winston Churchill suggested his theory that the Germans thought that the prime minister himself was aboard the plane: "The brutality of the Germans was only matched by the stupidity of their agents," he wrote. After long inquiries into the matter, British journalist Ian Colvin and Howard's own son Ronald Howard concluded that the actor had indeed been the target of the Germans, and that the order to shoot down

Leslie Howard signs autographs at a party for the US Eighth Air Force in Watford, England, on February 15, 1943.

Flight 777 came from Goebbels himself. Colvin and Ronald Howard even published separate books with their conclusions.

It is important to note, however, that several other VIPs were aboard Flight 777 who might have inspired just as much antipathy from the Germans, including Wilfred Israel, formerly the owner of one of the largest department stores in Berlin. Long since having relocated to Britain, Israel helped organize the Kindertransport: a program to get Jewish children out of Nazi-occupied territory. It's believed Israel saved more than ten thousand Jewish children from Germany and Austria alone. He had been in Lisbon on a two-month trip to help organize passage for Jewish refugees from the Nazis who'd made it to Spain and Portugal. He could very well have been the Germans' target. Biographer Estel Eforgan, in the 2013 book *Leslie Howard: The Lost Actor*, concluded that Howard was not the reason for the Germans' attack on Flight 777, and a first-person account of one from the Junkers 88 fighter pilots who shot it down suggests he at least did not know at all who was aboard. But the theorizing doesn't end there: Spanish author José Rey Ximena has suggested that Howard was a diplomat on a top-secret mission for Churchill to dissuade Franco from joining the Axis, and that his persuasion may very well have had an effect. Then there's British spymaster Sir William Stephenson. The head of UK Intelligence in the western hemisphere during the war and Ian Fleming's real-life inspiration for James Bond, Stephenson claimed that Churchill knew about the Germans' intent to shoot down Flight 777 but insisted that they had to let them shoot it down anyway. The reason? If they intervened and stopped Flight 777 from taking off, the enemy would become aware that Britain had

cracked the German Enigma code. Furthermore, former CIA agent Joseph B. Smith said that in 1957 he learned that Howard had even been aware prior to takeoff that his flight was to be attacked by German fighters, but, committed to not revealing Britain had broken the German code, he willingly sacrificed himself. Was that why he was so insistent upon taking the place of an eight-year-old boy on that flight? But there were also two other children aboard. And why did he buy stockings for his girlfriend back in London before boarding?

We may never know for certain the full story of Flight 777, but we do know one thing about Leslie Howard's wartime work: it had an impact. *"Pimpernel" Smith* even saved lives. As was the case with most British- and Hollywood-produced anti-Nazi films, *"Pimpernel" Smith* was banned in Sweden. "They couldn't show it openly in Stockholm, because it was anti-German," said Nina Lagergren, the half-sister of Swedish diplomat Raoul Wallenberg. "So they had a special cinema where we could see it, specially invited, at the British embassy. This was in 1942. And afterwards Raoul said: that is something I would like to do." Wallenberg meant it. As a diplomat to Hungary, he had seen how terribly the government there had treated Jews after joining the Axis. So he came up with a plan inspired by *"Pimpernel" Smith*: he rented a couple dozen buildings around Budapest, flew the Swedish flag over them, designating the properties as Swedish diplomatic territory, then issued Swedish passports to Hungarian Jews. They could then take sanctuary in these makeshift Swedish consulates. It's believed he saved tens of thousands of Hungarian Jews from deportation to Auschwitz.

Even after Howard died, his work went on.

SHERLOCK HOLMES AND LASSIE GO TO WAR

"*Pimpernel*" *Smith* took a beloved concept and updated it to face the Nazi threat. That film wasn't alone. Fighting Fascism became the new reality for a number of franchises. It was simply a reality that couldn't be ignored. In the third of their pairings as Sherlock Holmes and Dr. Watson, Basil Rathbone and Nigel Bruce brought Arthur Conan Doyle's beloved characters into the present day, where they helped Britain's war effort. An updated treatment wasn't in the cards from the beginning: the duo's first two Holmes-Watson films for Fox took place in the period in which Conan Doyle had set them: the late nineteenth century. A move to the minor studio Universal meant smaller budgets, which a present-day setting certainly accommodated; but when *Sherlock Holmes and the Voice of Terror* debuted on September 18, 1942, that contemporary setting also gave Holmes and Watson a greater urgency and relevance. A bit of onscreen text at the beginning, calling Holmes "ageless, invincible, and unchanging" and stating that he was needed now to solve "significant problems of the present day," accounted for the period shift. In this film, they investigate a Nazi propagandist who broadcasts messages into the UK over the radio for all to hear; at the conclusion of each broadcast, an act of terrorism follows. Does that mean that each time he takes to the airwaves, the "Voice of Terror"—the

villain's actual name in the film—gives some kind of code to activate spies embedded in Britain? Viewers would have recognized the concept of the "Voice of Terror" as being similar to Lord Haw Haw, the nickname for William Joyce, a British Fascist politician who defected to Nazi Germany and broadcast morale-undermining messages to the British public in his stiff, upper-crust accent throughout the war. Joyce was captured by the British at the war's end and hanged for treason in 1946.

The public loved this present-day take on Holmes even more than the nineteenth-century version, and Universal went on to produce eleven more films with Rathbone and Bruce playing their characters in a 1940s setting. They wouldn't battle Nazis in all of these, but a few had a distinct wartime theme: *Sherlock Holmes and the Secret Weapon* (1942) adapted the classic Conan Doyle story from 1903 "The Adventure of the Dancing Men" into a story about code-breaking and preventing a high-tech

Nigel Bruce's Watson and Basil Rathbone's Holmes take on the challenges of the 1940s—namely, Nazis.

bombsight from ending up in Nazi hands. *Sherlock Holmes in Washington* (1943) was a completely original story about foiling Nazi spies in America's capital. And though it didn't have an explicitly Nazi-centric story, their later adventure, *The Spider Woman* (1943), has a pivotal scene set at an English carnival where one of the games visitors can play is a shooting gallery, in which they're to take aim at metal effigies of the Axis leaders. "Try your luck on Mussolini, Hirohito, or Hitler!" the barker says. "Hit 'em where their hearts oughta be and listen to the hollow sound." Talk about the war influencing literally all forms of entertainment.

Other franchises followed suit: 1944's *The Thin Man Goes Home*, the fifth of the William Powell–Myrna Loy sleuth series and the only film Loy made

during the war years because she was so devoted to her work for the Red Cross, took on saboteurs in an aircraft factory. Drinking had been a cornerstone of the Thin Man movies, but this installment was almost dry—wartime liquor rationing meant Nick and Nora Charles nearly had to become teetotalers.

Son of Lassie (1945), released just three weeks before V-E Day and MGM's sequel to the smash hit *Lassie Come Home* (1943), provided a direct continuation of the original film's storyline. Joe Carraclough, originally portrayed by Roddy McDowall, has now grown up—Peter Lawford's taken over the portrayal—and is serving Britain in uniform, while his father runs a kennel to train "war dogs." Lassie herself, originally portrayed in a gender-bending performance by a male rough collie named Pal, has

Laddie stares down a German soldier in <u>Son of Lassie</u>.

now aged as well, with Joe instead turning much of his time and attention to Lassie's son Laddie (played by Pal, who has the unique distinction of playing both a mother and her son, though admittedly in different movies). Laddie can't bear Joe leaving home for boot camp, so he walks overland dozens of miles to find his master—ultimately sneaking on board Joe's reconnaissance plane as he sets out on a mission over Nazi-occupied Norway. Joe is shot down, and so now he is all alone in enemy territory with only Laddie as a companion. But of course, his dog is all he needs. Together, they're able to escape and find their way out of the country.

Other stars pivoted their schtick to war-related themes too: Norwegian skater turned actress Sonja Henie, usually associated onscreen with frothy snowbound frolics at Sun Valley or other ski resorts at which she could show off her fancy footwork on the ice, did her part. Eight months after Pearl Harbor, Henie, who was to figure skating what Esther Williams would later be to swimming, appeared with 20th Century Fox contract player John Payne in *Iceland* (1942). Britain had occupied the North Atlantic island in May 1940 to deny the Germans an attempt at controlling it. A year later, but still six months before Pearl Harbor, the United States took over the occupation, as the British forces were needed elsewhere. After America's entry into the war, more than thirty thousand army, navy, and marine personnel ended up being stationed there. *Iceland* created controversy in the country: it positively depicted an American marine captain (Payne) wooing an Icelandic girl (Henie). That was something that happened so often—it was "gall to the Icelanders," *The New York Times* said—because American and British men almost exceeded the male Icelandic population in some parts of the nation. Diplomatic strain and backlash ensued. There's even an Icelandic word for the phenomenon of American and British personnel courting away the country's women: Ástandið. *Iceland* was not popular in Iceland.

Abbott and Costello, who shot to fame in the late 1930s with their radio act, also made a wartime pivot. They battle Nazi spies in 1942's *Rio Rita*. Just a couple years earlier they had appeared on Broadway in *The Streets of Paris* opposite Carmen Miranda. Her box-office hit streak just kept going: her film *Springtime in the Rockies*, for which she received third billing, recorded $2.8 million in box-office rentals after debuting in November 1942. It's a mark of how inflated movie attendance was during wartime: just a couple years earlier, a $2.8 million gross would have placed *Springtime in the Rockies* in the year's top ten box-office winners. And then, climbing Hollywood's ranks, she received second billing in her next film a year later, *The Gang's All Here* (1943), which grossed a whopping $3 million. Busby Berkeley and Miranda were a director-actor pairing for the ages with this one: he choreographed "The Lady in the Tutti Frutti Hat," in which she played a banana xylophone wrapped around her waist like a Hula-Hoop—with dozens of scantily clad chorus girls behind her dancing with large bananas. It's an abstract tropical explosion; no one yet used the word "trippy," but this was trippy. As *The New York Times* put it, Miranda's numbers were staged "as if money was no object but titillation was. Mr. Berkeley has some sly notions under his busby. One or two of his dance spectacles seem to stem straight from Freud and, if interpreted, might bring a rosy blush to several cheeks in the Hays office." In short, *The Gang's All Here* was the ultimate Carmen Miranda movie.

Hollywood's contribution to the Good Neighbor Policy had been immense—but it was time to pivot outreach efforts elsewhere: starting with Russia. There had been a moment in 1939, with

Sonja Henie's Icelandic skater finds love with marine John Payne during the US occupation of her country in <u>Iceland</u>.

the signing of the infamous nonaggression pact between Germany and the Soviet Union, that Stalin, who enthusiastically invaded Poland from the east as Germany stormed in from the west, could be America's enemy sooner rather than later. But Hitler's astonishing betrayal with his invasion of the Soviet Union in June 1941 changed all that. By mid-1943, after the bloodiest two years of war in human history, Stalin's forces had gained the upper hand on Germany and finally began to push Hitler's legions back to the west. Stalin had pull with FDR and Churchill. What he wanted above all was for the United States and Britain to open up a western front to cause Hitler to reassign his forces and relieve the pressure on the USSR.

To drum up enthusiasm for helping aid the beleaguered Russians, Hollywood stepped up. One of the most stirring episodes, the fifth installment, of Frank Capra and Anatole Litvak's *Why We Fight* series was *The Battle of Russia* (1943). Born in Kiev but of Lithuanian heritage, Litvak was the primary director on this one. And to him, it was personal. He had become treasurer of the Russian War Relief association just a month after the German invasion, and helped get his *Confessions of a Nazi Spy* star Edward G. Robinson to make radio broadcasts celebrating the Russian defense. His *Why We Fight* installment was going to be a rousing tribute to everything great about his homeland: clips from Sergei Eisenstein films would illustrate its history (and previous battles with the Germans), Disney animation brought to life their valiant tactics against the Nazi horde, while Litvak commissioned the Russian-born Hollywood composer Dimitri Tiomkin to write the score.

The Battle of Russia was stirring not only to American viewers and servicemen, but to Russians themselves. Stalin personally decorated Litvak when the director returned to his homeland to introduce it, and the film was shown all around Russia. That wasn't common for American movies; Stalin had even banned *The Grapes of Wrath* (as well as the novel) because its vision of poverty still seemed better than the poverty many Soviet citizens were used to—at least the Joads had a truck. One heartwarming visit did occur on Litvak's trip: he was reunited with his mother, whom he hadn't seen in twenty years. The whole experience of *The Battle of Russia* had to have been so meaningful to Litvak: he had suffered a difficult setback the previous November when footage he'd shot of the American landing at Casablanca and the combat that followed was lost when the ship transporting it to London was torpedoed.

The Battle of Russia won the New York Film Critics Circle's Best Documentary prize and was the second *Why We Fight* film to receive a Best Documentary nomination at the Academy Awards. But to really drum up enthusiasm for the Russian cause after two decades of Stateside redbaiting required something more: a Russian *Mrs. Miniver*. It was an idea Nelson Poynter of the Office of

Mission to Moscow's kindly, unconnected-to-reality Joseph Stalin (Manart Kippen) denies to Ambassador Davies that he has dreams of global domination. So why does he have a giant globe?

War Information's Hollywood bureau had put forth after seeing Wyler's film: "Give us a *Mrs. Miniver* of China or Russia." But surprisingly the first dramatic pro-Russia feature out of Hollywood wasn't really that at all: it was Michael Curtiz's immediate follow-up to *Casablanca*, a shocking bit of Stalinist propaganda called *Mission to Moscow* (1943). Warner Bros.' film had almost nothing to do with the war itself; it was merely an attempt at rehabilitating the Soviet premier's image as something other than a bloodthirsty autocrat. Loosely based on former US ambassador to the Soviet Union Joseph E. Davies's memoir, it dramatized, in highly whitewashed fashion, the "show trials" and purges Stalin had carried out in the 1930s. The film

suggests that the military leaders Stalin had killed were pro-German spies. Robert Bruckner, *Mission to Moscow*'s producer, knew what this film was: "an expedient lie for political purposes, glossily covering up important facts with full or partial knowledge of their false presentation."

This film did not resonate in Russia, where the population certainly knew better. Dimitri Shostakovich said he had nothing but scorn for *Mission to Moscow*, and that not even Soviet propaganda would be so bold as to try to get audiences to swallow such extraordinary lies. Film historian Robert Osborne said decades later that when it was shown in Moscow during the war, the "people who saw it considered it a comedy—its portrayal of average, everyday life in the Soviet Union apparently way off the mark for 1943."

Slightly less off the mark was MGM's *Song of Russia* (1944). At least it didn't glorify Stalin, but this one did what Hollywood movies so often do: it told the story of Germany's invasion through the lens of how it affected the romance between two people. Robert Taylor plays an American conductor on a forty-city tour of Russia who falls in love with a Russian pianist (actress Susan Peters; audiences would have to wait until Tamara Toumanova in *Days of Glory* (1944) to actually have a Russian lead in one of these pro-Russia films), and the German sneak attack destroys their bliss.

The one that actually comes the closest to being a "*Mrs. Miniver* for Russia" is *The North Star* (1943), about life in a small Ukrainian village right before the invasion. Once again it's a cast of mostly American actors, plus Erich von Stroheim as the evil Nazi doctor who wants to drain the village's children of their blood and give it to wounded German soldiers. Until those horrors, it's an idyllic vision of countryside life—the most idealized vision of Ukrainian collective farms you could imagine— with an end-of-the-school-year party and several young kids planning a trip by foot to Kiev for their vacation. On the trip, the war breaks out, and the kids have to grow up fast.

All of these films did seem to have an effect. The American public was more pro-Russia than ever. But *The North Star* represented a shift in another way for its director, Lewis Milestone. He had previously made maybe the least glamorous depiction of battle, the most stirring antiwar cri de couer in Hollywood ever: *All Quiet on the Western Front* (1930). That film illustrated the waste and meaninglessness of World War I. But the stakes of World War II, this literal battle of good versus evil, had changed Milestone's mindset entirely. He was now making prowar films. Before *The North Star*, he had directed one of the most stirring World War II films of all, 1943's *Edge of Darkness*, about Norwegian resistance fighters. That film, somehow even more than the film set on a collective farm, emphasized the importance of sublimating individual desires to collective action: Judith Anderson's resistance fighter is in love with a German soldier—she still kills him to serve the cause.

Lewis Milestone, like so many, had followed a similar arc to Sergeant York's: a strong pacifist sense gave way to the knowledge that it would be necessary to take lives in order to save lives from evil. He was so interventionist that even a full two years before America's entry into the war he authorized *All Quiet on the Western Front* be recut by Universal to lay blame on Germany for its plans of "world domination," with a new bit of narration even invoking Hitler. Frank Capra allowed for his *Lost Horizon* (1937) to be similarly recut to deemphasize its original quasi-isolationist message and reframe the story as a tale of the Sino-Japanese War. Jean Renoir, director of the only movie to exceed *All Quiet on the Western Front* as an antiwar statement, *La Grande Illusion* (1937), made the same shift too: his *This Land Is Mine* (1943), starring Charles Laughton and Maureen O'Hara as teachers in a Nazi-occupied village, is a plea to fight at any cost. And Billy Wilder, long removed from his days hunched over his hot plate at the Chateau Marmont, was making *Five Graves to Cairo* (1943), another urgent wartime yarn (with von Stroheim as Rommel). The humane call for peace he had helped issue in the screenplay he cowrote for *Ninotchka* (1939) was now well in the past. This was no time for pacifists; if it seemed like everyone was on board, that's only because everyone was needed.

There was one audience, though, that Hollywood still needed to reach—and it would begin outreach efforts, however flawed, that it wouldn't match for decades.

A *WHY WE FIGHT* FOR AFRICAN-AMERICANS

He took off in the early morning hours of June 2, 1943, from Fardjouna Airfield in Tunisia. The mission? To contribute to the air assault of a small island thirty-seven miles off the Tunisian coast: Pantelleria, a thirty-square-mile dot in the middle of the Mediterranean and a critical stepping stone to the invasion of Sicily. As the volcanic island became visible through the cockpit of his P-40 Warhawk, so did light-to-medium air cover by the Italian forces. He tightened his grip on the controls and prepared to let loose a salvo.

Bullseye.

His name was Lieutenant Charles B. Hall, of Brazil, Indiana, and he was the first African-American pilot ever to shoot down an enemy aircraft. His 99th Fighter Squadron was part of a legendary group: the Tuskegee Airmen, the Black fighter pilots who trained at Alabama's Tuskegee University before entering combat over the Mediterranean in 1943 and, with three more squadrons comprising the 332nd Fighter Group, flew daring bomber escort missions from Ramitelli Airfield on Italy's Adriatic coast throughout 1944.

The Tuskegee Airmen had to fare for themselves too. Segregation was still strictly enforced in the Armed Forces, so their ground crews couldn't count on support from any white units, and their pilots had to develop their own tactics without input from white flyers. Yet white bomber crews would become so impressed by the Airmen that they'd frequently request them as their fighter escorts. Still, the officers' club was off-limits. And even after that

air assault on Pantelleria being so successful—the eleven thousand Italian military personnel stationed there surrendered before US troops even made a landing—the 99th Fighter Squadron's white group commander tried, and failed, to have the all-Black flyers drummed out of the service. In fact, there was also a growing problem across the Armed Forces: racist violence within the ranks inflicted by white servicemen on Black servicemen they encountered.

Hollywood could be useful to help make African-Americans feel like they were part of the American experiment too. But that hadn't previously been the case. The southern market was important to the film industry and that meant moguls wanted to keep Black representation onscreen to a minimum. With Washington liaison Lowell Mellett's directive to diversify, and a call from Walter Francis White of the NAACP to cast Black actors as more than just "comic relief," that began to change. There had certainly been independent productions by Black filmmakers featuring all-Black casts before: the films of Oscar Micheaux and Spencer Williams come to mind. But since MGM's *Hallelujah* (1929), that studio hadn't touched an all-Black musical.

Cabin in the Sky (1943) broke the barrier. MGM gave a healthy, if not spectacular, budget to this adaptation of the Broadway musical. It was certainly a fantasy not unlike that which the

----

Tuskegee Airmen at a briefing before flying a mission.

Eddie "Rochester" Anderson's Little Joe Jackson is trying to be a faithful husband in <u>Cabin in the Sky</u>. Lena Horne's Georgia Brown is making it difficult.

studio had made with all-white casts before, but given a level of specificity to suit its all-Black cast and target audience: producer Arthur Freed and director Vincente Minnelli, helming the first film of his luminous career, let officials at the NAACP read the script and suggest notes. This was the story of a married couple, played by Ethel Waters and Eddie "Rochester" Anderson, who hit the skids when Anderson's gambling fiend can't quite kick his habit—a misunderstanding with the temptress Georgia Brown, played by newcomer Lena Horne, doesn't help matters. Wounded in a gunfight, Anderson dreams he and his wife were both killed and are now to be judged before Heaven about whether he is worthy to ascend the stairway to its heights of glory. Of course, Rex Ingram's Lucifer Jr. had been trying to use Georgia Brown to lead him astray so he and Lucifer Sr. would have Anderson in their clutches "down below." Ingram has a great moment when he and his minions (including Louis Armstrong) are brainstorming ways to lead Anderson to his doom: "I'm stuck with a bunch of B-idea men. All the A-Boys is over there in Europe!"—presumably referring to the Nazis.

Cabin in the Sky is quietly radical. There is not a white person in sight. It's a celebration of Black joy, and one facilitated by having flung open the gates to Hollywood's most prestigious studio. This

Rex Ingram as Lucifer Jr. tries to lead Anderson's Little Joe Jackson astray. Ingram had an impressive run of movies across multiple genres in the 1940s.

was possibly a way to gain a new Black audience for Hollywood, make them feel included, and, of course, make them feel more invested in contributing to the war effort. After its release, one of the film's white writers claimed he'd received a letter from the NAACP "congratulating [them] on the treatment of this Black fable, which avoided cliches and racial stereotypes." A few months later Ingram had a standout part in Warner Bros.' *Sahara* (1943), as a Sudanese soldier serving in the British army. The reprehensiveness of Nazi racism is laid bare when Ingram goes to help a downed German pilot, and the flyer barks that he doesn't want "to be touched by an inferior race." The implicit message to the

audience: America doesn't want to be like them.

But the summer of 1943 showed just how far the United States had to go to address its racial inequities. Over several months, a wave of "race riots," as they were called at the time but usually instigated by white-on-Black violence, swept the country. The Alabama Drydock and Shipbuilding Company in Mobile had helped turn the city into one of the biggest shipbuilding centers in the country. But in May 1943, when the company tried to promote twelve Black employees to the position of welder, usually reserved just for white workers, the white employees began a riot—one so bad the mayor of Mobile asked Alabama's governor to send in the National Guard.

Tensions flamed elsewhere too, when servicemen and local white residents ganged up to injure 150 Mexican-American, Italian-American, Filipino-American, and Black youths in the Zoot Suit Riots of Los Angeles in early June. Similar conflagrations engulfed Detroit, Harlem, and Beaumont, Texas, in the months ahead. Detroit in particular had been a site of racist animosity against Blacks for some time. It had become one of the biggest hubs for the Ku Klux Klan in the Midwest, with a spin-off group called the Black Legion (which Warner Bros. had criticized in the film *Black*

Legion in 1937). Twenty-five Black lives were lost in Detroit during these days of violence.

Just a month later, on July 21, 1943, Fox opened its own all-Black musical extravaganza: *Stormy Weather*. Where *Cabin in the Sky* had Duke Ellington and his orchestra perform some songs, this one had Fats Waller, Cab Calloway, and the Nicholas Brothers, with the lead being played by dancer extraordinaire Bill "Bojangles" Robinson. Staged like a musical revue, with a thin through line about Robinson's character's rise to stardom, *Stormy Weather* was also the second showcase in just three

Bill "Bojangles" Robinson plays a World War I veteran trying to make it in showbiz in <u>Stormy Weather</u>. Lena Horne helps his career and falls in love with him. But there's a suave, tuxedoed entertainer as his competition.

months for Lena Horne, who sings the title song.

Horne first came to the attention of Hollywood when MGM composer Roger Edens saw her performing at Los Angeles's Trocadero in early 1942, after she'd spent years at Manhattan's Cotton Club. He brought her to the attention of Arthur Freed, who signed her to a contract that stipulated she would not have to perform illiterate comedy or portray a cook. Even before *Cabin in the Sky*, her first assignment was to sing two songs in 1942's *Panama Hattie*. But none of the MGM hairdressers would work on a Black woman's hair. So the studio's head of hair styling, Sydney Guilaroff—who'd created the Louise Brooks bob, dyed Lucille Ball's hair red, and given Claudette Colbert bangs—stepped in himself. "I will do Miss Horne's hair," the actress recalled him saying in his fake British accent. "Now Miss Horne, do you know a lady who can come in to help assist me so that when I'm busy on another set, she will know what I want done and will come and tell me?" Horne suggested her friend Tiny Kyle. Busy indeed—Guilaroff was the first MGM hair stylist ever to receive a credit, after which his name appeared on over one thousand films—he helped get the young Black hair stylist into the makeup and hair stylists union. 20th Century Fox hairdresser Helen Rose (best known as a costume designer today) claimed she stepped in herself to do Horne's hair on *Stormy Weather*, as well.

These films had made an impact, but the target Black audience for them still had to watch from the balcony in most movie theaters around the country, segregated as they were. For the most part, they still weren't shown at all in the South. On July 29, 1943, a white crowd gathered outside a movie theater in Mt. Pleasant, Tennessee, that dared to show *Cabin in the Sky*, calling for the manager to "pull the switch." After it had screened for only thirty minutes, the local sheriff had the projector shut off.

In 1944, *The Negro Soldier* documentary, which William Wyler had abandoned after concluding he couldn't imagine why Black soldiers would risk their lives at war for a country that supported institutional racism against them, finally premiered: it was the most direct plea yet for African-Americans to throw themselves into the war effort. Black writer Carlton Moss, who wrote segments for the radio show *Jubilee*, on which Butterfly McQueen had appeared, took over the script, structuring the movie as a literal sermon in which a Black pastor extols the virtues of serving in the Armed Forces to his congregation. The Office of War Information had made it clear: racism was not to be discussed, and the script still had to go through several iterations to make any potential white viewers comfortable. The resulting film was an un-whitewashing of history, though, making clear the contributions of Black lives to defending America and adding to the nation's progress since 1660. At a test screening for a Black audience in Harlem, Moss was asked afterward, "Are you going to show this to white people? . . . Because it will change their attitude." It played in just Black-only movie theaters in the South, though it did reach theaters with predominantly white audiences in New York and Detroit.

All of these efforts paid off for the Armed Forces: in 1944, there were eight hundred thousand Black men in uniform; in 1945, 1.2 million.

NEW STARS ARE BORN, AND OLD ONES BORN AGAIN

taly was finally out of the war. So it seemed for just a moment, anyway. On September 8, 1943, the provisional Italian government that had overthrown Mussolini back in July following the sudden Allied conquest of Sicily agreed to armistice terms. Five days earlier, General Montgomery's British troops had landed in Calabria, in the "toe" of Italy, and Taranto, in the "heel," encountering surprisingly little resistance. The door seemed open for the Americans to land in Salerno on September 9. But as it turned out, not all Italian troops heeded the armistice order. The fighting in this port town was fierce.

At the same moment, Germany swept in from the north and began its own outright occupation of the country, disarming any Italian troops they encountered who didn't now want to fight for the German forces—though about one hundred thousand Italian military personnel did join the Nazis and became the fighting outfit for a new German puppet state, the Italian Social Republic. On September 12, in a daring raid, ten German gliders full of paratroopers landed near the Hotel Campo Imperatore, high in the Apennine Mountains, and rescued Benito Mussolini. Hitler installed Il Duce as the leader of the new Social Republic, which included Rome and stretched further south down to just north of Naples, where an elaborate series

of fortified defensive lines—the Winter Line— were created. Everything south of that the Allies controlled. But the Germans and Italian Fascists were dug in. All of this fighting, not to mention continued grueling campaigns in New Guinea, New Britain, and Tarawa, in the Gilbert Islands, had turned inexperienced American troops everywhere into hardened warriors. It was now time for the next big objective: Operation Overlord, the invasion of France.

The hardships they had seen, the things they had been forced to do . . . it made the soldiers long for home even more, and the wave of home front films

Joan Leslie as "Miss Yankee Doodle Dandy" showing rationable items in 1943.

Arguably, Mickey Rooney gave his finest performance ever in <u>The Human Comedy</u>, which represented a high point in his career, culminating in an Oscar nomination for Best Actor. Sitting third from left is Van Johnson, representing the new wave of stars rising to fame during the war years as Rooney's was beginning to fade.

that followed *Mrs. Miniver* also proved successful. These were visions of how domestic life struggled on even with loved ones shipped out, with women putting in long hours in new jobs, and, of course, with that universal wartime reality: rationing. It wasn't life as usual, but it sure looked good to the troops overseas.

The first major American-set home front film, and arguably the best, is Clarence Brown's *The Human Comedy* (1943) for MGM. Set in the fictional California town of Ithaca, it stars Mickey Rooney as a high school kid, Homer, whose older brother (Van Johnson) is sent off to war. Their father, who died sometime before, provides God-like voiceover about what's happening to his family as he watches them from above. Developed by the

playwright William Saroyan, *The Human Comedy* is like a Norman Rockwell painting come to life. Homer goes about his frenetic day: school, practice for the 220-meter low hurdles race he hopes to win at the next track meet, his job at the local telegraph office. Of course, delivering telegrams means he has to give the news to unsuspecting families around town that a loved one of theirs has died. When he reads out the full telegram that her son has died to a Mexican-American woman, she collapses into her grief. But before he goes, she wants to give him a piece of candy. "All boys like candy." This is a film about the small acts of kindness that people are capable of in the midst of great stress or sorrow. And it's also an inclusive vision. One scene has Homer's boss (James Craig) taking his girlfriend (Marsha

Hunt) on a drive through a park: as they idle past, he points out all the different ethnic groups gathered there to celebrate their heritage—but, no matter their background, all are Americans.

The Human Comedy represents a high point for Rooney he'd never quite achieve again—and a glimpse of a couple of the new stars who'd ascend to the heights he once occupied. The movie earned $2.8 million in the United States and Canada, and Rooney received an Academy Award nomination for Best Actor. But criticism was starting to mount against him about why the twenty-three-year-old actor wasn't joining up. In part, it was because Louis B. Mayer refused to let his top star go. He had been the number one box-office draw of 1939, 1940, and 1941. Despite the best efforts of Mayer's "fixer" Eddie Mannix, Rooney was finally inducted in June 1944, and assigned to an entertainment outfit—his mission was to sing, dance, and put on comedy for the troops, and to do so while actually in uniform as opposed to being part of the USO. Did Mayer and Mannix succeed in fixing it so that Rooney wouldn't be in harm's way? Possibly. They certainly smoothed things over on his behalf when he went AWOL in Los Angeles during the summer of 1944 in an attempt to reconcile with his ex-wife, Ava Gardner.

Between *The Human Comedy* and his enlistment, Mickey Rooney had crammed in another four movies. But Mayer and Mannix weren't exactly off the mark in their fears: more than any other star who served, Rooney's absence from the screen due to his twenty-one months of service did hurt his career. When he next appeared onscreen in *Love Laughs at Andy Hardy,* in December 1946, he was twenty-six and his teenage schtick no longer resonated with the power it once had.

Robert Mitchum, far left, played his first named character, "Horse," in The Human Comedy. Donna Reed, still appearing in uncredited roles until the year before, is second from right.

The Human Comedy, however, introduces two new stars. Robert Mitchum is in one memorable scene where a couple of girls agree to do their patriotic duty and be dates for some guys in uniform. It was his first named role in a film—he plays a Texan named "Horse"—though he was still uncredited. Van Johnson, as Homer's older brother Marcus, makes a particular impression. After a successful run as Gene Kelly's understudy in *Pal Joey* ended in 1941, Johnson was signed to MGM. Johnson was intended to be a replacement for Lew Ayres when the actor left MGM's Dr. Kildare film series to serve as a medic in the war, since he was a conscientious objector. *The Human Comedy* followed, and then, as Johnson was filming his biggest part for MGM yet, as the young love interest in *A Guy Named Joe* (1943), disaster struck. He was in a terrible car accident. Hit by another driver who ran a red light, he was thrown from his vehicle. A significant swath of skin on the back of his head was ripped off, requiring the installation of a metal plate and muscle tissue taken from an arm to fill out the site of the injury. But he was determined to finish *A Guy Named Joe*, and costars Spencer Tracy and Irene Dunne said they'd walk off the film altogether if he was recast. The young actor finished the movie.

Johnson's injury undoubtedly helped make him a star: considering how well publicized his injuries had been, the soldiers who watched him in *A Guy Named Joe* bore him no ill will for being 4-F. This was no spurious 4-F, like they suspected was the case for Frank Sinatra. Johnson was indeed

----

Van Johnson famously has his leg amputated in Thirty Seconds Over Tokyo. That movie dramatized what this photograph of the real-life aftermath in China shows: two American flyers have been rescued and are being cared for by the Chinese forces fighting for their freedom.

a star who had risen to fame because other actors, especially Ayres, had left to serve. But he was one you felt good looking up to. And *A Guy Named Joe* and his follow-up, *Thirty Seconds Over Tokyo*, a thrilling account of the Doolittle Raid, were both among the top ten highest-grossing films of 1944. In many ways, as war fatigue began to set in, those two movies would be the last successful Hollywood films during the war years to explicitly show combat.

While other actors were away fighting, several other stars rose to prominence—or ascended to greater heights than ever before. For the first couple years of the war, Gregory Peck was already in high demand on Broadway as an actor whose health prevented him from joining up: he'd severely injured his back in a Martha Graham dance course sometime earlier. As he'd also been on the rowing team at UC Berkeley, 20th Century Fox later wanted to attribute his injury to that athletic background instead. "In Hollywood, they didn't think a dance class was macho enough, I guess," Peck said. "I've been trying to straighten out that story for years." Signed to Fox, Peck made his screen debut in *Days of Glory*, which premiered two days after D-Day. This was yet another Russian outreach film, about the valiant efforts of a group of partisan guerrillas

stuck behind enemy lines near the occupied city of Tula who are picking off Germans wherever they can. By that point, interest in these Russian-themed movies had waned, and the film quickly left theaters. More successful was his film from later in 1944, *The Keys of the Kingdom*. And in 1945 he'd shoot to absolute superstardom with the number three and number four highest-grossing movies of that year: *Spellbound* and *The Valley of Decision*.

Errol Flynn, suffering from venereal disease, alcoholism, and even having a heart attack during the making of his thrilling boxing drama *Gentleman Jim* (1942), received a much-needed career boost during the war. With that health, he certainly wasn't going to fight. So for many, he became the most daring onscreen soldier. While Van Johnson was an everyman, your ordinary G.I. Joe, Flynn was the kind of devil-may-care avenger you believed could win the war all by himself in movies like *Desperate Journey* (1942), *Edge of Darkness* (1943), *Northern Pursuit* (1943), *Uncertain Glory* (1944), and *Objective, Burma!* (1945). World War II was good for his box office. And he needed it: in 1942, Flynn had been continually in the news on account of being charged with statutory rape. He was acquitted, but the trial was a sensation—so much so that it nearly derailed his career. Ever after, he'd be regarded as a potentially dangerous rogue.

And though today we think of Bing Crosby as more of a mass media father figure, the crooner had been known to have a wild side himself during the early part of his career. He'd scored the biggest hit of all time with "White Christmas" in late 1942, but no one took him seriously as an actor: not in *Holiday*

OPESITE

Inn, nor in his trifling *Road* movies with Bob Hope. Back in 1929, his reputation for drinking led his friends to call him "Binge" Crosby, and when he was arrested for DUI after he rear-ended a car at the Hollywood Roosevelt Hotel's driveway—flinging both him and his female companion onto the pavement—he didn't face just a drunk driving charge but one for violating Prohibition. "Yes," Crosby told the judge, wearing his golf attire, evidently having just come from the course. He was aware alcohol was illegal nationwide. "But no one pays much attention to it." He spent forty days in jail.

So when Crosby played Father O'Malley in *Going My Way* (1944), it felt like he was showing range. Especially since everyone knew that after he had more or less given up the bottle, he'd been married and had four sons. A celibate priest he was not. This was a stretch, critics and award-giving bodies thought. It was also just a damn good performance. O'Malley is a jovial priest—one who lived a little life before being ordained—whom the New York City diocese sends in to help shake up the foundering parish of Father Fitzgibbon (Barry Fitzgerald), whose old Irish ways have ossified enough that the collection plate is suffering. Bankruptcy for his church seems inevitable, and it's up to O'Malley to turn it around. *Going My Way*, like the best home front films, is relatively episodic. There's the through-line plot about saving this downtrodden church and maybe reuniting Father Fitzgibbon with his aged mother, but mostly the film is a series of vignettes: O'Malley starts a boy choir, he helps a girl who's run away from home and teaches her the real meaning of singing, he runs into an old flame who's now starring at the Metropolitan Opera, he and Fitzgibbon and another priest play a game of golf. The war quietly looms over all of this, especially regarding the son of the stern banker who holds the mortgage on Fitzgibbon's church. He ends up marrying the girl who ran away from home because

----

OPPOSITE: Gregory Peck's first movie role was as a Russian freedom fighter leading a group of partisans behind enemy lines in <u>Days of Glory</u> (1944). He was 4-F in real life, due to a dancing injury.

The closing scene of <u>Going My Way</u>—where Bing Crosby and opera singer Risë Stevens (whose husband, Sergeant Walter Surovy, would visit the set in uniform) arrange for Barry Fitzgerald's elderly priest to see his mother (Adeline De Walt Reynolds) after forty-five years—is one of the most touching in the movies.

they both know he's about to be sent off to war and there's now no time to waste. When he is shipped out, his service ends after he's accidentally run over by a jeep in North Africa. Many of the casualties of the war didn't come from battle, and *Going My Way* is one of the few films to reflect that. In its gentle rhythm, its focus on small domestic moments with characters who feel like they exist when the cameras stop rolling and aren't just shoehorned into a plot, *Going My Way*, directed by Leo McCarey, very much followed the style and mood of *The Human Comedy*. It was a formula to be repeated later in the summer of 1944 with *Since You Went Away*, another home front film and one that featured Hattie McDaniel in a supporting role. That film ended up being number

three at the US box office in 1944—it was enough of a sensation that its director, John Cromwell, even cohosted the Oscars with Jack Benny in 1945. Imagine then how much of an impact *Going My Way* had . . . It was number one.

When Crosby won the Best Actor Oscar for playing Father O'Malley in *Going My Way*—the film also took Best Picture for 1944—it was the culmination of a storyline about a crooner with a wild streak who had matured into a role model for the nation. From then on, he'd be the number one box-office draw for each remaining year of the 1940s. But clutching his statuette, he demurred. He said he only won "because all the good actors were off at war."

HOW THE OSCARS CHANGED

The American people showed tremendous discipline in regards to rationing during the war years. Every household received a ration book with a number of stamps determined by the number of people in the family; each stamp could be redeemed for a different product. "Things taken for granted were now unavailable—sugar, coffee, chewing gum, cigarettes," Bob Hope said. "There were very few complaints. Sacrifice was part of everyone's contribution." Food was rationed to provide three square meals a day for servicemembers. But the most significant changes were related to driving: four days after Pearl Harbor, a commission of 7,500 local tire rationing boards were set up around the country to regulate who could receive a replacement tire if necessary. Rubber, not then available synthetically, had just become scarce due to Japan's invasion of Malaya, French Indochina, and the Dutch East Indies, home to much of the world's rubber supply. If someone had extra tires lying around, they were confiscated.

All the new gasoline restrictions were primarily geared to discourage driving so that people wouldn't need new tires. Unless you could prove you served some war-essential function or drove a truck for a living, you had to rely on just three to four gallons of gas a week. Driving for pleasure or sightseeing was now banned. So was the Indianapolis 500 and all racing events. The federal government imposed a nationwide 35 mph speed limit. These restrictions became so familiar that MGM even released a Wallace Beery comedy in 1944 called *Rationing*.

The Academy Awards needed to ration too. The 1942 ceremony, two and a half months after Pearl Harbor, caught Hollywood in the midst of a transition; the full austerity mindset of the war years to come hadn't sunk in completely. The next Oscars occurred on March 4, 1943, at the Ambassador Hotel's Cocoanut Grove. And though it was still a small, luxurious dinner, with actors sitting at large party tables, the war was acknowledged and

At the 1943 Academy Awards (honoring the best films of 1942), the Oscar statuettes made of Britannia were replaced with plaster versions, spray-painted gold. The one in Greer Garson's hand doesn't quite have the usual gleam. No one at this time was saying "Oh, it's so heavy" about the little gold knight—the usual reaction of surprise by winners when grasping the 8.5-pound statuette. These were Wiffle-ball light. Van Heflin (in uniform and about to head to the Ninth Air Force in Europe as a combat cameraman) and Teresa Wright hold what was originally standard for Supporting Actor and Actress winners: plaques instead of trophies.

integrated into every aspect of the show. The most important difference concerned Oscar himself: the 13.5-inch, 8.5-pound little crusader knight was filled with an alloy called Britannia (a mix of tin, antimony, and copper) onto which gold plating was applied. These were now considered essential metals for the war effort, so the winners of 1943—among them Greer Garson and Teresa Wright for *Mrs. Miniver*—picked up temporary plaster statuettes that could be exchanged for real Oscars after the war.

That 1943 Oscars ceremony unfolded over five hours, extended in part because of all the conspicuous patriotism on display: Jeanette MacDonald sang the national anthem to open the proceedings, and Tyrone Power and Alan Ladd appeared in uniform, a year after Jimmy Stewart had done the same. The duo announced that 27,677 members of the film industry now served in the Armed Forces. One humorous moment occurred when Irving Berlin presented the award for Best Original Song. He was nominated in the category for "White Christmas," and of course

Barry Fitzgerald—with Ingrid Bergman (Best Actress winner for 1944's <u>Gaslight</u>) and Bing Crosby—had a frightful thing happen to his plaster Oscar statuette for Best Supporting Actor. While practicing his golf swing, he accidentally sent the delicate Oscar's head flying into the air. Like all Oscar winners during the war years, Fitzgerald was able to exchange his for the genuine article once the war was over.

he won. "I'm glad to present the award," Berlin said. "I've known the fellow for a long time."

The next year's Academy Awards, held on March 2, 1944, established the template for the ceremony that it's stuck to ever since. This time it wouldn't be a banquet at all, as those more intimate affairs had a whiff of being exclusionary and insular. For this sixteenth Academy Awards, the proceedings took place at Grauman's Chinese Theatre, with the majority of its 2,258 seats given free to servicemembers—plus ten rows of bleacher-style seating on stage for those in uniform too. Jack Benny was the host and the ceremony was broadcast over Armed Forces Radio for those fighting overseas. Documentary Short Subject was awarded to the contentious *December 7th: The Movie*, while the British *Desert Victory* (1943) won Best Documentary Feature, which some perceived as a slight to all the efforts American filmmakers were putting into documentaries during 1943, such as the nominated *Report from the Aleutians* and *The Battle of Russia*. This was also the first year that the Supporting Actor and Actress winners received full-size statuettes (still plaster, though, of course) as opposed to plaques, which had been the norm for the Supporting categories since they were introduced in 1937. Fox's *The Song of Bernadette* (1943) won the most awards, with four total, but most considered it to be *Casablanca*'s night. As Humphrey Bogart and his wife Mayo Methot got out of their car, they were swarmed with fans, many yelling, "Here's looking at you, kid!" Twelve police officers were needed for Bogie and wife to dodge the throng. Once they got inside, the movie won three Oscars: for Best Screenplay, Best Director (Michael Curtiz), and Best Picture.

There was definitely a segment of Hollywood that wanted the old elegant dinner party version of the Oscars to continue. It's probably not a coincidence then that the first Golden Globe Awards was held a few weeks before 1944's reformatted Oscar ceremony. This event, a luncheon held on the 20th Century Fox lot by the Hollywood Foreign Correspondents Association (later renamed the Hollywood Foreign Press Association), was a return to the insular banquet of Oscars past. (After drinks and a lavish meal, hitting the dance floor was *de rigueur* at the Globes well into the 1960s.) The HFCA also wanted to make a statement: as they represented press outlets in other countries, and foreign markets had been largely cut off to Hollywood during the war years, this soiree was to show that those territories were waiting for the day when Hollywood films could open there again. In the decades since, the Golden Globes have been the naughty younger sibling of the Oscars—a banquet to this day, stars are known to get soused, and the taste of its cadre of voters, as well as their impartiality, is questionable. That was the case even in 1944, when the winners received not globes as their prizes but scrolls. *Casablanca* didn't win a single award at that first Golden Globe Awards. *The Song of Bernadette* won the top prizes. Is it because it was a 20th Century Fox film and the event was held on the Fox lot? Hollywood appeared to be ready for even more glamour in 1945, when the Golden Globes became a gala event at the Beverly Hills Hotel. Wartime austerity be damned—many wished for a return to business as usual.

THE RISE OF YOUTH CULTURE
. . . AND THE PINUP

Who was the most hated man of World War II? According to historian William Manchester, perhaps slightly in jest, it wasn't Adolf Hitler. It was Frank Sinatra. And that hate was coming from men in uniform fighting overseas. They saw the crooner as the ultimate example of a star designated 4-F under spurious circumstances who got to use the war years to increase his wealth and seduce all the gals back home. But that hate only existed because it was balanced by an equally strong love: from the legions of bobby soxers, the name for teenage girls still in their childhood socks and flats who gathered at theaters where he'd be performing hours before he'd take the stage. Sinatra had had the first-ever number one hit on the Billboard singles chart, with "I'll Never Smile Again," for Tommy Dorsey's band, on July 27, 1940, and ever since then his fame had only grown. By the end of 1942, more than one thousand Sinatra fan clubs had sprung up around the country. When he performed at New York City's Paramount Theatre in 1944, the bobby soxers began lining up at 3:00 a.m. Since the Paramount didn't clear the theater between shows, most stayed for all five performances Sinatra gave

Bobby soxers lining up outside Times Square's Paramount Theatre for Sinatra's October 12, 1944, set of shows.

each day. His publicist George Evans even parked an ambulance outside the Paramount in case any of the girls, in their hysteria over their idol, should require medical attention. That was Sinatra's effect on women.

If you asked an ordinary GI if he believed that bit of mythmaking, he'd probably say yes. Sinatra's low stature in the military was solidified in the *Stars and Stripes* newspaper when a piece on his sex appeal concluded, "Mice make women faint too." Was he a draft dodger? He first received a deferment for having an infant daughter—future star Nancy. Then he was deferred again for having a perforated eardrum and for being only 119 pounds, four pounds under the minimum requirement for a five-foot-seven guy. That report also listed him as "emotionally unstable." Was this a payoff? Soldiers suspected so, while the bobby soxers didn't care in the least.

Sinatra's rise to superstardom during the war

years was a profound signifier of a cultural shift: the rise of youth culture. With those in their late teens or twenties off fighting, the teenagers left behind were the ones now plunking nickels into the jukeboxes and buying movie tickets. Van Johnson credited the bobby soxers as powering his early success too. Teenage girls were known to storm the gates of MGM in hopes of meeting the young star; if they caught up to Johnson, the bobby soxers were known to pull the buttons off his clothes so they'd have a memento. And he had to keep getting his car repainted as fans kept scrawling love notes on it. These fans knew they had power: they were responsible for Johnson and Sinatra's success, which meant they felt a degree of ownership over them.

A strange movie from 1943 cowritten by *Why We Fight* scribe Leonard Spigelgass captures this explosion of youthful energy: MGM's *The Youngest Profession* (1943), directed by Edward Buzzell. It

Servicemen on November 10, 1941, ask Rita Hayworth to autograph their copies of Time magazine, on which she'd just made the cover.

stars Virginia Weidler and Jean Porter as teenage best friends who are the founding members of a film fan club in New York City. They spend their time outside of school finding out what movie stars may be in town and strategizing how to meet them. The two most valuable autographs in Weidler's collection? Jimmy Stewart and Clark Gable, of course, "because they're in the army," and thus unavailable. Weidler's younger brother is obsessed with *The Lone Ranger* and other serialized radio dramas; people couldn't get enough of them before the mass introduction of television. While they're at a movie theater watching William Powell and Hedy Lamarr in *Crossroads* (1942)—another MGM film, because a movie like this served as an excellent bit of advertising for the whole MGM stable, with star cameos abounding—the kid even turns on his radio. "Hi-yo, Silver!" rings out to the befuddled movie audience as Powell lays a passionate kiss on Lamarr. The theatrical experience! But also indicative of how young kids during the war years, with their parents and older siblings so focused on how they could contribute to the conflict, developed their own world.

Not that their older brother in uniform was that much older or any less interested in his own version of youth culture. While their younger siblings back home had their radio shows and jukebox music, soldiers turned to visual media. Comic book readership exploded on account of the GI. In 1941, ten million comics were sold a month. By 1944, twenty million were being sold every month. Captain James Stewart was one of those readers: his favorite was *Flash Gordon*.

Stylized art and photography became soldiers' favorite pastime, and there was nothing they cherished more than their favorite pinup. These were sexy photos of glamorous female stars posed seductively, and often scantily clad. The name "pinup" itself came because these photos or posters, pinned up in their lockers, were the first things soldiers

wanted to see when they opened their locker door. For two years, the single most requested pinup was a photo of Rita Hayworth taken by Bob Landry that appeared in the August 1941 issue of *Life* magazine. In the famous shot she is posed invitingly on a bed while wearing a negligee. Servicemen awarded made-up honorifics to certain female stars, such as when navy personnel declared Hayworth "The Girl We'd Most Like to Get Shipwrecked With." Two years later, a pinup of Betty Grable, posing in a bathing suit, her legs insured by 20th Century Fox for $1 million, became every bit as much a sensation. George Stevens remarked on the effect Grable had on the American soldiers who saw her in *I Wake Up Screaming* (1941) while in Cairo in November 1942. "It just wasn't my cup of tea," the director said of the early noir. "But I sat there with 20,000 other guys, and I saw the Passion Play! . . . There was a good sister and a bad sister . . . Betty Grable was the good sister because she's glossy and cute and the G.I.'s dream." And because the men were so starved for any connection to normal life back home—let alone women—the film had "fifty times the weight on the individual" viewer than it might have had on someone watching it back home.

20th Century Fox immediately capitalized on the success of Grable's swimsuit photo by building their Technicolor musical *Pin-Up Girl* (1944) around it. More overt sexuality was the order of the day: after the navy turned down her wartime inventing work, Hedy Lamarr starred in a movie that traded almost entirely on sex, even being considered a "dirty picture" to give the troops a thrill: *White Cargo* (1942), in which she played the sultry native girl Tondelayo. And mores began to change

----

Hayworth leaned into her pinup status, continuing to take more "cheesecake" photos throughout the war years.

as well. *The Miracle of Morgan's Creek* (1943), which astounds viewers to this day for how it somehow got past the Production Code Administration, is a mature, judgment-free view of premarital sex during wartime.

Pinups found their way onto airplanes as well. More artistically minded airmen painted Hayworth or Grable on their planes, in what became known as "nose art." Lana Turner quickly joined them as a favorite subject of these amateur artists, and the crew of one B-17 based in England as part of the Eighth Air Force named their Flying Fortress "Tempest Turner" in honor of the star. Uncle Sam or Yankee Doodle appeared as nose art on some as well, as did even Humphrey Bogart's Sam Spade from *The Maltese Falcon*.

Also popular as nose art? Cartoon characters: Bugs Bunny, Popeye, and Donald Duck—a reminder of how young these airmen usually were. Soldiers especially ate up the war-themed Warner Bros.' Looney Tunes and Merrie Melodies shorts, which were heavy on jokes, had a touch of the surreal, ran for just seven minutes, and were as graphically simple as the comic books they loved. Some of these haven't aged well and are shocking for their racism against the Japanese. But one that stands the test of time as a World War II spoof worthy of *The Great Dictator* and *To Be or Not to Be* is *Herr Meets Hare* (1945), in which Bugs runs afoul of Hermann Göring. The rabbit ultimately causes the Wehrmacht leader to flee deep into the Black Forest when he dresses up as Joseph Stalin—presented as one person who really does strike terror

into the Nazis. Pipe in hand, the mustachioed Bugs as Stalin quips, "Does your tobacco taste different lately?" which every soldier would know was the slogan of Sir Walter Raleigh pipe tobacco. Maybe not the most sophisticated comedy, but indicative of how the soldier audience was still largely kids, even if they'd had to grow up incredibly fast.

Warner Bros.' wartime cartoons were basic appeals to already widely held views of the Axis powers. They didn't exactly seek to influence public policy. Walt Disney felt that he could go further.

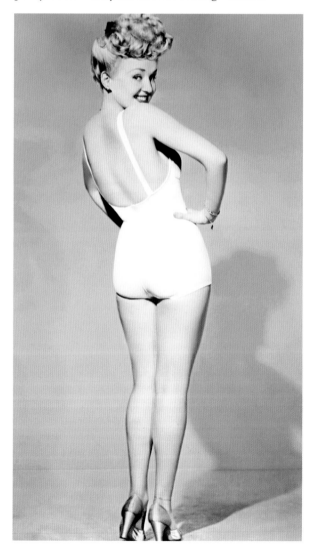

The famous Betty Grable pinup taken by Frank Powolny while she made <u>Sweet Rosie O'Grady</u> (1943). It became the most popular pinup of the war; at the time, she was married to band leader Harry James.

DRAWING UP PROPAGANDA

Walt Disney had made informational shorts, such as the pro–income tax *The New Spirit* (1942), and training films, but he'd resisted propaganda, other than for the animated segments he'd helped produce for the *Why We Fight* films. Like so many Americans, he had a negative feeling about propaganda after the experience of World War I, in which both sides were drowning in persuasive images to rally their populaces into a war-hungry frenzy. Disney knew the cost of war. At the age of sixteen he joined the Red Cross as an ambulance driver—being underage, he forged the date on his birth certificate to appear older—but didn't make it to France until after the Armistice. He saw that Europe lay devastated and . . . for what?

But after America was at war for nearly a year, Disney began to change his mind. Government contracts had kept his studio afloat. The last completed feature of his that hadn't been made possible through a subsidy was *Bambi* (1942)—and like *Pinocchio* (1940) and *Fantasia* (1940), it bombed, losing $200,000. Luckily, it was offset by *Saludos Amigos* (1942), a surprise success, grossing over $1.1 million in the United States and South America combined. That contrast pointed Disney in the direction he needed to go: he needed to put not just his time and energy into war-themed work, but his heart and soul into it too. So propaganda it would be.

Donald Duck has a nightmare in the Disney short Der Fuehrer's Face. He's living in Nazi Germany! All the state allows him for breakfast is "aroma of bacon" and bread so hard he has to cut it with a hacksaw.

On January 1, 1943, Disney attached the short *Der Fuehrer's Face* to RKO features playing in cinemas nationwide. The title and concept came from a song written by Disney composer Oliver Wallace. It opens the short, which features a group of oddly shaped Aryan supermen singing as part of a Nazi oompah band:

When Der Fuehrer says we is *der master race*
We heil (pfft), heil (pfft) right in Der
    Fuehrer's face
Not to love Der Fuehrer is a great disgrace
So we heil (pfft), heil (pfft) right in Der
    Fuehrer's face

Then Donald Duck wakes up in a house nearby. He's living in Nazi Germany, but his life is not his own. His alarm clock, with swastikas in place of numbers, wakes him up—swastikas adorn his wallpaper as well, if it isn't clear already that this is going to be an animated take on *The Great*

Dictator and *To Be or Not to Be* territory. After a meager meal, including coffee made from one bean tied to a string, to show how poorly the Axis powers treated their own people, he goes to a job at a munitions factory making shells. "Attention, vurkers! Through the kindness of the Phoor-er, now comes the vacation mit pay!" The vacation in question is just the chance to stare at a poster of the Alps for a few minutes before getting back to pounding shells. Finally, Donald wakes up and realizes that it was all a terrible nightmare. He's in the good ol' USA after all. He hugs the little Statue of Liberty by his bedside in gratitude.

If *Der Fuehrer's Face* has a particular acid wit, that's due to its cowriter Joe Grant, who was Jewish, which helps account for the particular Borscht Belt style of the comedy in this short. It has a bite that other Disney shorts lack. He also wrote another propaganda effort, released just two weeks later, that's as serious as *Der Fuehrer's Face* is funny: *Education for Death* (1943), a grave-as-a-heart-attack dissection of how a young boy can be taught to hate in the Hitler Youth until he's ready to be sent off to die in war. Animated in the rich style of *Pinocchio*, it's a chilling thing to watch. And then Grant cowrote the best of these by far: *Reason and Emotion* (1943). This short takes us inside an ordinary guy's brain: lurking inside that noggin are two very different characters vying to sit in the driver's seat and control his actions—Reason, who looks as studious as Mr. Chips, and Emotion, dressed like a caveman. When Emotion bops Reason over the head with his club, he takes the driver's seat and catcalls a "classy dish," something Reason would never do. The woman slaps him. Then we get inside her head to see her Reason and Emotion—Emotion in her case thinks the guy was "kinda cute . . . Do you wanna be an old maid?" This concept keeps building until it becomes a metaphor for Nazism. Hitler had succeeded so completely in ruling through fear that inside his

Reason and Emotion, from 1943, is a precursor to Disney-Pixar's 2015 release Inside Out. Where that film personified five different emotions living in our brains, Reason and Emotion focuses on just two abstractions, making a point about how the people living in the Axis powers had allowed emotion to overwhelm their reason.

followers' brains Emotion had completely cowed Reason into submission. The result is war and mass suffering.

While Grant, who continued working on Disney films until 2004, lent his stamp to those shorts, Disney himself was obsessed with making another feature that he hoped would actually change the direction of the war. He had been captivated by Russian aviator Alexander P. de Seversky's book *Victory Through Air Power*, published in 1942. It made the case that the war could, and would, be won largely through long-range bombers . . . which at that point had not yet been invented.

Disney not only wanted to turn this book-length argument into a film, he wanted Seversky to be its host, laying out his case in his own words as animated graphics illustrated his points. He hoped Churchill and FDR would then see this movie and alter their war strategy accordingly. How many other moguls have ever thought they could influence public policy in this way? And Disney made this film entirely with his own money. To cut costs, he made it in black and white, making it the only theatrically released Disney animated feature not to be in color. Other filmmakers also had found that their commitment to the war effort overrode any personal financial imperatives: in 1944, Alfred Hitchcock hitched a ride on a bomber to London to make two propaganda films about the Free French, *Bon Voyage* (1944) and *Aventure Malgache* (1944), for the salary of £10 a week. "I knew that if I did nothing, I'd regret it the rest of my life," Hitchcock later said.

Disney seems to have felt the same way. *Victory Through Air Power* (1943) is compelling to watch just for how much of an oddity it is, and for some of its crazy suggestions: among them, using the airstrip at Adak in the Aleutians to fly long-range bombers

---

Victory Through Air Power has some animated sequences—though drawn in color, they were processed in black and white to cut down on costs as Disney didn't make this movie to turn a profit—but mostly it comes across like a kind of PowerPoint lecture six decades before PowerPoint was introduced.

to attack Japan itself, something the makeshift airfield was fundamentally incapable of facilitating.

But one idea in the *Victory Through Air Power* movie became a reality: Royal Navy Captain Edward Terrell actually invented a bomb Seversky suggested in the film, which, once dropped from a plane, would fire a rocket engine so as to fall faster than free-fall—all the better to be a bunker buster. The Disney bomb, as it was called, was a 4,500-pound beast with a rocket engine that would hit the ground at 990 mph, when typical free-fall velocity would be just 750 mph. The first Disney bombs were dropped on a fortified Nazi dock in the Netherlands in February 1945. When has another mogul and studio ever had a bomb named for them?

On top of that, it seems Churchill not only did watch *Victory Through Air Power*; he actually recommended it to Roosevelt as well. That must have been some small consolation for the fact that Disney's usual distributor RKO, so puzzled over his choice to make this movie, declined to release it. Disney had to turn to United Artists to release it, instead.

It lost $500,000 in theaters.

HOLLYWOOD WAS THERE ON D-DAY

Victory Through Air Power got one thing right: it was essential to establish air superiority before the invasion of Fortress Europe could commence. That meant spending months in advance softening up targets in Germany and France with concerted aerial bombardment. In mid-November 1943, Captain James Stewart, commanding from the plane *Tenovus*, led his squadron of B-24 Liberators on takeoff from Miami. Their route was the long southern route to England: from Miami to San Juan, then Georgetown, Guyana, then Belém and Natal, and across the Atlantic to Dakar. From there up to Casablanca, and from Casablanca finally to England. It was a five-day trip. The B-24s had a longer range and a larger payload (up to 8,800 pounds of bombs) than the B-17 Flying Fortress, but in every other respect they were inferior aircraft, prone to equipment failures with little notice.

In England, Stewart and his fellow pilots and ten-person crews settled into a base at the small East Anglia town of Tibenham. It was cold. The men lived in meager, drafty, brick-and-concrete dormitories. Stewart had been in the Army Air Forces for two and a half years, and now he commanded over one hundred flyers, plus the two hundred ground crew who had made the trip to England aboard the *Queen Mary*. On December 13 he commanded his first mission, leading his men, the 703rd Squadron of the 445th Bombardment Group of the Second Combat Wing of the Second Bomb Division of the Eighth Air Force, on a daring bombing raid to destroy the

James Stewart was promoted to lieutenant colonel three days before D-Day.

U-boat yards at Kiel. A week later, Stewart commanded another, this time over Bremen. Destroying Germany's production capacity was essential so that when the Allied invasion happened, destroyed German equipment couldn't be so easily replaced.

All in all, Stewart commanded over twenty bombing missions, sometimes taking the controls himself as pilot. Over twenty thousand feet in the air at 230 mph, the B-24s, unpressurized, could reach 45 degrees below zero. You had to check that the tube to your oxygen tank wasn't getting clogged with ice formed from your breath. And then there was the antiaircraft fire. After Stewart's first mission, "There were a dozen holes big enough to slide his hand through in the left side of the ship alone, and pockmarks on the bottom of the wing," historian Robert Matzen writes. But they had dropped their payload and made it back alive. To protect against the antiaircraft rounds—or flak—the airmen wore flak jackets, and sometimes put a flak jacket over the seat to provide a little extra protection since the projectiles would be coming from below. Airmen were known to get "flak happy," the aerial version of being shell-shocked. For that reason, a rotation for flyers was capped at twenty-five missions. (And the base's medical officer would prep "four or five finger shots of Irish or Scotch Whiskey" for any flyer who wanted it after landing.) In late 1943 and early 1944, each plane had about a 50 percent chance of being shot down on a mission. Airmen only had a one-in-three chance of surviving all twenty-five missions. And many were mustered out well before that due to psychological stress. More than in any other job in the Armed Forces, being a flyer also meant you could disappear without a trace.

Promoted to major, Stewart flew his first mission over Berlin on March 22. Plans at this point were well underway for D-Day, the start date for the invasion of France. The only delay was the wait to gather enough landing craft to ferry the 156,000 soldiers the Allies intended to set ashore. Dwight D. Eisenhower and Bernard Montgomery, the architects of the invasion, had carefully studied the most brutal amphibious landing of the war, at the Battle of Tarawa. The American soldiers who jumped into the surf there were instantly met with an overwhelming barrage of Japanese fire. They also learned how important it was to monitor the phases of the moon and the tides—landing troops right at low tide could expose any obstacles, including possibly mines, on the beach—as well as the weather. The invasion was finally set for June 5, but the weather was so bad on June 4 that it was decided to push it back a day. The forecast suggested bad weather would endure for many more days, which meant that the German commanders along the French channel coast actually withdrew to conduct war games elsewhere.

Not long after midnight on June 6, nearly 7,000 ships set out from the south coast of England: over 1,200 warships (nearly 900 of which were Royal Navy) and over 4,000 amphibious landing craft among them. It was the largest seaborne invasion in history. On board one of the vessels, the USS *Barton*, was Lieutenant Commander Robert Montgomery, returning to France for the invasion when four years earlier he was driving an ambulance in support of the retreating British and French armies before Dunkirk.

Three days before D-Day, Stewart had been promoted to lieutenant colonel. At 2000 hours (8:00 p.m.) on June 5 the word came down that the next day would be the invasion. Stewart's role this time was not up in the air but to coordinate his new bomb group of several squadrons, the 453rd, and their strategy, from the ground. The cost of a promotion. And in a way, it was even more nerve-racking: imagine being responsible for all those lives and being able to do nothing but give them a plan and wait.

Lieutenant Commander Robert Montgomery had been there for both the evacuation of the British Army leading up to Dunkirk and D-Day, the triumphant, if costly, return. Here he's awarded the Bronze Star.

Sitting in a cockpit gave you at least a bit of control.

The biggest target for the men he commanded was a fortified installation of heavy guns and forty soldiers about three hundred yards in from the sea overlooking the strip of Normandy coast now being codenamed Omaha. Across fifty miles, there would be five beachheads total: from west to east they were Utah and Omaha (the two to be taken by American soldiers), and Gold, Juno, and Sword (to be taken by British and Canadian troops). The 453rd took off after 0300 and they dropped their payloads before 0628, the cutoff for the bombers targeting objectives near the beach—but they missed that critical German fortification due to low cloud cover. At that part of Omaha, the men on the ground would have to take out that bunker themselves. Of the five beaches, this was the most challenging because the men would have to ascend high cliffs in order to reach the German fortified position. The first boots splashed into the water at 0630, two minutes after the American bombs stopped falling. It was a wall of bullets they faced and by 0900 over two thousand lay dead on Omaha Beach.

John Ford was on the destroyer USS *Plunkett* off Omaha. He recalled how rough the sea was, sailors being overcome by nausea, and soldiers in the landing craft using their helmets to bail sea water lapping over the sides. Ford didn't actually set foot on the beach until days later. Director George Stevens, who was now part of Frank Capra's Army Pictorial Service and aboard the HMS *Belfast*, actually did set foot on Juno Beach later on D-Day. Accompanying him on the *Belfast* were his *Talk of*

the Town screenwriter Irwin Shaw and *The Human Comedy* writer William Saroyan.

The war was unfolding with lightning speed now. Just the previous day, June 5, Rome finally fell to the Allied forces after a nine-month slog of all-out fighting that inched its way up the Italian peninsula. Marlene Dietrich, who arrived as an entertainer for the troops shortly after the city fell, said the Allied troops rolling in was "like an Easter parade . . . the boys threw cigarettes and chocolate." And on June 19, at the Battle of the Philippine Sea, the US Navy sank the fifth of the six Japanese carriers that had attacked Pearl Harbor two and a

US soldiers hurry through the water after leaving their landing craft at Omaha Beach on D-Day.

half years earlier. The one place where the fighting was much slower than anticipated was in Normandy. The Allied death total on D-Day was 4,414. The plan had been to unify all five beachheads in a single front by the end of D-Day and to take the town of Caen. The Allies didn't manage to link all five beachheads until six days later, and fighting in Caen continued until July 21.

Ford collapsed into a days-long bender after D-Day, all but ending his military service. Stewart resumed flying missions, though Matzen says the stress he felt in the months ahead kept building until the only foods that could get him through were peanut butter and ice cream. Luckily, for Stewart and for everyone else, the end was finally in sight.

PART V A NEW WORLD, A NEW HOLLYWOOD

1944-

Frank Sinatra and Gene Kelly in <u>Anchors Aweigh</u> (1945) epitomized the celebratory spirit of V-E Day and V-J Day.

RAISING MONEY, RAISING HOPES

Movie stars kept on serving coffee and doughnuts, doing dishes, and wearing out the dance floor at the Hollywood Canteen. At the one-year anniversary party, on October 31, 1943, Bette Davis unveiled the Hollywood Hall of Honor, a wall on which appeared photos of many of Tinseltown's finest who were now in uniform themselves.

That Christmas, Davis starred in a patriotic short called *A Present with a Future* (1943), playing a mother preparing everything for her two kids on Christmas morning. The tykes come down to the living room and see the tree all decorated. "Mother! Where are our stockings?" "Children, sit down a minute." Davis's Christmas present for her "children"? "War Bonds . . . Well, gee, thanks a lot, Mom," the son says. The daughter isn't as copacetic: "I wanted a bicycle." Mom has to explain why it's important to contribute, even in lieu of Christmas presents. "Just think. If Daddy were wounded, one single war stamp might pay for the medicine that would save him from pain . . . even save his life." Sure, this family could afford both war bonds and a bicycle. But what if everyone felt that way? "If everybody bought everything they wanted, it would take thousands of people to make the goods and to sell them, and those people are needed to make essential things for the war." With "Silent Night" lilting in the background, it's a glorious simulacrum of domesticity as Davis, somehow knowing that being arch even here would lead to this message being more memorable, interacts with these child performers and barely attempts

to acknowledge them as anything but actors. For an extra Brechtian touch, the short ends by cutting to Davis, herself again, in her dressing room, to give us a direct message: "Ladies and gentlemen, I think what the mother said in that scene I played today was right. Any bond that you or I give as a present is much more than a gift. It's a Christmas blessing."

Not long before Davis filmed that Yuletide greeting, Orson Welles opened his own rival to the Hollywood Canteen: *The Mercury Wonder Show*, which also welcomed soldiers for a night of Hollywood entertainment. Welles's romance with Rita Hayworth had deepened, and he trained her

The Red Cross unleashed a lavish campaign to feature Bette Davis's wartime work for the charity.

to be his magician's assistant. She learned to act like she had psychic abilities and pretended to be sawed in half. But Harry Cohn, head of Columbia, which had Hayworth under contract, threatened to void her contract if she did something so plebeian as to appear in a magic show. Always ambivalent about her movie career, Hayworth considered letting him just go ahead and do that. But Welles talked her out of it, and replaced her with Marlene Dietrich. *The Mercury Wonder Show* opened on August 3, 1943, in an 80-by-120-foot tent at 9000 Cahuenga Boulevard. The plan was for it to only last a month, but Welles personally invested $40,000 of his own money into it. After his disastrous departure from RKO, he'd recovered financially a bit by starring in *Jane Eyre* (1943) for 20th Century Fox. Wearing a fez and a striped sorcerer's coat, Welles entertained a thousand soldiers each night. "Welcome, suckers!" he'd bellow at the crowd. All proceeds from the four hundred or so civilians allowed in each night (who were charged $5.50 a ticket) went to the War Assistance League. It wrapped up on September 9— two days before that, he'd made Hayworth his wife.

Meanwhile, the Canteen itself had entered a groove. Different studios claimed nights at which to feature their talent: Tuesdays were Warner Bros.

Marlene Dietrich performs as Orson Welles's assistant for a magic trick in <u>Follow the Boys</u> (1944), much like in the magic act they put on in real life at <u>The Mercury Wonder Show</u>.

Soldier Dane Clark dances with Joan Crawford in the <u>Hollywood Canteen</u> movie.

night. Thursdays were for RKO starlets. Paul Henreid, though an "enemy alien" subject to the 8:00 p.m. curfew, enjoyed volunteering on those Tuesdays. "He was very much involved in the Hollywood Canteen," his daughter Monika Henreid said. "He was really impressed by the young military guys he met there. The Hollywood Canteen made them real human beings because you met them and talked to them, and they were either just on their way to being shipped out or just on their way back."

Henreid was also in the movie *Hollywood Canteen*, which tried to put into a two-hour story the unique experience that had been this coming together of stars and soldiers. He appears in an apron doing dishes and gives some love advice to Dane Clark's sergeant character. The movie, released in December 1944 and directed by Delmer Daves for Warner Bros., is a skewed representation of the actual Canteen as it's mostly a showcase for Warner Bros. stars. The movie does show and celebrate that the Canteen was an integrated space, though. The message here is clear—the unity that comes out of being inclusive is the key to defeating the homogenous Axis powers. Joe E. Brown even sings as much in one showstopping number:

You can always tell a Yank
By the way his glass will clank
With a guy from Rome and a guy from Pinsk
And a guy from Shanghai, Wales, and Minsk
You can always tell a Yank

You can always tell a Yank
By his friends on either flank
There's a guy called Slim and a boy named
   John
And a kid called Chang and his friend Ivan
You can always tell a Yank

That's a vision of Hollywood at its best. And though the movie is silly in many respects—Dane Clark's sergeant, who walks around with a cane after an injury, literally seems to be healed by his experience at the Canteen—it was a mission statement for a more open and engaged film industry. In the movie, the lead character, a soldier played by Robert Hutton, has a massive crush on *Yankee Doodle Dandy* star Joan Leslie; he comes to the Hollywood Canteen in the first place just so he can meet her. Bette Davis and John Garfield go out of their way to play matchmaker for the two of them: they arrange for him to receive a kiss from Leslie, then they award him the prize of "One Millionth Visitor" to the Canteen (with a little chicanery), which allows him to go on a date outside the Canteen with the actress. The film ends with them being engaged right before Hutton is sent back to war.

"It kind of got me," his friend Dane Clark says. "All them famous people being friendly and democratic. Democratic . . . democracy, that's what it means, Slim. Everybody equal like tonight! All them big shots listening to little shots like me and being friendly." In real life, some stars truly did go out of their way: Kay Francis was known to pick up wounded soldiers at various hospitals around the Los Angeles area and drive them up to fifty miles so they could find some fun at the Canteen. This was a vision of a more engaged Hollywood that wouldn't go away after the war; on some level ever since, Hollywood stars would have to admit that their lives are something of an open book to the public—it's the public that makes them stars, after all.

The Canteen was the best that Hollywood could be. It was a shame, though, that only soldiers passing through Los Angeles could be a part of it. Luckily, there was evermore Hollywood talent gearing up to put on shows overseas.

FRONTLINE ENTERTAINMENT

arlene Dietrich appeared at the Hollywood Canteen as well as *The Mercury Wonder Show*, of course. Partly the gusto she brought to her wartime work was to prove how American she was. She had become a US citizen in 1939, but the FBI kept a file on her in the early part of the war years, as, by birth anyway, she was still an "enemy alien" in their eyes. Partly, she became so enthusiastic for performing for the troops and selling war bonds because she was so aghast at what her homeland had unleashed upon the world and was legitimately fighting for a new and better Germany.

The Treasury Department acknowledged, via a citation presented by the governor of California, that she had personally sold the most war bonds of any star during 1942–1943. But her methods were scandalous to some: she was known to go as far as sitting on the laps of deep-pocketed potential donors in nightclubs while G-men made certain their checks to the Treasury Department for large war bond purchases actually cleared. President Roosevelt was concerned. He called her to Washington for a meeting and said, "I hear what you're doing to sell bonds, and we're grateful to you for it. But I won't allow this

LEFT: Marlene Dietrich dances with a soldier at El Morocco in New York in 1944. **RIGHT:** Dietrich, held aloft by servicemen at a USO show.

sort of prostitution technique. You will henceforth no longer appear in nightclubs. This is an order."

So Dietrich reinvented her war work again. Her work on MGM's *Kismet* (1944) complete, Dietrich donated her salary for that film, plus proceeds from an auction of many of her valuables, to finance a USO trip. For this purpose, the army even outfitted her with a special military uniform. She appeared in North Africa in April 1944, then Italy, and introduced her version of a song that became a smash with both the Allied and Axis forces: "Lili Marleen," written in 1915 and a nostalgic ode for all that one had before facing an uncertain present. Goebbels had banned it after Stalingrad, but not even he could hold back Dietrich's version. Yes, he considered her a traitor. Yes, her version of "Lili Marleen" was also being sponsored by the War Department as part of its psy-ops radio broadcasts called MUZAK, to make German troops wish to return to civilian life. But the German forces ate it up so completely, Goebbels had to relent and un-ban it. German soldiers across Europe could tune in to the US Armed Forces Radio to hear her perform, and on one occasion she even broke into a bit of German—knowing they were listening. "Boys!" she cried, in her mother tongue. "Don't sacrifice yourselves! The war is shit! Hitler is an idiot!" According to the CIA, "the United States Strategic Bombing Survey discovered that the programs were just as devastating to German morale as an air raid." She even helped interrogate German prisoners of war. Dietrich so wore herself down with her efforts that, while touring Italy in that summer of 1944, she required treatment with the new antibiotic drug penicillin for a case of pneumonia. She also dealt with lice and dysentery, and recalled how she'd hear rats scurrying near her sleeping bag

at night. The soldiers' struggle was her struggle; the glamour of Hollywood was far away, but she made the soldiers feel like they had a connection to home. This level of sacrifice ensured she was awarded the French Légion d'honneur after the war, as well as the US Medal of Freedom.

Then on August 25, 1944, the Allied forces, which had only just broken out of the pocket of Normandy they controlled at the start of the month, liberated Paris. Dietrich was there, signing autographs in lipstick in front of her favorite store, Hermès, a symbol of the once-prosperous City of Lights that could be again.

Dietrich showed the power of the USO so clearly. General Patton said of her shows, performed near the front lines, that the soldiers would "tell themselves the situation can't be so bad if Marlene Dietrich's there." He also gave her a pearl-handled revolver, in case the Germans made a sudden breakthrough. She was obviously meant to commit suicide rather than be captured. And other entertainers put themselves near the action too. Mickey Rooney ended up winning the Bronze Star for entertaining the troops near battle lines in France. During this time he suggested that shows could be set up quickly and easily by him and other performers putting on

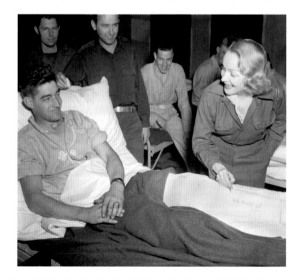

Dietrich signs a wounded serviceman's cast in Belgium in November 1944.

Private Mickey Rooney, performing for troops in the German town of Kist, on April 13, 1945.

their acts from flatbed jeeps. Thus the "Jeep Show" was born. He hadn't had an easy time since he finally entered uniform after all of MGM's attempted deferments; Rooney ended up logging considerable hours in KP ("kitchen patrol"), peeling potatoes and other grunt jobs, but he didn't complain.

Though widely criticized for pursuing his movie career rather than enlisting himself, John Wayne embarked on a USO tour to Australia and the South Pacific in December 1943. When he appeared before the troops, they booed him for never having made it into uniform. But according to his biographer Scott Eyman, an old buddy of Wayne's was colonel of a battalion in New Britain and allowed the movie star a chance to playact as a soldier for a few days,

even dropping some mortar shells on the Japanese position from an artillery spotting plane. He snuck aboard for a second mission a few days later. His friend recalled, "I was up in the head of one of the landing craft. I looked around and here alongside of me, here's Duke. And I said, 'What the Devil are you doing here?' And he said, 'I want to go and see what's going on.'"

Bob Hope, the best-known face of the USO, got up close to the action himself. A first glimpse of what was to come appeared when he checked into Claridge's in London for a stay in the summer of 1943 and the severity of Britain's rationing regimen surprised and impressed him. "Sorry, sir, there is no soap in the King's bathroom either," the hotel

OPPOSITE: Gene Kelly selling war bonds in 1945. **ABOVE:** Betty Hutton shares a meal with members of the 49th Combat Engineers Battalion before a USO show near Reims, France, in 1945. **BELOW:** Betty Hutton in a chow hall for sailors and marines in the Marshall Islands in 1944.

concierge told him. Before long, he'd be dodging air raids while performing for troops in Morocco. Then he flew to entertain marines in the Pacific and developed a case of jungle rot. In August 1944, Hope was flying to Brisbane, Australia, when the right motor of his aircraft gave out. The pilot told everyone to quickly throw all of their belongings out of the plane so they could stay aloft: this was a pontoon plane and they were over land. After pushing his luggage out like a payload dropped from the sky, Hope braced himself: the plane came in for a hard landing on a river and everyone had to jump out immediately, lest the fuel should ignite. During all of this, Hope was only being paid $10 a day. The cause was everything. Even this trauma didn't make him skip a beat: Hope quickly resumed answering every military fan letter he received, as he would do for much of the rest of his life.

The female equivalent of Bob Hope for the sheer logging of miles on USO tours had to be Carole Landis, who had risen to stardom in 1940 with her United Artists film *One Million B.C.* and became another popular pinup during the war years. But if you were in uniform, she was a pinup you could see in person: she performed in Britain and North Africa in 1943 and the South Pacific during 1944, traveling over one hundred thousand miles to entertain the troops, the most of any female star. Her experiences were already so vast as of January 1944 that she published a book about her travels: *Four Jills in a Jeep*, which 20th Century Fox acquired in advance and turned into a movie in 1944 starring Landis and her actual touring buddies on all those USO shows: Martha Raye, Kay Francis, and Mitzi Mayfair.

The initiative that Landis took here went well beyond what had been expected of female movie stars before the war: she was now showing that sex appeal and professional accomplishment were by no means at odds. And that combination expressed

Four Jills in a Jeep starred, and was based on the actual wartime experiences of, from left, Carole Landis, Martha Raye, Mitzi Mayfair, and Kay Francis. Landis wrote a book of the same name that became the basis for the film.

itself in the fashions that were becoming more popular with women at the moment: "natural beauty" was the order of the day in makeup, and fashions were becoming more and more professional in their look. Unless a starlet was literally taking a pinup photo, she'd mostly be photographed wearing tailored skirt suits, which was the usual attire you'd see Landis wearing at the Hollywood Canteen or at her USO shows. Call it early business attire, culminating in the shoulder pad–heavy look Joan Crawford would make famous in *Mildred Pierce* (1945). And then there was something new entirely: the idea of "sporty chic" as promulgated by Esther Williams.

The MGM swimming star is sometimes thought of as a peculiarity of the era, but in every respect Williams was a transformational image of a woman: where female stars of old had been expected to be passive and look pretty, Williams was active— an Olympic athlete turned *Aquacade* star turned inventor of the "swimming musical" subgenre turned sportswear progenitor. Her existence all but spurred the invention of waterproof makeup. Not to mention how much she promoted swimming and fitness. Williams's first major starring role, after cameos in several previous films, was *Bathing Beauty* in 1944. She instantly became a pinup. Like Landis,

she visited with soldiers as well, but in a different respect: instead of frontline shows, the USO asked Williams to undertake hospital tours. These still involved stage performances, and Williams spent her days listening to Hope's and Benny's routines on the radio to try to perform them herself for convalescing servicemen. One feature of her act was to put on mock screen tests, in which she'd act out a scene opposite one of the recuperating men; these would inevitably end with Williams in a swimsuit and, of course, with a kiss.

Around the same time, Lena Horne, who came up with Williams at MGM at roughly the same time, was doing her part to entertain the troops. But as was so often the case, the pride she took in her war work was offset by the bitterness of trying to raise money and hopes in a still deeply segregated America.

ABOVE: Four Jills in a Jeep doesn't shy away from how much wartime entertainers had to "rough it."
BELOW: Esther Williams—and her cutout—crashes the set of Anchors Aweigh (1945). Gene Kelly and Frank Sinatra are amused.

BLACK EXCELLENCE

MGM called Lena Horne their "Negro Ambassador" for the war effort. After her twin successes of *Cabin in the Sky* and *Stormy Weather*, she spent the rest of 1943 performing at USO shows and dancing with soldiers at the Hollywood Canteen—Black soldiers who attended didn't always find many Black women to dance with there. She appeared on Carlton Moss's African-American-targeted radio show *Jubilee*, and she would use those opportunities to dedicate records to each soldier who wrote to her—of which there were many. Instead of answering the letters by mail, she let her radio shout-outs be her form of reply. Hearing her recognize you must have been a ray of hope to Black soldiers, who were under extraordinary pressure during wartime. Facing censure or violence from white soldiers "a lot of places where they were, [Black soldiers] couldn't put Betty Grable's picture in their lockers, see, but they were safe with my picture," Horne said decades later. "They made my career." If they were caught fantasizing about white women, such as Grable, they faced violent reprisals and even official reprimand. But the white gatekeepers who controlled much of American image making did not consider that there might be an audience for more than one Black pinup than Horne. "The men who fantasized about me, MGM gave me to them; they didn't choose me," she said.

Serving the war effort as an entertainer didn't

An example of the kind of Lena Horne photo, from 1944, Black soldiers would have felt comfortable putting in their lockers.

mean an escape from segregation. Near Alabama's Tuskegee airfield in February 1944, just after she finished a show for the airmen, she stopped in an airport diner to get a cup of coffee. "I'm sorry, I can't serve you," the waitress said. Then a teenage kid ran out from the kitchen to ask for her autograph. As Horne's biographer James Gavin put it, "The moment pointed out one of the painful ironies of her life. She was an MGM star, with more fan mail than she could answer, but couldn't order a cup of coffee in a southern airport." One time in Arkansas, she thought she was going to sing for an integrated crowd, but only the white soldiers and airmen ended up being invited. The next morning she gave a special performance in the Black mess hall. On another occasion, Horne was playing an integrated crowd, she thought, until she realized that all the white people were sitting up front with Black folks in the rear—and the white audience members were German POWs. The Armed Forces thought even captured soldiers who'd served the Nazis were more worthy of being close to the stage than their own Black personnel.

All the Black entertainers who helped with the war effort faced similar struggles. Eddie "Rochester" Anderson usually didn't tour with Jack Benny when the comedian brought his radio show on tour—if Anderson and Benny appeared together at military bases, they'd inevitably be forced into separate accommodations. On one occasion in 1945 when Anderson was touring with Benny, the radio show arrived in St. Joseph, Missouri. The entire cast and crew were welcomed into the Hotel Robidoux— except Anderson. "If he doesn't stay here, neither do I," said Benny, also threatening not to perform

his show the next day. The hotel relented, gave Anderson a room, and never barred Black guests again. Benny made good on his threats too. Several years earlier on a trip to New York City, the manager of their hotel asked if Anderson could stay elsewhere. A couple from the South had complained about his presence. Benny said that Anderson would leave the next day. What he didn't mention was that accompanying Anderson in his departure would be the entire cast and crew of forty-five, who all agreed to leave in protest.

Hattie McDaniel continued her work too, first by launching her own all-Black revue, a kind of parallel to the Hollywood Victory Caravan, to entertain the all-Black 10th Cavalry. At Camp Young, near Indio, California, she led another group of Black entertainers to put on a show and found

Lena Horne putting on a show at the Los Angeles Coliseum for Generals Patton and Doolittle after V-E Day.

Eddie "Rochester" Anderson, Lena Horne, boxer Max Baer, and jazz musician Lionel Hampton performing on the Armed Forces Radio show Jubilee in 1943.

herself in stunning danger when a dust storm with 80-mph winds suddenly descended. At one event in June 1943, she even reached her target for that performance: $175,000, the cost of a B-17 Flying Fortress. She had helped the Army Air Forces buy another bomber. On top of this she appeared in the Warner Bros. film *Thank Your Lucky Stars* (1943) and donated her salary to the Hollywood Canteen. And Lena Horne and her *Cabin in the Sky* costar Ethel Waters eventually joined McDaniel's road-show. The only white performer who joined them to perform for Black audiences? Bette Davis.

Hollywood was not a welcoming place for Black talent, and wouldn't really be for decades after. But though there weren't many Black movie stars, the ones who were there deserve the highest of praise for what they did onscreen and how they served the war effort. They may not have been appreciated by the industry—or by a large swath of the white moviegoing audience—then, but they can be seen and admired now. Their presence was the living dream of a more inclusive Hollywood, even if it would take so very long for that dream to be realized. And for the Black soldiers serving at home and overseas, they were a lifeline, an inspiration.

———

As Horne, Anderson, and McDaniel were playing for crowds of Black soldiers, the Tuskegee Airmen provided critical bomber escort support following the fall of Rome. The Allies inched ever higher up the Italian peninsula, while the British and American forces that liberated Paris met up with a separate Allied invasion force that took

A Black soldier of the 12th Armored Division standing guard over a group of Nazi soldiers in April 1945.

southern France—Lieutenant Commander Douglas Fairbanks Jr. commanded the HMS *Aphis* during those landings—and pushed deep into Belgium and finally Germany in December 1944. The Germans attempted one last offensive to retake their lost territory in Belgium; though it resulted in astonishing loss of life, the Battle of the Bulge ended up as the last time the German army would be on the attack during the war. With the British and the Americans closing in from the west and the Russians breathing down their necks in the east, the Third Reich was quickly collapsing into itself. And helping with that collapse was the all-Black 761st Tank Battalion, which steamrolled through France, Belgium, and into Germany with Patton's Third Army, capturing thirty towns in the process. During

the Battle of the Bulge, German soldiers actually posed as American soldiers—wearing US uniforms, adopting Yankee accents—for particularly effective infiltrations and sneak attacks. But Black soldiers would never be a part of the German forces, so Patton ordered the 761st into positions where they alone were to hold territory, with orders to shoot any white men who acted suspiciously.

In the Pacific, the US forces began their reconquest of the Philippines. Japanese strongholds in the Gilbert Islands, Marshall Islands, and Marianas had fallen, and the United States was beginning its own constricting move on the Japanese home islands. The next stop? A barren isle 750 miles south of Tokyo: Iwo Jima.

VICTORY

Major Clark Gable went on inactive duty shortly after D-Day. He still had a war documentary to edit and he felt he could do a better job of that out of uniform. Captain Ronald Reagan signed his discharge papers in Culver City. Gable ended up narrating *Combat America* himself, and it debuted in theaters in January 1945. It wasn't going to have any impact on the war effort, but the film was nonetheless a remarkable sixty-two-minute color portrait of what it was like for the Allies to bring the war to Fortress Europe in the year leading up to D-Day.

Gable then began the process of negotiating a new contract with MGM. That resulted in one of the most moving days in the history of the studio. The grieving actor hadn't sat in his fabled chair at the commissary since before Carole Lombard's death. And while he was in the army, the staff had placed the chair upside down upon the table to indicate that no one else would sit in his place of honor. As the ink dried on a seven-year contract extension, Gable, wearing his uniform, took his seat at the head of the table once more: an act of faith that, despite tragedy and trauma, it could be possible to get back to normal. "Everybody got up and applauded and cried," said publicist Eddie Lawrence. "Richard the Lionheart didn't get a better reception when he came back from the Crusades."

The King had returned.

In February and March 1945, the Battle of Iwo Jima raged. The United States gained control of this island so they would have an airstrip they could use to further a sustained, relentless bombing campaign of the Japanese home islands, expanding the initial bombing efforts the Army Air Forces had undertaken from Saipan, Tinian, and Guam using the new long-range B-29 bombers four months earlier. Future star Charles Bronson flew twenty-five missions over Japan in one of those B-29s and earned the Purple Heart for one of them. Seversky's *Victory Through Air Power* dream of winning the war from the skies was beginning to come true. On the night of March 9 and 10, the United States carried out the single most devastating air raid in history with those B-29s in the firebombing of Tokyo.

More than one hundred thousand civilians were killed and over a million left homeless from the one raid—higher totals than the atomic bombings of Hiroshima and Nagasaki. This battle on the black sand of Iwo Jima was practically down to the last man for the Japanese forces, because Japan knew how many lives back home would be lost if America gained this volcanic isle. Of the twenty thousand Japanese soldiers who defended Iwo Jima, more than eighteen thousand died in combat, three times as many as the number of American soldiers and marines killed in action during the battle. During the six-week engagement, Lieutenant Tyrone Power, a marine flyer, made endless missions in an R5C transport to pick up wounded marines on Iwo Jima and deliver supplies to those still fighting.

Jimmy Stewart was still flying B-24 bombers over Germany. Among the men he'd give briefings to was a young radioman-gunner named Sergeant Walter Matthau. Meanwhile, future TV producer Norman Lear was in the skies over Italy as a radio operator and gunner in a B-17. In December 1944, Stewart was promoted to full colonel—he flew his last mission on March 21, 1945, at which point a new threat greeted the Eighth Air Force: the

Germans had invented a futuristic jet fighter plane, the Messerschmitt Me 262, which basically could only be destroyed if still grounded. Stewart had flown more than twenty missions over Germany and France, and wrote more condolence letters than he probably ever imagined he'd have to. The stress of combat and command had taken its toll: he had aged visibly during his four years in the Army Air Forces. "It wasn't ever official," said General "Hap" Arnold about his decision to ground Stewart. "But I just told him I didn't want him to fly any more combat. He didn't argue about it."

When victory came in Europe, it was a time of relief and celebration, but also abject horror. As the American, British, and Russian troops stormed into Germany, they liberated the concentration camps the Nazis had been operating. No one was prepared for what they saw: thousands of emaciated corpses piled like firewood at Bergen-Belsen; rooms full of confiscated shoes and eyeglasses, human hair, and children's toys—a Soviet cameraman caught a glimpse of a stuffed Mickey Mouse—at Majdanek; the horrors of the gas chambers and crematoria at Auschwitz. The full extent of the Holocaust was not known outside Nazi territory until the Allied soldiers saw it for themselves.

On April 28, 1945, a crowd of anti-Fascists shot Mussolini in the street and hung him upside down alongside his mistress. Hitler committed suicide two days later. And on May 7, the new leader of the Third Reich, Admiral Karl Dönitz, signed an unconditional surrender. A shocking wave of mass suicide erupted around Germany as those who couldn't imagine life without National Socialism chose death instead—at least seven thousand were believed to have taken their own lives in Berlin alone.

The Nazi menace was gone. But the consequences of the regime would endure forever.

In the last months of the Third Reich, Hitler and his architects of the "Final Solution" for European Jews were so committed to their policy of murder, they diverted resources to keep the camps going and ensure the killings continued even as German forces were losing ground on all sides. Before the Red Army could liberate Auschwitz, the Germans marched any able-bodied prisoners halfway across Europe to other camps in Germany to continue their torment. Director George Stevens, present for the liberation of Dachau, just north of Munich, was changed forever by what he saw. "It was like wandering around in one of Dante's infernal visions," he said, adding later that the camp was "where I learned about life." The prisoners who were still alive had been denied food and medical care for so long that most could not be moved. As was the case at other camps, many would end up staying there for months on end until they were medically fit to travel—but the fact was, many did not even know where they would go. More than twenty thousand Jews refused to leave Belsen because they didn't know where their next home would be. When finally able to leave the former concentration camps, many then ended up in displaced persons camps, as the United States and Britain would not accept these refugees as immigrants. Most of the refugee camps remained in operation until 1948, when many of the Jews within elected to settle in the new state of Israel. The last two camps—one in Germany and one in Austria—didn't close until 1957 and 1959, respectively.

British film producer and future Granada TV founder Sidney Bernstein coordinated the editing of footage shot by British, American, and Soviet cameramen into a film intended to serve as a definitive record of Nazi atrocities in the camps. The immediate propaganda objective of the occupying forces in Germany was to elicit contrition—and compliance—from the German people. Military commanders who liberated the camps rounded up the local populations nearby and forced them to parade through to see the devastation they had allowed to happen on their doorstep. At Bernstein's request, Alfred Hitchcock returned to London in June 1945 to serve as "supervising director" of the film, tentatively titled *German Concentration Camps Factual Study*. One of his editors on the project, Peter Tanner, said, "I can remember [Hitchcock] strolling up and down in his suite at Claridge's, and saying, 'How can we make this convincing?' We tried to make shots as long as possible, so that there was no possibility of trickery." The fact was, the images were so horrific—piles of bodies being buried by a bulldozer, corpses so skeletal they looked out of a Hollywood horror film—that there was a real fear audiences, especially the German audience, wouldn't believe they were real. Germans who revered Hitler might think this was the work of Jewish Hollywood, after all. So Hitchcock did everything he could to show there was no manipulation of the footage: this was the way it really was.

But as the summer of 1945 wore on, American and British policy changed enough that *German Concentration Camps Factual Study* became a political inconvenience. Film and video archive curator Kay Gladstone of the Imperial War Museum said, "The evidence on the ground in occupied Germany, both in the American and British sectors, was indicating that the Germans had already been so bombarded with the message of their guilt that there was no longer a need for a film like this at this time." Pamphlets were distributed all over Germany with atrocities put right on the cover accompanying headlines such as "These Shameful Deeds: Your Fault!" The Americans and British might need these defeated Germans as allies against the Soviet Union, after all. Not to mention that Britain was in no mind to allow an independent Israel to be formed from its colonial holdings in Palestine, enthusiasm for which they feared would grow if the public saw on film how much Jews had suffered during the

Holocaust. Hitchcock and Bernstein's documentary was shelved—it wasn't shown until 2014. Bernstein instead joined Hitchcock in Hollywood to produce his films *Rope*, *Under Capricorn*, and *Stage Fright*.

Billy Wilder, however, picked up the gauntlet and reedited some of the footage that was in Hitchcock's film into a much shorter documentary titled *Death Mills* (1945). He was allowed to do this one because it had a much more simple message of scolding the Germans into obedience, whereas Hitchcock and Bernstein's film plumbed a depth of existential despair from which there might not have been any path forward. Wilder had had his breakout smash *Double Indemnity* the year before. Now he was bringing a genre filmmaker's sensibility to this devastating material, leaning into some of the more salacious aspects of the atrocities: regarding the Nazis' female camp guards, Wilder's narrator said, "Amazons turned Nazi killers were merciless in their use of the whip, practiced in torture and murder, deadlier than the male." The particularly punchy, visceral nature of this film might have had something to do with this: Wilder's mother, grandmother, and stepfather had all been murdered in the camps.

In 1988 Wilder recalled his motivation at the time: "We must show it to as many Germans as possible. This was 1945. They will say: 'It's a lie. These are extras with make-up. This is Hollywood . . . made by Jews.' But where would we have got them from? They were just skin and bone! Let's preview it in Wurzburg. A preview like they do in Hollywood. They were showing an operetta with Lillian Harvey. Afterwards I said: 'Please remain seated, and have a look at this.' There were 500 in the audience. At the end only about 75."

Back home in America, audiences certainly weren't interested in dwelling on the sadness of the past four years. William Wellman's *The Story of G.I. Joe* (1945), starring Captain Burgess Meredith, late of the Army Air Forces himself, was a glimpse,

It's a sign of how much moviegoers were ready to move on from the war that the only military-themed movie to end up as one of the top ten box-office successes of 1945 was <u>Anchors Aweigh</u>.

through the experiences of the war correspondent Ernie Pyle in North Africa and Italy, of how war was hell. It made little waves at the box office. It had only been seven months since *Thirty Seconds Over Tokyo* was a smash, but movies about combat and hardship were not what audiences wanted to see now. Compounding the depressive air around that movie, Pyle himself had been killed during the Battle of Okinawa in April. When *They Were Expendable* (1945), John Ford's elegiac tribute to those servicemembers who lost their lives in the Philippines during the earliest days of the war, opened in December, it pretty much bombed. Moviegoers did not want to revisit those early defeats. The general feeling of V-E Day and its aftermath was one of wanting to quickly put the war in the rearview mirror.

The film about military personnel in uniform that was a smash in 1945? The dancing sailors MGM musical *Anchors Aweigh*, starring Lieutenant Gene Kelly, fresh from his stint helping to make war documentaries as a US naval aviator in Washington, DC. Instead of sober reflections on all that the nation had been through, this was a Technicolor extravaganza in which Kelly danced onscreen with Jerry the Mouse. And it costarred Frank Sinatra, now earning $800,000 a year, making him the highest-paid entertainer in the world. How much Hollywood was done with war movies was underscored when the movie that won the Oscar for Best Picture of 1945 was Billy Wilder's *The Lost Weekend*, an issue movie about alcoholism with virtually no reference to the war at all. In a sign of how energized and ready he was to resume his movie career, Jimmy Stewart cohosted that Academy Awards ceremony with Bob Hope.

Of course, even after V-E Day there was a whole other war to win. The conflict raged on in the Pacific. Tyrone Power now flew supply and retrieval missions to Okinawa. Future director Robert Altman copiloted B-24s on fifty missions to Borneo and the rest of the East Indies. Future star Paul Newman was a turret gunner on a torpedo bomber assigned to the carrier USS *Bunker Hill*. But when his pilot was grounded with an earache, the assignment was delayed; lucky thing since the USS *Bunker Hill* was damaged and 352 crew killed by two kamikazes shortly thereafter. Lieutenant Henry Fonda's quarters aboard the USS *Curtis* were completely destroyed and thirty-five crew killed during that ship's own kamikaze attack. It took over fifteen hours to put out the fires. Since Fonda was in intelligence, he applied himself to figuring out where the kamikazes that attacked his ship were coming from: he figured out the suicide flyers were based at an airstrip on Pagan Island in the Marianas. An air raid soon eliminated the navy's kamikaze problem in the area. In early August 1945, Fonda met the crew of the *Enola Gay* while at a stop on the island of Tinian. He knew the B-29 was carrying something important, but not exactly what.

As the fall approached, Japan had been completely encircled, but the prospect of invading the Japanese home islands was daunting. Where the invasion of France began on a day codenamed D-Day, there would be two separate invasion days for Japan: X-Day (the invasion of the southernmost home island, Kyushu, as a diverting action) and Y-Day (the invasion of Honshu, the main island, on a plain near Tokyo). The casualties were estimated as being beyond anything yet experienced by the United States during the war. Over five hundred thousand Purple Heart awards were manufactured to be ready for when the fighting began. They weren't needed. And all the Purple Hearts that have been issued to soldiers in every one of America's wars since have come from that stockpile, mass produced as the medals were in 1945 for the fateful invasion of Japan that never came.

On August 6, the *Enola Gay* dropped the first atomic bomb ever used in combat on the city of Hiroshima. Three days later, the United States used another A-bomb on Nagasaki as well, and the Soviet Union declared war on Japan. World War II came to its close as a nuclear war. Japan finally surrendered on August 15. During the official ceremony in Tokyo Bay on September 2, the director Merian C. Cooper, years after first helping form the Flying Tigers, stood on the deck of the USS *Missouri* as the capitulation was formalized. Future star Tony Curtis watched from his submarine tender—the USS *Proteus*—about a mile away. He had signed up in part because he was inspired by the Cary Grant submarine thriller *Destination Tokyo* (1943).

The war was over. And it had come to an end so quickly. So much more quickly than anyone thought. After all, servicemen had invented slogans like "Out of the Sticks in '46," "Not Done Till '51," and "Keep Alive Till '55" that suggested just how unclear everyone was about how long the conflict would continue. At the very earliest, X-Day wouldn't have happened until November; Y-Day, not until March 1946. Instead, Times Square filled with celebrants. Ticker tape fell from the skies. The Hollywood Canteen closed its doors on Thanksgiving Day. Colonel Jimmy Stewart returned to his family home at Indiana, Pennsylvania. His ascent from private to colonel in less than four years is one of the fastest promotional tracks of anyone during the war. Meanwhile, Henry Fonda won the Bronze Star. So had Robert Montgomery, Tyrone Power, and Mickey Rooney. Above all, they and the whole country wanted to return to normal as quickly as possible.

At last it was a world without war.

Fred Astaire with a spoil of war: a German Iron Cross a US soldier gave him during a USO tour in 1944.

COMING HOME TO NEW BATTLES

assie had PTSD.

So did hundreds of thousands of soldiers returning from the war. But the term "post-traumatic stress disorder" was not even coined by the US Committee of Reactive Disorders until 1978, as a way to describe the devastating psychological effects of the Vietnam War on that generation's soldiers. "Shell shock" had been a term used to describe a debilitating emotional state during World War I, but World War II didn't yield any such term, other than "flak happy" for airmen. Counseling was not widely available for returning servicemen, who were encouraged, and often desired themselves, to deny any mental distress and return to normal as quickly as possible. Images of PTSD sufferers were few and far between in movies about returning soldiers. John Huston's *Let There Be Light*, a documentary about the still-unnamed condition for the War

In <u>Courage of Lassie</u> (1946), the Collie suffers from debilitating combat stress after serving as a war dog during the Aleutians campaign.

Department, was thought to be so demoralizing that the US government withheld its release for thirty-five years.

One of the only Hollywood movies to address the condition was, remarkably, *Courage of Lassie* (1946). The third installment in MGM's canine franchise starred Elizabeth Taylor as a girl in the Pacific Northwest who adopts an orphaned collie she names Bill. Played by the star of the Lassie movies, the extraordinary collie named Pal, Bill is separated from young Liz when he's hit by a military truck and taken by the servicemen aboard to their war dogs kennel for treatment. Not knowing who he belongs to, the soldiers conscript Bill once he's well again. He becomes a war dog and accompanies a battalion sent to reinforce the US presence in the Aleutians. (Few Hollywood features addressed PTSD; but this may be the only one to depict the Aleutians campaign, unless you count John Huston's *Report from the Aleutians* documentary for the army.)

The staging ground is cold, forbidding, and miserable. Then Bill is sent into the Battle of Attu, the fierce eighteen-day struggle to retake the American island the Japanese had conquered. A group of US soldiers gets trapped on a bluff behind enemy lines during the final Japanese banzai charge—an offensive that in real life ended up in shocking hand-to-hand combat and resulted in only twenty-eight of the 2,900 Japanese soldiers present being taken prisoner (a mortality rate of over 99 percent). More than five hundred American soldiers were killed in action during the battle as well. During the fighting, Bill has to crawl through the mud and keep his head low to make his way back to the American lines to carry a message that his unit is still trapped in enemy territory. It's one of the ultimate "Lassie's trying to tell us something!" moments, and indeed Bill leads a rescue party back to where the soldiers are huddled and somehow holding out. But upon his return to Elizabeth Taylor

after all this, Bill is not the same. He's suffering from PTSD and prone to violent outbursts, even raiding neighboring farms' chicken coops.

A case is brought before the local magistrate about whether this dog should be put down as a menace. What emerges in the courtroom battle is actually a thoughtful consideration of how those who fought in the war may need time to let go of all they've been through and find peace again. Frank Morgan is Bill's defense counsel at the hearing and he notes how his own son is still recuperating from his war wounds at a hospital. "From what he writes, I guess he's going through something like what Bill here went through," Morgan says. "And it just occurred to me that perhaps a lot of our boys will be coming back not quite ready to take up where they left off. They'll have gone through more than most of us could ever think of, and they're going to need patience and love and understanding from us. And most of all perhaps they'll need time. You know, they didn't become soldiers in a day and we can't expect them to become civilians in a day either." Somehow the "dog movie" packaging made it easier to address these delicate issues.

Courage of Lassie opened thirteen days before the movie that best addresses the hardships faced by returning soldiers: *The Best Years of Our Lives* (1946). Congress had authorized unprecedented legislation to assist returning servicemembers in getting jobs, college educations, and loan guarantees: the GI Bill. Though that satisfied the basic necessities of life, it didn't provide for counseling, and *The Best Years of Our Lives* shows the emotional challenges facing the returning soldier. The difficulty of resuming your role as father and head of your family. The flaws you now see in your marriage you didn't recognize before. The adjustment required to factor your new disability into your daily routine. That last point is illustrated by a real-life soldier who lost his hands in an accident while serving as an instructor in

Harold Russell is the only actor ever to win two Oscars for a single performance (in <u>The Best Years of Our Lives</u>): one for Best Supporting Actor and another Honorary Oscar.

demolition work in North Carolina. Harold Russell was a nonprofessional actor suddenly finding himself being directed by one of Hollywood's greatest filmmakers, William Wyler, who himself had lost much of his hearing while making a documentary about P-47 Thunderbolt fighters.

The Best Years of Our Lives was a smash, making over $10 million in 1946 and winning Best Picture at the Academy Awards. It was the direct, cathartic working-through of unresolved emotions from the war that audiences needed. The movie also anticipated the new Cold War reality: that some people in the United States might try to suggest that the

Russians were the great enemy that really needed to be fought, even expressing regret that the United States hadn't aligned with Nazi Germany against the threat of Communism. In one scene, Dana Andrews's discontented returning vet, back to his old job as a soda jerk, confronts a patron who insists Hitler wasn't so bad and that our real enemies were "the Limeys and the Reds." A Fascist thought like that expressed in America? It wasn't unlikely, and filmmakers began to express a new anxiety: What if ex-Nazis, or their ideology, began to burrow their way into the Americas? Orson Welles's immediate postwar film was *The Stranger* (1946), in many ways a director-for-hire job for Sam Spiegel's International Pictures, but one with its own resonance: Welles himself plays Franz Kindler, a Nazi war criminal who helped steer the Final Solution, who's now posing as a professor in a small Connecticut town. Edward G. Robinson, coming full circle from *Confessions of a Nazi Spy*, is the Nazi-hunting G-man tracking him down.

More likely even than Nazis coming to the United States was the idea of Nazis seeking refuge in South America, something that actually did happen. Thousands of ex-Nazis made it first to Spain, and then from there via "ratlines" to South America, particularly Argentina, where a Fascist-leaning strongman, Juan Perón, came to power in 1946 and gave cover to several prominent German war criminals. One of the first Hollywood noirs of the postwar era was Edward Dmytryk's *Cornered* (1945), about an ex-flyer tracking down to Buenos Aires the Nazi commandant who killed his French wife. Alfred Hitchcock's *Notorious*, which opened just sixteen months after V-E Day, imagined a cabal of wealthy ex-Nazis plotting in the Argentine capital to build their own atomic bomb—keeping radioactive material in wine bottles—in an attempt to retake power. Even *Gilda* (1946) makes more than a few hints about what the title character's Germanic husband did during the war to achieve the wealth and position he currently holds in Buenos Aires.

These were early stabs in the film noir genre that asked what America had been fighting for. Most later noirs would end up without any connection to the war—though some would, such as Fred Zinnemann's *Act of Violence* (1949), about an ex-GI avenging a betrayal that had occurred at a German POW camp where he had been held—but all critically examined the promises of the American Dream that had been on the line during the war. What if those promises weren't always met?

The Stranger, grossing more than three times its budget, was a much-needed hit for Welles after the calamity of *The Magnificent Ambersons* and *It's All True*, and he'd follow it up with another arty noir, this time with his wife Rita Hayworth at her studio, Columbia: *The Lady from Shanghai* (1947). But his career had been undoubtedly damaged by World War II. And he wasn't the only one. Frank Capra's *It's a Wonderful Life* (1946) grossed only about a third of *The Best Years of Our Lives*. Capra's new outfit, Liberty Films, suffered a crippling blow from that relative box-office failure (made all the worse due to Capra's excessive salary), and the director emerged, along with Welles and Mickey Rooney, as someone whose career had withered during the war. But movie lovers and scholars of the wartime years who'd watch the *Why We Fight* films in subsequent years suggested that it had all been worth it—those films turned propaganda into art and retained their power even after the cannons stopped firing.

Carmen Miranda's star was also fading. She was the highest-paid female entertainer when 1945 began, making over $200,000 a year. But she had peaked. Her last two films, *Greenwich Village* (1944), in which she was a co-lead, and *Something for the Boys* (1944), in which she played a lead role as a defense plant worker, grossed much less than her earlier hits. Her exotic appeal had connected so much at a time when Americans' view was directed outward and millions of men and women were shipped to ports of call they'd never imagined visiting. Now, audiences' gaze turned inward. Visions of home were what they wanted. And suddenly there wasn't a place for Carmen Miranda any longer. She had made enough money to be set for life, and experienced a mini-revival with the introduction of television, a medium better suited for the kind of one-and-done appearances she specialized in, but the tutti-frutti queen now had a smaller kingdom. After appearing visibly exhausted, even falling to her knees, on an episode of *The Jimmy Durante Show* on August 4, 1955, she died of a fatal heart attack in the early morning hours of the next day. She was forty-six.

Unlike some other stars, Marlene Dietrich was able to evolve, morphing her career into character parts that ensured she'd continue working. Dietrich was in for a shock, though. After V-E Day, she continued with the Allies into Germany and reunited with her mother. She helped vouch for her sister Elisabeth not being a Nazi so that she could receive work during the period of "denazification" when ex-Nazis were shut out of most available jobs. But she also discovered that Elisabeth had run a cinema to entertain the SS guards at Bergen-Belsen. For the last forty-seven years of her life, Dietrich insisted she was an only child, and never once mentioned Elisabeth in her 1989 memoir.

Hattie McDaniel, after her wartime work and appearance in the smash-hit home front drama *Since You Went Away* (1944), found that job offers began trickling in a bit more infrequently after the war. The studios that had invested in films with all-Black casts immediately abandoned those films when wartime outreach no longer incentivized them. McDaniel appeared in Disney's *Song of the South* (1946), but her roles in postwar movies grew smaller and smaller. She always said that she'd rather play a maid onscreen than be one, but in her last movie, *The Big Wheel* (1949), even her name was misspelled in the credits. And in the immediate aftermath of the war, she was in for a shock. Since 1938 she'd lived in a seventeen-room mansion in the Los Angeles neighborhood of West Adams Heights. She'd held meetings of the Hollywood Victory Committee there throughout the war. Clark Gable was a regular at her parties. But in 1945 her white neighbors had succeeded in crafting a lawsuit against her and other Black homeowners that sought to expel them from the area altogether. It invoked an unenforced 1902 deed restriction that prevented "non-Caucasians"

from owning homes in the area. But thankfully, Judge Thurmond Clarke threw the case out. "It is time that members of the Negro race are accorded, without reservations or evasions, the full rights guaranteed them under the 14th Amendment to the Federal Constitution," he ruled. "Judges have been avoiding the real issue too long." McDaniel replied, "Words cannot express my appreciation."

But if there was ever a reminder of the tenuous place of African-Americans in virtually all areas of American life—even for an Academy Award winner—that was it. She was only able to keep her home due to a fair-minded judge being selected for her case. In other parts of the country, even more visceral horrors awaited Black soldiers, who believed they had been fighting for a "Double Victory": against Fascism and racism abroad and, through the extraordinary heroism and patriotism they'd exhibited, to claim their rights at home. Instead, the NAACP found itself having to champion the tragic case of Isaac Woodard, a twenty-six-year-old Black returning veteran who found himself having some heated words with a bus driver in South Carolina when he asked if the bus could wait while he used the bathroom. The driver alerted the police, who hauled Woodard off the bus supposedly for being "drunk and disorderly," though there was no evidence that he had been. The police jailed him and the local sheriff, Lynwood Shull, blinded him by repeatedly jabbing in his eyes with his billy club.

The case ignited a national outcry. Woody Guthrie wrote the song "The Blinding of Isaac Woodard" so that listeners "wouldn't be forgetting what happened to this famous Negro soldier less than three hours after he got his Honorable Discharge." He later recalled, when he sang the song for thirty-six thousand people at New York City's Lewisohn Stadium, "I got the loudest applause I ever got in my whole life." Orson Welles campaigned on-air during his *Orson Welles Commentaries*

radio series for ABC to get Shull arrested for the crime, saying of the sheriff, "All America is ashamed of you. If there's room for pity, you can have it, for you are far more blind than he."

Shull freely admitted to his crime but was acquitted of any wrongdoing by an all-white jury. He outlived Woodard by five years, dying in 1997 at age ninety-five.

Ex-soldier Isaac Woodard, blinded by South Carolina police, is assisted by officials from the NAACP with filing his disability claim with the Veterans Administration.

HOLLYWOOD'S COLD WAR RETREAT

On July 1, 1946, a B-29 bomber dropped the fourth atomic bomb ever detonated. The target of the government nuclear test was the uninhabited Bikini Atoll in the Marshall Islands. The bomb was named *Gilda*, after the Rita Hayworth noir that had opened across the country a little over two months before. It also bore an image of Hayworth, taken from the June 1946 issue of *Esquire*. She had literally become a bombshell. "Rita used to fly into terrible rages all the time," her husband Orson Welles said. "But the angriest was when she found out that they'd put her on the atom bomb. Rita almost went insane, she was so angry

. . . She wanted to go to Washington to hold a press conference, but [Columbia president] Harry Cohn wouldn't let her because it would be unpatriotic." The day before the bomb test, Welles took to the air on his *Orson Welles Commentaries* radio show and said, "I want my daughter to be able to tell her daughter that grandmother's picture was on the last atom bomb ever to explode."

The bomb was now a reality of everyday life. Just one more sign that the postwar world was to come with an astonishing array of new anxieties: the Cold War had dawned. And with it, Hollywood abandoned much of the progress it had made during

In addition to having her image painted on an atomic bomb, Rita Hayworth appeared as nose art on a B-29 equipped to carry atomic bombs.

the war years. The spirit of unity that had seized the industry, and much of the country, was gone, including the desire to be more inclusive. The prewar isolationism was gone too. America was a superpower now and one that wished to flex its muscles on the world stage. But the world was now defined by bipolar spheres of interest: America's, and that of the Soviet Union. And fear of the USSR—not unjustified, as Stalin's gobbling up of Eastern Europe in the immediate aftermath of V-E Day showed—resulted in new suspicions within America.

There were Red Scares in the United States ever since the Bolshevik Revolution, and "foreign influences" in Hollywood—a euphemism with anti-Semitic overtones—had spurred the Nye Committee and Martin Dies's House Un-American Activities Committee (HUAC) to investigate the film industry before the war. The fear then was that Hollywood was driving America to interventionism and war. The fear in the late 1940s was that Hollywood wouldn't be hawkish enough against the Soviet Union, and maybe people who worked as directors, writers, or actors even supported the Communist state.

Of particular suspicion were those who had agitated against Fascism in the Hollywood Anti-Nazi League and other groups in the 1930s. Why were they anti-Nazi before the Nazis declared war on America? The term the House Un-American Activities Committee was now using to describe these individuals, such as Edward G. Robinson, was "prematurely anti-Fascist." Boxed into a corner, he renounced his previous Leftist connections in an

article for *American Legion Magazine* titled "How the Reds Made a Sucker Out of Me." Lena Horne renounced Communism too, but her connections to Communist-affiliated civil rights groups earlier in the forties meant she was blacklisted. She was pretty much fed up with Hollywood, anyway. Under contract to MGM, the only lead role the studio ever gave her was in *Cabin in the Sky*. After that one, they reverted to the prewar policy of just putting a Black performer in one scene that could be easily cut out for the Southern audience. Her most desired role was the mixed-race character Julie LaVerne in the 1951 production of *Show Boat*. It went to her friend Ava Gardner instead. Paul Robeson ended up blacklisted too. And so was Irving Pichel, the director of *The Man I Married*. Edward Dmytryk, the director not only of *Cornered* but of *Crossfire* (1947), another noir and one about anti-Semitism in the army, actually became one of the Hollywood Ten, a group of writers and directors cited for contempt of Congress for refusing to testify before HUAC. As a result, Dmytryk served four months and seventeen days in prison. He later testified and thus reclaimed his career. And Charlie Chaplin, maybe the ultimate premature anti-Fascist, ended up being banned from the United States.

Edward G. Robinson performing for troops in Normandy with the USO in the summer of 1944. After the war he was labeled "prematurely anti-Fascist" for campaigning against Nazism during the 1930s.

HUAC particularly examined the creation of the Russian-themed movies that were made as overtures to the Soviet Union during the war: *Mission to Moscow*, *The North Star*, and *Song of Russia*. The committee even brought in Ayn Rand to watch these movies and write up her feelings about how they represented Communist infiltration in Hollywood. Called to testify, Robert Taylor disowned *Song of Russia* and said he had been forced to make it under duress. Samuel Goldwyn, as an independent producer, was able to retain some control over *The North Star*, but he reedited the film extensively and even tacked on commentary about the Hungarian Uprising against the Soviets in 1956.

Rand contributed a guiding set of principles to a group of Hollywood talent that wished to cooperate with HUAC: the Motion Picture Alliance for the Preservation of American Ideals (MPA). Walt Disney was one of the founding members. His experience with the animation strike and his employees unionizing certainly pushed him further to the right. He testified before HUAC, and always believed that Communists had tried to undermine his business. So did John Wayne, who particularly targeted *The Best Years of Our Lives* as "a dangerous vehicle for left-wing propaganda."

Hollywood faced a shifting landscape. Some filmmakers, like rising director Elia Kazan, wanted to explore social problems that still festered in America. But the moguls retreated into a new conservatism due to several threats to the industry. First, HUAC could completely revive the prewar idea that Hollywood was immoral and driven by foreign or un-American interests. Also, television

was on the horizon as a potential game-changing competitor. Actors were gaining more power over the terms of their contracts following Olivia de Havilland's successful employment lawsuit against Warner Bros. and the ever-increasing rise of the agency MCA and power agents such as Charles Feldman, who helped negotiate nonexclusive agreements and profit-sharing deals for stars. And the Justice Department's Paramount Consent Decrees fundamentally changed the business model of the industry—it ended the practice of studios owning movie theaters. Now the studios would have to compete for screen space and split revenue with independent theater owners.

So that push-pull between wanting to carry the momentum of the war years into real social change and the fear produced by all these industry threats resulted in a wishy-washy effort like *Gentleman's Agreement* (1947). Kazan's cinematic exploration of anti-Semitism in America does feature Jewish actor John Garfield in a supporting role, but most of the movie is a touristic view of prejudice in which Gregory Peck's journalist character acts like he's Jewish for a while to see what kind of treatment he receives. The point of view is not with Jews but with a WASP coming to realize how blind he was to anti-Semitism before. A movie like this is watered down, handling its audience with kid gloves. Yet despite that, the Jewish moguls of Hollywood beseeched Darryl F. Zanuck to reconsider making the movie for fear it would stir up trouble. "Of all the studio heads he was the only gentile at the time and they were all against him doing it," his son Richard Zanuck said. "'Darryl, don't go there.' But he felt it was a good story, he had a responsibility, and it was an important issue."

The movie, one of the top ten box-office hits of 1947, appealed to an audience that often didn't respond to issues of prejudice unless it affected them directly: Zanuck himself only got the idea for the

Through a combination of timidity, indifference, and a feeling that the horrors of the Holocaust could not be appropriately portrayed onscreen, there was no major Hollywood depiction of what happened to European Jews during the war until <u>The Diary of Anne Frank</u> in 1959. The film was directed by George Stevens, and it was a passion project born out of how he had witnessed the liberation of Dachau.

movie when the Los Angeles Country Club refused him membership because it was assumed, incorrectly, that he was Jewish. Even *Crossfire*, seemingly the more potent of 1947's two films about anti-Semitism, had hedged: the original Richard Brooks novel it was based on was actually about homophobia and the murder of a gay man—but that was too incendiary to touch at all, while anti-Semitism seemed at least like a possibility to put onscreen.

Kazan and the entire lead cast of *Gentleman's Agreement* were still called to testify before HUAC, even though the director himself later said of the movie that it "skated over the surface of an issue that needed a more penetrating treatment." For HUAC it

was still too potent—it did go on to win Best Picture at the Academy Awards, after all. Kazan, famously, later named names, an act that tarnished his legacy forever despite his directing an entire movie, *On the Waterfront* (1954), to justify his actions. At those hearings, John Garfield testified but didn't name names. He had never been a Communist himself, but his wife Roberta Weidler had. Pressure mounted on him to testify against her. Their marriage strained beyond the breaking point when he agreed to write an "I Was a Sucker" essay for *Look* along the lines of Edward G. Robinson's in which he distanced himself from leftist ideology. Permanently separated from Weidler, Garfield was found dead of a heart attack in a new love's bed in 1952. He had been blacklisted from work for a whole year prior. He was thirty-nine. The days of his great contribution to the war effort, the Hollywood Canteen, seemed long ago.

It had seemed like Hollywood abandoned the unity and inclusiveness of the war years. And some, given over to blacklisting and naming names, indeed had done so. But with any progress, there are always steps backward. After the explosion of Black joy that was the one-two punch of *Cabin in the Sky* and *Stormy Weather*, there'd only be a handful of all-Black studio efforts in the next couple decades: Otto Preminger's *Carmen Jones* (1954) and *Porgy and Bess* (1959) stand out. But that level of joy in those Lena Horne starrers might not have appeared onscreen again

until 1978's *The Wiz*, directed by Sidney Lumet (who married Lena Horne's daughter, Gail Jones). The great director was a World War II veteran himself, serving from 1942–1946 as a radar repairman in India and Burma. If the right-wing attacks on *The Best Years of Our Lives* had diminished its reputation slightly by the end of the 1940s, future actors and filmmakers who saw it and had served during the war years brought its cinematic values with them into the future. Lumet said of *Best Years* that it was a "magnificent movie, and I came into it as I think any veteran would, a little suspicious. We'd been through an earth-shattering, life-changing experience of our own and we weren't going to accept any bullshit version of what that experience was like. Well, it not only didn't have any bullshit, it portrayed what we felt right to the core of our being." That turn of phrase, describing *The Best Years of Our Lives*, could

Rita Hayworth leads a line of sailors in the bunny hop at a USO show.

also describe the New Hollywood Lumet helped launch twenty years later. He and other future stars and creators—Kirk Douglas, who helped end the blacklist by giving Dalton Trumbo a credit on *Spartacus* (1960); Robert Altman, who put the rebel spirit of the counterculture in his movies; Norman Lear, who would revolutionize TV—remembered the immediacy, the relevance, and the sense of purpose in the war movies they watched while they were in uniform.

World War II proved forever that movies mattered. During the four war years, box-office gross rentals for the cumulative top ten movies of each year averaged $44 million. That was a 57 percent increase over the average box office for the top ten movies of the four previous years, 1938 to 1941. Hollywood's loss of its foreign markets barely mattered at all. The four years after the war (1946–1949) averaged $48 million for each year's cumulative top ten, a 73 percent lift over the four years leading up to US involvement in the war. It was undeniable now: movies were the American art form, the entertainment that brought together a country with many divisions.

Once Hollywood moviemaking proved it could survive the advent of television, the dismantling of the studio factory system, and the blacklist, and could become something other than an industry too big to fail, it was then able to evolve into an industry more accommodating of iconoclastic voices. And those voices wanted to make the big statements they had seen onscreen during the war years. From then on, Hollywood wouldn't just be a mirror held up to America. It'd be a steering wheel, helping to set the overall cultural agenda of the nation. Without *The Great Dictator* or *To Be or Not to Be*, you wouldn't have *Dr. Strangelove* or *The Producers*. Without *Confessions of a Nazi Spy*, you wouldn't have *The Parallax View* or *All the President's Men*. Without *The Stranger*, you wouldn't have *Marathon Man*. Without *Going My Way*, which normalized and celebrated Catholic life at a time of ongoing persecution against Catholics, you wouldn't have had *Fiddler on the Roof* for Jewish life. Without Van Johnson losing his leg in searing fashion in *Thirty Seconds Over Tokyo*, you wouldn't have the physical and emotional traumas of *The Deer Hunter*. Without *The Best Years of Our Lives*, you wouldn't have the exacting domestic dramas of the New Hollywood, from *Who's Afraid of Virginia Woolf?* to *Coming Home*. Without *Casablanca* and its unique characterization of its twin heroes as embodying idealism and cynicism, you wouldn't have Luke Skywalker and Han Solo in *Star Wars*.

The roots for the Hollywood to come were all there because of the war years. Inclusivity would take much longer to achieve and is something that the industry still struggles with to this day. As far as openness, though, Hollywood stars, by dancing with soldiers or performing for soldiers or becoming soldiers themselves, had proven they were more like ordinary moviegoers than ever before. What resulted was what historian Steven Cohan notes was "a patriotic identification with America through entertainment." Garfield's life ended in tragedy, but the democratization of Hollywood he'd pioneered with Bette Davis in the Hollywood Canteen changed the relationship of stars to fans forever.

Think of this: have you ever heard anyone at all, who was in uniform or out of it, associated with the movie business or not, say they regretted contributing to the good fight of World War II? Davis said, "There are few accomplishments in my life that I am sincerely proud of. The Hollywood Canteen was one of them."

For all the traumas of World War II, no one in Hollywood looked back on their participation in it with anything but a sense that it had been necessary and righteous.

That's the spirit that fuels victory—in any age, in any way.

ACKNOWLEDGMENTS

Writing *Hollywood Victory* during a pandemic that changed the world was a singular experience. Many a time it was quite easy to get lost in the 1940s, a time when unity of purpose seemed to coalesce so much more naturally than it does today. But it's critical to remember how actually difficult that unity was to achieve, and for how long it seemed like the forces that stood against tyranny didn't know what to do. There are so many lessons to be learned from World War II and the bravery and sacrifice of the men and women who fought for freedom, and that is one of them. The defeats at Bataan and Corregidor are as instructive as D-Day. This book is dedicated to everyone, in uniform or not, who risked their lives and their careers to give birth to the world we've known ever since.

In the twenty-first century there are some individuals without whom this book wouldn't have been possible: my fantastic editor, Cindy Sipala, who refined my proposal, gave it a new sense of narrative urgency, and always believed I had a story to tell, then helped me tell it; Fred Francis, who handled its production and knows how to keep the trains running with meticulous precision; John Malahy at Turner Classic Movies, whose encouragement and attention to detail always show just why Turner Classic Movies is so beloved of film fans everywhere; Aaron Spiegeland at Parham Santana, who always asks smart questions and sees the big picture; Eileen Flanagan, for helping me navigate TCM's deep photo archives; Bill Warhop, maybe the most talented copy editor I've ever encountered, for his extraordinary cleanup effort; designer Joshua McDonnell, for turning this book into a work of art; and my publicists, Seta Zink at Running Press and Taryn Jacobs at TCM, for promoting the hell out of this project. Plus Seth Adam and The Lead PR for their support and encouragement. To the whole team at TCM who helped make this book a reality, you have earned the deep loyalty shown by your fans with everything you do to promote classic film every day.

Thanks go also to the many people who contributed to my research. Among them: Gerrit Thies from the Deutsche Kinemathek in Berlin; David L. Cobb at the University of Kentucky Press for his help in connecting me with Emil Jannings's biographer Frank Noack to refine the story that opens this book; Noack himself for giving me an English translation of the chapter of his biography (auf Deutsch) about Jannings's interaction with the US troops who occupied his estate; and of course, Monika Henreid, who shared with me vivid recollections, passed down from her father, about the making of *Casablanca* and what it was like for refugees from Germany and Austria in the Hollywood of the 1930s and '40s.

So many authors influenced the shape of this book, but credit certainly goes to Mark Harris, Thomas Doherty, Jody Rosen, and Robert Matzen, whose work not only served as key references for *Hollywood Victory* but set a bar of literary skill to which I aspired. Special thanks to Robert Matzen for his support and encouragement and for clarifying for me what others have gotten wrong: James Stewart did not fly a mission on D-Day.

A whole lot of friends supported this book along the way: Jeremy Berman, a great cinephile and a greater friend, who let me prattle on at length about it; Caryn James, for her enthusiasm and support; Erich Schoeneweiss, who was always so excited to read this book, and whose Zoom lunches have been among my favorite things in pandemic life; Kristin Baver and James Floyd, whose gatherings over Zoom provided some fun and encouragement throughout; and Heather Antos, for providing some important advice right before I started on this journey.

And then there are my colleagues at IndieWire. The entire staff is incredible, and if I could name every one, I would. But, as relates to this project: Dana Harris, the best Editor in Chief in the business, and Eric Kohn, as enthusiastic a champion of film culture as anyone today, both of whom supported this book from the beginning; Kristen Lopez, who's the one-woman cheer squad classic film needs and who connected me with Monika Henreid in the first place; and my own team, the indefatigable trio of Zack Sharf, Leah Lu, and Ryan Lattanzio, who bring hard work, energy, and skill to everything they do and make my life as Managing Editor so much better.

But there's no one else who should wrap up this list than my mom, Dianne. Living together during the pandemic and during the writing of this book, she never knew what to expect from me: maybe one day upon waking she'd walk in and find me obsessively studying a map, with me immediately launching into "So you see the Allies actually took almost two months to break out of their beachhead in Normandy and . . ." Or me firing up a five-hour playlist of Bing Crosby's '40s hits. Or demanding we watch *Hollywood Canteen* a second time. Or randomly quoting one of the zingers from a Bob Hope joke book I kept handy. Or suddenly breaking into song with "White Christmas"—in July. You were on this journey too. Every step of the way. As you always have been my whole life. I wouldn't be here without your love, support, and encouragement during the highs, the lows, and everything in between.

NOTES

INTRODUCTION

ix   while the Third Reich fell: Frank Noack, "The Grey List," *Emil Jannings: Der Erste Deutsche Weltstar* (Munich: Rolf Heyne Collection, 2012), Chapter 21: "The Grey List" translated into English. Special thanks to Noack for sending this English translation to me directly over email. This story of Jannings holding his Oscar before him as if to shield him from American troops is one that's been spread in recent years by a few British publications, including the following: Martin Chilton, "The Nazi Shame of the First Ever Best Actor Winner at the Oscars," *The Independent*, January 14, 2020. That story and others get fundamental details wrong. Jannings was not in Berlin at the end of the war but at his estate in Strobl, Austria. It was Soviet forces who took Berlin, not American troops, who were positioned west of the Elbe, so it seems odd that Chilton and others would think that an Oscar would impress Russian troops. Noack notes that Joseph Goebbels was very upset with Jannings for avoiding Berlin, and the bombings that wrecked it, the last couple years of the war. Did Jannings say, "I have Oscar!"? Noack notes to the author that there is no evidence of any such quote.

ix   For the twelve million American soldiers: "US Military by the Numbers," National World War II Museum, New Orleans, https://www.nationalww2museum.org /students-teachers/student-resources/research-starters/research-starters-us-military-numbers.

HOLLYWOOD OPENS ITS ARMS . . .

1   "Billy—What kinda name is that": Maurice Zolotow, *Billy Wilder in Hollywood* (London: Pavilion Books, 1988), 55.

From 1933 to 1941, more than ten thousand: Kevin Starr, Chapter 13 opener *The Dream Endures: California Enters the 1940s* (Oxford, England: Oxford University Press 2002).

Among those, over 750: Steven J. Ross, *Hollywood Left and Right: How Movie Stars Shaped American Politics* (Oxford, England: Oxford University Press, 2011), 97.

One of his Columbia coworkers: Zolotow, 56.

When his six-month contract: ibid., 57.

2   "I'll decide who's Jewish!": Patricia Ward Biederman, "Infamous but Seldom-Seen Films of the Third Reich

Will Get a Rare Screening," *Los Angeles Times*, February 3, 1991. This story has been told many times—it's even included in Jean-Luc Godard's *Contempt*, in which Lang appears as himself. As with the accounts of many directors of the period—most given to self-mythmaking—it should not be taken at face value.

(photo caption) In reality, Lang's passport: David Thomson, *The Big Screen: The Story of the Movies* (New York: Farrar, Straus and Giroux, 2012), 64–65.

3   One night at a dinner party in 1937: Alexandra Dean's *Bombshell: The Hedy Lamarr Story* presents the most coherent version of this story.

"Oh, I want to be in that": From Fleming Meeks's interview tapes with Lamarr, which formed the basis of a May 14, 1990, *Forbes* interview with the star—the interview that first revealed to many Lamarr's second life as an inventor—and gives Dean's *Bombshell* documentary its backbone.

. . . BUT CLOSES ITS MIND

4   "I think one of the most important things": "Warriors and Peacemakers," *Moguls and Movie Stars*, episode 5, 2010.

5   "He had this idea of, 'I want to create the America'": ibid.

in November 1936, 95 percent of Americans: Ross, 90, but originally sourced from George Gallup and Claude Robinson's polling in *Public Opinion Quarterly* no. 2 (July 1938).

6   "The Silver Shirts and the Bundists": Ross, 98.

"Italy has always produced great men": ibid., but the original quote was printed twice in *The New York Times*, on March 24, 1934, and on October 18, 1936.

"seems to be a very great fellow too": ibid., but original quote was printed in the *New York World Telegram* on May 3, 1937.

"They were very wary of rocking the boat": ibid.

"A lot of Jews will lose their lives": Ross, 100.

7   (photo caption) Budd Schulberg claimed Mayer: *The Tramp and the Dictator* (2002), documentary directed by Kevin Brownlow and Michael Kloft.

The mogul pivoted: Patricia Geiger, "Laemmles Bürgschaften retteten vielen das Leben," *Schwäbische Zeitung*, November 4, 2012.

Once a major silent screen star, Gloria Swanson: Tricia Welsch, *Gloria Swanson: Ready for Her Close-Up* (Jackson: University Press of Mississippi, 2013), 299–301.

SOUNDING THE ALARM ABOUT JAPAN

8   "The artist must take sides": "Spanish Relief Efforts: Albert Hall Meeting £1,000 Collected for Children," *Manchester Guardian*, June 25, 1937.

9   she published a lengthy editorial: Graham Russell Gao Hodges, *Anna May Wong: From Laundryman's Daughter to Hollywood Legend* (London: Palgrave Macmillan, 2004), 105.

"Why is it that the screen Chinese": Shirley Jennifer Lim, *A Feeling of Belonging: Asian American Women's Public Culture, 1930–1960* (New York: New York University Press, 2005), 58, from the original 1933 article "I Protest" in *Film Weekly*.

10   "If you let me play O-Lan": Hodges, 136.

SAVING HER HOMELAND FROM ITSELF

11   Dietrich was particularly targeted: Steven Bach, *Marlene Dietrich: Life and Legend* (New York: William Morrow, 1992), 186.

"I sometimes wonder": Bach, 289.

12   It had to have been a blank check too: Bach, 220. There's some debate about the exact salary Dietrich received. In an article by Jeremy Arnold for TCM.com simply titled "Knight Without Armour," Arnold says the figure was $350,000. The $450,000 figure makes sense to me because Korda wanted to say that he had paid Dietrich twice the extravagant $200,000 salary David O. Selznick had paid her for *The Garden of Allah* (1935).

"QUARANTINE HITLER"

13   John Ford mounted the stage: "Martin Dies," Spartacus Educational, https://spartacus-educational.com/USAdies.htm.

That had drawn international indignation: Shirley Temple Black, *Child Star: An Autobiography* (New York: McGraw-Hill, 1988), 253.

"capitulation to Hitler": Thomas Doherty, *Hollywood's Censor: Joseph I. Breen and the Production Code Administration* (New York: Columbia University Press, 2007), 210.

14   "The world is faced": Ross, 89.

CONFESSIONS OF A NAZI SPY

15   "strive for pictures that provide something more": Ross, 104.

"the blood of a great many Jews": "Confessions of a Nazi Spy," *AFI Catalog of Feature Films*, https://catalog.afi.com/Catalog/moviedetails/908.

"the Jews" as being purveyors of immorality: Thomas Doherty, "Was Hollywood's Famed Censor an Anti-Semite?," *Forward*, December 11, 2007, https://forward.com/culture/12234/was-hollywood-s-famed-censor-an-antisemite-00948/.

"screaming madman": ibid.

"against slurring a friendly country": Paul Buhle and David Wagner, *Radical Hollywood: The Untold Story Behind America's Favorite Movies* (New York: The New Press, 2002), 212–213.

18   lived at the studio for the duration: "Confessions of a Nazi Spy," *AFI Catalog*.

"One day an overhead light came crashing": "Warner Bros. Led the Movie Industry's Fight Against Fascism 80 Years Ago," Warner Bros. website, May 6, 2019, https://www.warnerbros.com/news/articles/2019/05/06/confessions-nazi-spy-80th-anniversary.

filed a $5 million libel suit: *Hollywood Reporter*, May 13, 1939, 1.

as many plainclothes policemen: Clive Hirschhorn, *The Warner Bros. Story* (New York: Crown Publishing, 1986), 198.

"active militant propaganda agency": *Hollywood Reporter*, September 6, 1939, 1, 10.

vowed to make his own series: *Los Angeles Examiner*, June 6, 1939.

TURNING APATHY INTO ENGAGEMENT

21 a Gallup poll found 79 percent: Nancy Snow, "Confessions of a Hollywood Propagandist: Harry Warner, FDR, and Celluloid Persuasion," *Warners' War: Politics, Pop Culture and Propaganda in Wartime Hollywood*, ed. Martin Kaplan and Johanna Blakley (Pasadena, CA: Norman Lear Center Press, 2004).

an April 1938 Gallup poll: Daniel Greene and Frank Newport, "American Public Opinion and the Holocaust," Gallup, https://news.gallup.com/opinion/polling -matters/232949/american-public-opinion-holocaust .aspx.

Right after Kristallnacht: ibid.

THE GREAT DICTATOR

23 "It is an ironical thought": "An Old Friend Leaves Us," *New York Times*, September 29, 1937, section 1, page 22.

24 Of Chaplin it remarked: Ivor Montagu, *With Eisenstein in Hollywood* (New York: International Publishers, 1969), 94.

"The Hitler-like moustache": Louella Parsons, *Los Angeles Examiner*, October 18, 1938.

25 Chaplin's then assistant Dan James said: *The Tramp and the Dictator*.

President Roosevelt himself loved: Jeffrey Vance, *Chaplin: Genius of the Cinema* (New York: Abrams Books, 2003), 237.

"for the Jews of the world": Theodore Huff, *Charlie Chaplin* (New York: Henry Schuman, 1951), 263.

26 "Leaders with tenth-rate minds": Robert Van Gelder, "Chaplin Draws a Keen Weapon," *New York Times Magazine*, September 8, 1940, 8.

"Had I known of the actual horrors": Charles Chaplin, *My Autobiography* (New York: Simon & Schuster, 1964), 426.

27 "At the start of the show": *The Tramp and the Dictator.*

Did Hitler actually see *The Great Dictator*?: Peter Steffens, "Chaplin: The Victorian Tramp," *Ramparts* 3, no. 6 (March 1965): 21. Budd Schulberg also gives his corroboration in *The Tramp and the Dictator* documentary.

BOMBS, BULLETS, AND BANANAS

30 According to historian Brian O'Neil, Whitney: Brian O'Neil, "Carmen Miranda: The High Price of Fame and Bananas," in *Latina Legacies*, eds. Vicki L. Ruiz and Virginia Sanchez Korrol (Oxford, UK: Oxford University Press, 2005), 195.

He offered her an eight-week contract: Amanda Ellis, "Captivating a Country with Her Curves: Examining the Importance of Carmen Miranda's Iconography in Creating National Identities" (master's thesis, State University of New York at Buffalo, 2008).

31 invited to perform for President Roosevelt: Woodene Merriman, "On Trail of Miranda Museum," *Pittsburgh Post-Gazette*, May 30, 1988, page 25.

DOWN SOUTH AMERICAN WAY WITH DISNEY

32 "I was asked by the government": "Walt Disney Interview" (episode of *Telescope*, originally aired 1963 on the Canadian Broadcasting Corporation), interview conducted by Fletcher Markle.

45 percent of its revenue potential: John Culhane, *Walt Disney's Fantasia* (New York: Abrams Books, 1983), 30–31.

33 It started the year $4.5 million in debt: *Walt & El Grupo* (2008), produced by Kuniko Okubo; written and directed by Theodore Thomas.

"There he is, the Great Man!": Tom Sito, *Drawing the Line: The Untold Story of the Animation Unions from Bosko to Bart Simpson* (Lexington, KY: University Press of Kentucky, 2006), 130.

34 "Some people came in today from Peru": *Walt & El Grupo.*

HOLLYWOOD ON DEFENSE

38 "green with envy": Dan Ford, *Pappy: The Life of John Ford* (Englewood Cliffs, NJ: Prentice Hall, 1979), 151.

"I think it made its point": Peter Bogdanovich, *John Ford*, revised and enlarged ed. (Berkeley and Los Angeles: University of California Press, 1978).

"All carry themselves with military carriage": Mark Harris, *Five Came Back* (New York: Penguin, 2014), 56.

39 "hate film": H. Mark Glancey, *When Hollywood Loved Britain* (Manchester, UK: Manchester University Press, 1999), 58.

A SUNDAY IN DECEMBER

45 and he hid in a corner of the studio: Jody Rosen, *White Christmas: The Story of an American Song* (New York: Scribner, 2002), 126.

That morning, listeners heard: Concert program, December 7, 1941, Program ID 1637, New York Philharmonic Leon Levy Digital Archives, https://archives.nyphil.org/index.php/artifact/b753cbcd-7915-4435-9a0c-fa13fe7b5309-0.1.

47 "The sound stages were filled": Ginger Rogers, *Ginger: My Story* (New York: HarperCollins, 1991), 241.

"And we went right on working": Robert F. Boyle, *An Oral History with Robert F. Boyle* (Los Angeles: Academy of Motion Picture Arts and Sciences, Oral History Program, 1998), 55.

"This is a time for energetic": Barbara Leaming, *Orson Welles: A Biography* (Winona, MN: Limelight Editions, 2004), 230–231.

48 "Walt, the army is moving in on us": Steven Watts, *The Magic Kingdom: Walt Disney and the American Way of Life* (Columbia: University of Missouri Press, 1997, rev. ed. 2013), 228.

Its leader, William Dudley Pelley: Associated Press, "Pelley of Silver Shirts Must Serve Prison Term," *San Bernardino Daily Sun*, January 21, 1942, 1.

"Your President has wanted this war!": Andrew Nagorski, *1941: The Year Germany Lost the War* (New York: Simon & Schuster, 2019), 283.

WHY WE FIGHT

49 more than six thousand studio employees: *Moguls and Movie Stars*, episode 5.

"That was the first bad thing": Joseph McBride, *Frank Capra: The Catastrophe of Success* (New York: Simon & Schuster, 1992; rev. ed. 2000), 443.

"Two Signal Corps officers": Frank Capra, *The Name Above the Title* (New York: Macmillan, 1971), 318.

50 "In any discussion of film": McBride, *Frank Capra*, 457; a version of this story is also recounted by George

Stevens Jr. in *Moguls and Movie Stars*, episode 5, with the wording slightly different and Stevens's assertion that the army chief of staff General George Marshall was in attendance.

"You Hollywood big shots are all alike": Capra, 318.

From his suite at Claridge's: Leonard Mosley, *Zanuck: The Rise and Fall of Hollywood's Last Tycoon* (New York: McGraw-Hill, 1985), 200.

51 "within a few weeks of the Pearl Harbor attack": Watts, 229.

"The first time I saw that picture": Thomas Patrick Doherty, *Projections of War: Hollywood, American Culture, and World War II* (New York: Columbia University Press, 1993), 20, 23.

52 Each being paid $20 a day: McBride, *The Catastrophe of Success*, 459.

"We had to go back to *Casablanca*": ibid., 460.

MOBILIZING STAR POWER

54 38.8 percent signed up voluntarily: "US Military by the Numbers," National World War II Museum.

In 1939 there were 334,000: ibid.

56 it only took sixty-three minutes: Scott Eyman, *Hank and Jim* (New York: Simon & Schuster, 2017), 139.

with more than 450,000 parts: Tim Trainor, "How Ford's Willow Run Assembly Plant Helped Win World War II," *Assembly Magazine*, January 3, 2019.

CAROLE LOMBARD: A STAR LOST

57 Suspicious of the possibility that Gable: Warren G. Harris, *Clark Gable: A Biography* (New York: Harmony Books, 2002), 245.

Gable convened a meeting of the actors: ibid., 243.

58 Hank's four-year-old daughter Jane: Marc Eliot, *Jimmy Stewart: A Biography* (New York: Harmony Books, 2006), 177.

59 Gable thought a soft glow: ibid., 249.

All Mannix could find was a strand of blonde hair: Gene Sherman, "Nine Air Crash Dead Removed," *Los Angeles Times*, January 18, 1942. It was Mannix who officially identified Lombard's remains with the Las Vegas coroner as well.

Benny's own father walked out: Jack Benny and Joan Benny, *Sunday Nights at Seven: The Jack Benny Story* (New York: Warner Books, now Grand Central Publishing, 1990), 232.

60 "a Berlin-born director who finds fun": Annette Insdorf, *Indelible Shadows: Film and the Holocaust*, 3rd ed. (Cambridge: Cambridge University Press, 2003), 67.

"Why did Ma have to go?": Warren G. Harris, 250.

THE WAR OUGHTA BE IN PICTURES

61 "A world-shaking tragedy comes into our lives": Mary Astor, *A Life on Film* (New York: Doubleday, 1972), 167–168.

"We're going to have to make the goddamndest": Patrick McGilligan, *Cagney: The Actor as Auteur* (London: Tantivy Press, 1976), 147.

WOULD AMERICA BE INVADED?

63 *Life* magazine published elaborate: *Life*, March 2, 1942, from Time Inc., now held by Meredith Corporation.

65 Davis wanted to have the Oscars: Robert Osborne, *75 Years of the Oscar: The Official History of the Academy Awards*, 4th ed. (Abbeville, SC: Abbeville Press, 2003).

"laying bare the vicious character": Mason Wiley and Damien Bona, *Inside Oscar: The Unofficial History of the Academy Awards*, 10th anniversary ed. (New York: Ballantine, 1996), 119.

hisses and boos were heard: Dan Glaister, "Oscar Won by Orson Welles for All-Time Favourite 'Citizen Kane' Fails to Sell at Auction," *The Guardian*, December 11, 2007.

ITCHY TRIGGER FINGERS

67 He moved the filming of scenes: Todd McCarthy, *Howard Hawks: The Grey Fox of Hollywood* (New York: Grove Press, 2000), 337–339.

68 "Bogie will know how to get out": John Huston, *An Open Book* (New York: Alfred A. Knopf, 1980), 88.

FIGHTING FOR FREEDOM ABROAD WITH NONE AT HOME

69 As early as February 1942, Lowell Mellett: Mark Harris, 134.

70 Japan did attempt to reach African-Americans: Saul K. Padover, "Japanese Race Propaganda," *Public Opinion Quarterly* 7, no. 2 (1943): 191–204.

"Notorious lynchings are a rare practice": Sato Masaharu and Barak Kushner, "'Negro Propaganda Operations': Japan's Short-Wave Radio Broadcasts for World War II Black Americans," *Historical Journal of Film, Radio and Television* 19, no. 1 (1999): 5.

"evoked a variety of responses": ibid., 26.

72 "They are fine and clean and brave": Carlton Jackson, *Hattie: The Life of Hattie McDaniel* (New York: Madison Books, 1989), 84.

"I didn't mind playing a maid the first time": "Butterfly McQueen, 84, 'Gone with the Wind' Actress, Dies from Burns," *Jet*, January 15, 1996, 60.

FIFTY MOVIE STARS BOARD A TRAIN . . .

73 "They had no trouble getting stars": "Hitting the Road with the Hollywood Victory Caravan," National World War II Museum, New Orleans, https://www.nationalww2museum.org/war/articles/hitting-road-hollywood-victory-caravan.

staged an elaborate photo shoot on the front lawn: "Entertaining the Troops" exhibit, part of *Hope for America: Performers, Politics and Pop Culture*, Library of Congress Exhibits, Washington, DC, 2010 (ongoing as of 2020).

76 "popular songs, dances, comedy sketches": Bob Hope with Linda Hope, *Bob Hope: My Life in Jokes* (New York: Hyperion, 2003), 49–50.

"We all came in on a special train": ibid., 50.

The tour had raised over $800,000: "Entertaining the Troops," Library of Congress Exhibits.

To start, she sold two kisses: "Lana's Kisses Really 'Sell,'" *Eugene* [OR] *Register-Guard*, June 12, 1942, 1.

she'd raise $5.25 million: "Lana's Kisses Sell Bonds Without Her Fancy Speech," *Pittsburgh Press*, June 25, 1942, 1.

THANKS FOR THE MEMORIES

79 "I would have won the Academy Award": Hope, 40.

"We soon discovered you had to be pretty lousy": William Robert Faith, *Bob Hope: A Life in Comedy* (New York: Putnam, 1982; rev. ed. Hachette, 2009), 149. Citations refer to the Hachette edition.

"We made a great point of researching": Hope, 41.

82 One time when he was standing over a gunner's shoulder: Mark Harris, 190.

THE GOOD NEIGHBOR POLICY VS. *THE MAGNIFICENT AMBERSONS*

84 A copy of the speech in her handbag: Gene Sherman, *Los Angeles Times*, January 18, 1942.

"Personally believe you would make": Joseph McBride, *What Ever Happened to Orson Welles? A Portrait of an Independent Career* (Lexington: University Press of Kentucky, 2006), 65.

85 "*It's All True* was not going to": Leaming, *Orson Welles*, 253.

"I went to the projection room": Orson Welles and Peter Bogdanovich, *This Is Orson Welles*, ed. Jonathan Rosenbaum (New York: HarperCollins, 1992), 115.

He'd give in-person lectures and talks: Richard Wilson, "It's Not Quite All True," *Sight & Sound* 39, no. 4 (Autumn 1970).

It's also possible he had a covert additional role: Catherine L. Benamou, *It's All True: Orson Welles's Pan-American Odyssey* (Berkeley: University of California Press, 2007), 245.

86 "The ambassadorial appointment would be": ibid., 46.

87 "And they absolutely betrayed me": Leaming, *Orson Welles*, 245.

88 "So I was fired from RKO": Mark W. Estrin, ed., *Orson Welles: Interviews* (Jackson: University Press of Mississippi, 2002), 66.

"did more to cement a community of interest": Alfred Charles Richard Jr., *Censorship and Hollywood's Hispanic Image: An Interpretive Filmography, 1936–1955* (Westport, CT: Greenwood, 1993), 274.

VICTORIES ONSCREEN AND AT SEA

90 "I jumped at it": William Wyler interviewed by Catherine Wyler, 1981, in Gabriel Miller, ed., *William Wyler Interviews* (Jackson: University Press of Mississippi, 2009), 112.

"Wyler took it upon himself": David Thomson, interviewed by Paul Gambaccini, "*Mrs. Miniver*," BBC Radio 4, August 2015.

"It's very sympathetic to them": Mark Harris, 120–121.

FLEEING NAZIS, ONLY TO PLAY NAZIS

95 When he was nineteen: Aljean Harmetz, *The Making of Casablanca: Bogart, Bergman, and World War II*, rev. ed. (New York: Hyperion, 2002), 211.

96 Veidt wrote that he was Jewish: David Stewart Hull, *Film in the Third Reich* (New York: Simon & Schuster, 1973), 90.

"dragged off to Auschwitz, but got sick": Stephen D. Youngkin, *The Lost One: A Life of Peter Lorre* (Lexington: University Press of Kentucky, 2005) 234–235.

HOW CHINESE- AND KOREAN-AMERICAN ACTORS FOUGHT JAPAN

101 Around the same time, she wrote the preface: Karen J. Leong, *The China Mystique: Pearl S. Buck, Anna May Wong, Mayling Soong, and the Transformation of American Orientalism* (Berkeley: University of California Press, 2005), 95.

THE HOLLYWOOD CANTEEN

104 John Ford's wife, Mary: Hollywood Canteen File, Federal Bureau of Investigation archive, Washington, DC, made public March 15, 1994.

105 After which you'd take a spin around the dance floor: Marsha Hunt anecdote from *Moguls and Movie Stars*, episode 5.

106 Why hadn't Welles been drafted?: "Orson Welles Rejected by Army," *Los Angeles Times*, May 6, 1943.

"I felt guilty about the war": Barbara Leaming, *If This Was Happiness: A Biography of Rita Hayworth* (New York: Viking, 1989), 86.

HOLLYWOOD'S ROSIES

107 "I remember sitting up in a bare attic": interview with Loder in Dean, *Bombshell.*

108 "And today we have Wi-Fi and Bluetooth": ibid.

Rosalind P. Walter, the most likely inspiration: Leah Asmelash and Alec Snyder, "Rosalind P. Walter, Who Inspired the 'Rosie the Riveter' Song, Has Died at 95," CNN.com, March 6, 2020, https://www.cnn .com/2020/03/06/us/rosalind-p-walter-rosie-the -riveter-song-death-trnd/index.html.

the longest to be employed was Elinor Otto: Nadra Nittle, "'Last Rosie the Riveter,' Elinor Otto of Long Beach, to Be Honored," *Long Beach Press-Telegram*, October 26, 2014.

111 One of the long-since-retired Rosies, Mae Krier: Kellie B. Gormly, "94-Year-Old 'Rosie the Riveter' Once Made Warplanes and Red Bandannas. Now She Makes Face Masks with the Same Cloth," *Washington Post*, July 21, 2020.

did happen to hundreds of women: Kevin, Starr, *Embattled Dreams: California in War and Peace, 1940–50* (Oxford, UK: Oxford University Press, 2002), 128.

"I almost caused a national crisis": John Lanouette Brenner, "Veronica Lake Gives Telegraph Exclusive Personal Interview," *Nashua* [NH] *Telegraph*, August 26, 1967, 9.

REAL-LIFE REFUGEES GIVE *CASABLANCA* ITS POWER

114 "practically guaranteed him instant stardom": Monika Henreid interview, conducted by the author, August 25, 2020.

117 the Nazis were putting Dalio's face on posters: Associated Press, "Marcel Dalio, 83, Film Actor, Dead," November 23, 1983.

"It must have been a . . . heartbreaking reunion": Richard Pells, *Modernist America: Art, Music, Movies, and the Globalization of American Culture* (New Haven, CT: Yale University Press, 2011), 251.

118 "There was little safe haven for them in Hollywood": Monika Henreid interview.

four individuals who wrote the script: *Casablanca: An Unlikely Classic* (2021), produced, written, and directed by Gary Leva.

"During the day": Al Alleborn to Tenny Wright, Warner Bros. interoffice communication, July 17, 1942, USC Warner Bros. Archives, Los Angeles, CA.

119 "The Warners . . . have a picture": Bosley Crowther, "'Casablanca,' with Humphrey Bogart and Ingrid Bergman, at Hollywood," *New York Times*, November 27, 1942, 27.

AND MAY ALL YOUR CHRISTMASES BE WHITE

121 "I want you to take down a song": Laurence Bergreen, *As Thousands Cheer: The Life of Irving Berlin* (New York: Hachette, 1996), 386.

"It aired on Armed Forces Radio": Rosen, 141–142.

"'White Christmas' was no 'Over There'": ibid., 143.

His earliest memory was at age four: ibid., 70.

STARS IN UNIFORM

123 "I felt that if he wanted combat duty": Robert Matzen, *Mission: Jimmy Stewart and the Fight for Europe* (Pittsburgh: GoodKnight Books, 2019), 102.

125 This ship had been damaged by a Japanese dive-bomber: "USS Curtiss, Report of Pearl Harbor Attack," Naval History and Heritage Command archive, Washington, DC, report written December 16, 1941, history.navy.mil.

"Mister, we can't have the ship smelling": Henry Fonda with Howard Teichmann, *Fonda: My Life* (New York: New American Library, 1981), 149.

In addition to training carrier-based pilots: "Robert Taylor ends Navy duty," *Free Lance-Star* (Fredericksburg, VA), November 6, 1945, 2.

126 He spent time learning the art of: F. L. Schultz and L. O'Doughda, "An Interview with Douglas Fairbanks, Jr.: 'A Hell of a War,'" *Naval History* 7, no. 3 (October 1993).

GABLE FINDS PURPOSE, HOWARD BECOMES A MARTYR

127 $3,750 a week: Warren G. Harris, 273.

129 "Oh, we've licked that": ibid., 272.

131 "The brutality of the Germans": Winston Churchill, *The Second World War: The Hinge of Fate* (New York: Houghton-Mifflin, 1950), 695–696.

132 first-person account of one of the Junkers 88 fighter pilots: Sönke Neitzel and Harald Welzer, *Soldiers: German POWs on Fighting, Killing, and Dying*, trans. Jefferson Chase (New York: Vintage Books, 2013), 139.

If they intervened and stopped Flight 777: William Stevenson, *A Man Called Intrepid: The Incredible World War II Narrative of the Hero Whose Spy Network and Secret Diplomacy Changed the Course of History* (Guilford, DE: Lyons Press, 1976, reissued 2000), 179. Citations from the reissued edition.

"They couldn't show it openly in Stockholm": Ray Furlong, "Wallenberg Family Mark Centenary with Plea for Truth," BBC News, August 3, 2012, https://www.bbc.com/news/world-europe-19101339.

SHERLOCK HOLMES AND LASSIE GO TO WAR

133 A move to the minor studio Universal: Mattias Boström, *From Holmes to Sherlock*, trans. Michael Gallagher (New York: Mysterious Press, 2017), 241.

135 "gall to the Icelanders": Bosley Crowther, "Iceland, Starring Sonja Henie, Romantic Film Picturing US Expeditionary Troops, Opens at the Roxy Theatre," *New York Times*, October 15, 1942.

"as if money was no object": "At the Roxy," *New York Times*, December 23, 1943.

137 Stalin had even banned *The Grapes of Wrath*: Stuart W. Leslie, review of "Industrialism in John Steinbeck's The Grapes of Wrath by Louise Hawker," *Steinbeck Review* 8, no. 1 (2011).

138 "Give us a *Mrs. Miniver* of China or Russia": Mark Harris, 138.

"an expedient lie for political purposes": Todd Bennett, "Culture, Power, and *Mission to Moscow*: Film and Soviet-American Relations during World War II," *Journal of American History* 88, no. 2 (September 2001): 508.

Dmitri Shostakovich said he had nothing but scorn: Jonathan Miles, *The Dangerous Otto Katz* (New York: Bloomsbury, 2010), 255.

"people who saw it considered it a comedy": Robert Osborne commentary on showing *Mission to Moscow*, broadcast June 4, 2014, on TCM, 1:00–3:15 a.m. ET.

A WHY WE FIGHT FOR AFRICAN-AMERICANS

140 MGM gave a healthy, if not spectacular, budget: *The Eddie Mannix Ledger*, Margaret Herrick Library, coll. 198, Academy of Motion Pictures Arts and Sciences, Los Angeles.

143 "congratulating [them] on the treatment of this Black fable": "What Blacks Thought of 'Cabin in the Sky,'" *New York Times*, February 2, 1983.

145 "I will do Miss Horne's hair": James Gavin, *Stormy Weather: The Life of Lena Horne* (New York: Atria, 2009), 108.

he helped get the young Black hair stylist: Lena Horne and Richard Schickel, *Lena* (New York: Doubleday, 1965), 181.

20th Century Fox hairstylist Helen Rose: Helen Rose, *"Just Make Them Beautiful"* (Los Angeles: Dennis Landman, 1976), 54.

On July 29, 1943, a white crowd gathered: *Motion Picture Daily* 53, no. 21 (July 30, 1943).

"Are you going to show this to white people?": "The New Pictures," *Time*, March 27, 1944.

NEW STARS ARE BORN, AND OLD ONES BORN AGAIN

149 "In Hollywood, they didn't think a dance class was macho enough": Welton Jones, "Gregory Peck," *San Diego Union-Tribune*, April 5, 1998.

151 "Yes," Crosby told the judge: Mark Bailey, *Of All the Gin Joints: Stumbling Through Hollywood History* (Chapel Hill, NC: Algonquin Books, 2014), 99.

HOW THE OSCARS CHANGED

153 "Things taken for granted were now unavailable": Hope, 44.

154 The duo announced that 27,677 members: Osborne, 74.

155 many yelling, "Here's looking at you, kid!": Ronald Haver, "*Casablanca*: The Unexpected Classic," Criterion, January 11, 1989, https://www.criterion.com/current/posts/791-casablanca-the-unexpected-classic.

THE RISE OF YOUTH CULTURE . . . AND THE PINUP

157 "Mice make women faint too": James Kaplan, *Frank: The Voice* (New York: Doubleday, 2010), 247.

Then he was deferred again: ibid., 187.

158 In 1941, ten million comics were sold: Ian Gordon, *Comic Strips and Consumer Culture: 1890–1945* (Washington, DC: Smithsonian Institution Scholarly Press, 1998), 139.

"It just wasn't my cup of tea": Paul Cronin, ed., *George Stevens Interviews* (Jackson: University Press of Mississippi, 2004), 112–113.

DRAWING UP PROPAGANDA

163 "I knew that if I did nothing, I'd regret it": Francois Truffaut with Helen G. Scott, *Hitchcock/Truffaut* (New York: Simon & Schuster, 1984), 159.

Royal Navy Captain Edward Terrell actually invented: Edward Terrell, *Admiralty Brief: The Story of Inventions That Contributed to Victory in the Battle of the Atlantic* (London: Harrap, 1958), 197–212.

The first Disney bombs were dropped: Pat Spillman, "The Disney Bomb Project," *92nd Bomb Group (H): Fame's Favored Few* (New York: Turner Publishing Company, 1997).

HOLLYWOOD WAS THERE ON D-DAY

165 "There were a dozen holes": Matzen, 155.

sometimes put a flak jacket over the seat: ibid., 162.

"four or five finger shots": Eyman, *Hank & Jim*, 129.

166 He recalled how rough the sea was: Mark Harris, 312–313.

"like an Easter parade": Bach, 293.

167 were peanut butter and ice cream: Matzen, 288.

RAISING MONEY, RAISING HOPES

170 *The Mercury Wonder Show* opened August 3, 1943: Sam Abbott, "Welles Dishes Magic, Sawdust at Mercury Bow," *Billboard*, August 14, 1943.

172 "He was very much involved in the Hollywood Canteen": Monika Henreid interview.

FRONTLINE ENTERTAINMENT

173 "I hear what you're doing to sell bonds": Monika Henreid interview.

174 "Don't sacrifice yourselves!" ibid., 292.

According to the CIA: "A Look Back . . . Marlene Dietrich: Singing for a Cause," CIA News & Information (2008), https://www.cia.gov/news-information/featured-story-archive/2008-featured-story-archive/marlene-dietrich.html.

"tell themselves the situation can't be so bad": Emily Yellin, *Our Mothers' War* (New York: Free Press, 2010), 92; quote originally appears in Marlene Dietrich, *Marlene* (New York: Grove Press, 1989).

He also gave her a pearl-handled revolver: Bach, 298.

175 "I was up in the head of one of the landing craft": Scott Eyman, *John Wayne: The Life and Legend* (New York: Simon & Schuster, 2014), 134.

"Sorry, sir, there is no soap in the King's bathroom either": Richard Zoglin, *Hope: Entertainer of the Century* (New York: Simon & Schuster, 2014).

177 The pilot told everyone to quickly throw: Robert William Faith, *Bob Hope: A Life in Comedy* (London: Granada Publishing, 1983), 163.

179 One feature of her act was to put on mock screen tests: Esther Williams, with Digby Diehl, *The Million Dollar Mermaid* (New York: Simon & Schuster, 1999), 102.

BLACK EXCELLENCE

180 "a lot of places where they were, [Black soldiers]": John Meroney, "The Red-Baiting of Lena Horne," *The Atlantic*, August 27, 2015.

"The men who fantasized about me": Gavin, 161.

181 "If he doesn't stay here, neither do I": "He Broke the Racial Bar," *St. Joseph (MO) News-Press*, March 4, 1977.

Benny made good on his threats too: Gerald Nachman, *Raised on Radio* (Berkeley: University of California Press, 2000), 64–65.

VICTORY

184 Captain Ronald Reagan signed his discharge papers: Chrystopher J. Spicer, *Clark Gable* (Jefferson, NC: McFarland, 2002), 223.

"Everybody got up and applauded and cried": Warren G. Harris, 273.

Among the men he'd give briefings to: Eyman, *Hank & Jim*, 125.

185 "It wasn't ever official": Matzen, 296.

"It was like wandering around": Mark Harris, 370.

"where I learned about life": ibid., 371.

186 "I can remember [Hitchcock] strolling up and down": *Night Will Fall* (2014), produced by Sally Angel and Brett Ratner; written by Lynette Singer; directed by Andre Singer.

"We must show it to as many Germans as possible": ibid.

COMING HOME TO NEW BATTLES

194 She helped vouch for her sister Elisabeth: Toby Helm, "Film Star Felt Ashamed of Belsen Link," *The Telegraph* (London), June 24, 2000.

"It is time that members of the Negro race": "Victory on Sugar Hill," *Time*, December 17, 1945.

"wouldn't be forgetting what happened": Robert Shelton, ed., *Born to Win: Woody Guthrie* (New York: Macmillan, 1965), 73.

"I got the loudest applause": ibid.

HOLLYWOOD'S COLD WAR RETREAT

196 "Rita used to fly into terrible rages": Leaming, *If This Was Happiness*, 129.

197 Her most desired role was the mixed-race character: *That's Entertainment! III* (1994), produced, written, and directed by Bud Friedgen and Michael J. Sheridan.

199 "Of all the studio heads, he was the only gentile": *Moguls and Movie Stars*, episode 5.

201 "magnificent movie": ibid.

202 "patriotic identification with America": Steven Cohan, *The Road Movie Book* (Abingdon, UK: Routledge, 1997), 116.

BIBLIOGRAPHY

Armstrong, Richard. *Billy Wilder, American Film Realist*. Jefferson, NC: McFarland, 2000.

Bach, Steven. *Marlene Dietrich: Life and Legend*. New York: William Morrow, 1992.

Bailey, Mark. *Of All the Gin Joints: Stumbling Through Hollywood History*. Chapel Hill, NC: Algonquin Books, 2014.

Benny, Jack and Joan. *Sunday Nights at Seven: The Jack Benny Story*. New York: Warner Books (now Grand Central Publishing), 1990.

Buhle, Paul, and David Wagner. *Radical Hollywood: The Untold Story Behind America's Favorite Movies*. New York: New Press, 2002.

Capra, Frank. *The Name Above the Title*. New York: Macmillan, 1971.

Capua, Michelangelo. *Anatole Litvak: The Life and Films*. Jefferson, NC: McFarland, 2015.

Chaplin, Charles. *My Autobiography*. New York: Simon & Schuster, 1964.

Cohan, Steven. *The Road Movie Book*. Abingdon, UK: Routledge, 1997.

Cronin, Paul, ed. *George Stevens Interviews*. Jackson: University Press of Mississippi, 2004.

Doherty, Thomas Patrick. *Hollywood and Hitler, 1933–1939*. New York: Columbia University Press, 2013.

———. *Projections of War: Hollywood, American Culture, and World War II*. New York: Columbia University Press, 1993.

Dunning, John. *On the Air: The Encyclopedia of Old-Time Radio*. Rev. ed. New York: Oxford University Press, 1998.

Eliot, Marc. *Jimmy Stewart: A Biography*. New York: Harmony Books, 2006.

Eyman, Scott. *Hank & Jim*. New York: Simon & Schuster, 2017.

———. *John Wayne: The Life and Legend*. New York: Simon & Schuster, 2014.

Faith, Robert William. *Bob Hope: A Life in Comedy*. London: Granada Publishing, 1983.

Fonda, Henry, with Howard Teichmann. *Fonda: My Life*. New York: New American Library, 1981.

Ford, Dan. *Pappy: The Life of John Ford*. Englewood Cliffs, NJ: Prentice Hall, 1979.

Friedrich, Otto. *City of Nets: A Portrait of Hollywood in the 1940's*. New York: HarperCollins, 1984 (rev. ed. 2014).

Gabler, Neal. *Walt Disney: The Triumph of the American Imagination*. New York: Alfred A. Knopf, 2006.

Gavin, James. *Stormy Weather: The Life of Lena Horne*. New York: Atria, 2009.

Gordon, Ian. *Comic Strips and Consumer Culture: 1890–1945*. Washington, DC: Smithsonian Institution Scholarly Press, 1998.

Harmetz, Aljean. *The Making of Casablanca: Bogart, Bergman, and World War II*. Rev. ed. New York: Hyperion, 2002.

Harris, Mark. *Five Came Back: A Story of Hollywood and the Second World War*. New York: Penguin Books, 2014.

Harris, Warren G. *Clark Gable: A Biography*. New York: Harmony Books, 2002.

Hodges, Graham Russell Gao. *Anna May Wong: From Laundryman's Daughter to Hollywood Legend*. London: Palgrave Macmillan, 2004.

Hope, Bob, with Linda Hope. *Bob Hope: My Life in Jokes*. New York: Hyperion, 2003.

Horne, Lena, and Richard Schickel. *Lena*. New York: Doubleday, 1965.

Jackson, Carlton. *Hattie: The Life of Hattie McDaniel*. New York: Madison Books, 1989.

Kaplan, James. *Frank: The Voice*. New York: Doubleday, 2010.

Leaming, Barbara. *If This Was Happiness: A Biography of Rita Hayworth*. New York: Viking, 1989.

———. *Orson Welles: A Biography*. Winona, MN: Limelight Editions, 2004.

Leong, Karen J. *The China Mystique: Pearl S. Buck, Anna May Wong, Mayling Soong, and the Transformation of American Orientalism*. Berkeley: University of California Press, 2005.

Lertzman, Richard A., and William J. Birnes. *The Life and Times of Mickey Rooney*. New York: Gallery Books, 2015.

Lim, Shirley Jennifer. *A Feeling of Belonging: Asian American Women's Public Culture, 1930–1960*. New York: New York University Press, 2005.

Matzen, Robert. *Mission: Jimmy Stewart and the Fight for Europe*. Pittsburgh: GoodKnight Books, 2019.

McBride, Joseph. *Frank Capra: The Catastrophe of Success*. New York: Simon & Schuster, 1992; rev. ed. 2000.

———. *What Ever Happened to Orson Welles? A Portrait of an Independent Career*. Lexington: University Press of Kentucky, 2006.

Mosley, Leonard. *Zanuck: The Rise and Fall of Hollywood's Last Tycoon*. New York: McGraw-Hill, 1985.

Mullenbach, Cheryl. *Double Victory: How African American Women Broke Race and Gender Barriers to Help Win World War II*. Chicago: Chicago Review Press, 2013. (This is a "young adult" text geared for high school students, but it's remarkably comprehensive, well sourced, and indicative of the scholarship that can take place even in books for younger readers. If you're a parent or a teacher of thirteen- to sixteen-year-olds, introduce them to World War II with this book first.)

Noack, Frank. *Emil Jannings: Der Erste Deutsche Weltstar*. Munich: Rolf Heyne Collection, 2012. (In German.)

Osborne, Robert. *75 Years of the Oscar: The Official History of the Academy Awards*. 4th ed. Abbeville, SC: Abbeville Press, 2003.

Packer, Sharon. *Movies and the Modern Psyche*. Santa Barbara, CA: Praeger Publishing, 2007.

Pells, Richard. *Modernist America: Art, Music, Movies, and the Globalization of American Culture*. New Haven, CT: Yale University Press, 2011.

Rhodes, Richard. *Hedy's Folly: The Life and Breakthrough Inventions of Hedy Lamarr, the World's Most Beautiful Woman*. New York: Doubleday, 2011.

Richard Jr., Alfred Charles. *Censorship and Hollywood's Hispanic Image: An Interpretive Filmography, 1936–1955*. Westport, CT: Greenwood, 1993.

Rifkind, Donna. *The Sun and Her Stars: Salka Viertel and Hitler's Exiles in the Golden Age of Hollywood*. New York: Other Press, 2020.

Rose, Helen. *"Just Make Them Beautiful."* Los Angeles: Dennis Landman, 1976.

Rosen, Jody. *White Christmas: The Story of an American Song*. New York: Scribner, 2002.

Shearer, Stephen Michael. *Beautiful: The Life of Hedy Lamarr*. New York: Thomas Dunne, 2010.

Sito, Tom. *Drawing the Line: The Untold Story of the Animation Unions from Bosko to Bart Simpson*. Lexington: University Press of Kentucky, 2006.

Spada, James. *More Than a Woman: An Intimate Biography of Bette Davis*. New York: Bantam, 1993.

Starr, Kevin. *Embattled Dreams: California in War and Peace, 1940–50*. Oxford, UK: Oxford University Press, 2002.

Thomson, David. *The Big Screen: The Story of the Movies*. New York: Farrar, Straus and Giroux, 2012.

Tranberg, Charles. *Robert Taylor: A Biography*. Albany, GA: BearManor Media, 2015.

Tucker, Sherrie. *Dance Floor Democracy: The Social Geography of Memory at the Hollywood Canteen*. Durham, NC: Duke University Press, 2014.

Vance, Jeffrey. *Chaplin: Genius of the Cinema*. New York: Abrams Books, 2003.

Vieira, Mark A. *Into the Dark: The Hidden World of Film Noir, 1941–1950*. Philadelphia: Running Press, 2016.

Watts, Steven. *The Magic Kingdom: Walt Disney and the American Way of Life*. Columbia: University of Missouri Press, 1997 (rev. ed. 2013).

Welles, Orson, and Peter Bogdanovich. *This Is Orson Welles*. Edited by Jonathan Rosenbaum. New York: HarperCollins, 1992.

Welsch, Tricia. *Gloria Swanson: Ready for Her Close-Up*. Jackson: University Press of Mississippi, 2013.

Williams, Esther, with Digby Diehl. *The Million Dollar Mermaid*. New York: Simon & Schuster, 1999.

Youngkin, Stephen D. *The Lost One: A Life of Peter Lorre*. Lexington: University Press of Kentucky, 2005.

Zoglin, Richard. *Hope: Entertainer of the Century*. New York: Simon & Schuster, 2014.

Zolotow, Maurice. *Billy Wilder in Hollywood*. London: Pavilion Books, 1988.

Documentaries and Other Supplementary Video

(Not including the narrative feature films or documentaries produced during the war that are mentioned throughout the book)

Bombshell: The Hedy Lamarr Story (2017), produced by Alexandra Dean, Katherine Drew, and Adam Haggiag, written and produced by Alexandra Dean.

"Carmen Miranda: The South American Way" (episode of *Biography*, originally aired 1996 on A&E), produced by Kerry Jensen-Izak; written by Doug Green and Lester Shane; directed by Elizabeth Bronstein.

Casablanca: An Unlikely Classic (2012), produced, written, and directed by Gary Leva. Appears on the seventieth-anniversary edition *Casablanca* DVD/Blu-ray set.

Cinema's Exiles: From Hitler to Hollywood (originally aired 2009 on PBS), produced, written, and directed by Karen Thomas.

Leslie Howard: The Man Who Gave a Damn (2016), produced by Thomas Hamilton, Tracy Jenkins, and Alistair Wyllie; written and directed by Thomas Hamilton.

Moguls and Movie Stars (2010), produced by Jon Wilkman and Tom Brown, with Hadley Gwin as director of production for Turner Classic Movies.

Night Will Fall (2014), produced by Sally Angel and Brett Ratner; written by Lynette Singer; directed by Andre Singer.

That's Entertainment! III (1994), produced, written, and directed by Bud Friedgen and Michael J. Sheridan.

The Tramp and the Dictator (originally aired 2002 on TCM), produced by Thorsten Pollfuss, Patrick Stanbury, and Tom Karsch for TCM; written by Kevin Brownlow and Christopher Bird; directed by Kevin Brownlow and Michael Kloft.

"Walt Disney Interview" (episode of *Telescope*, originally aired 1963 on CBC), interview conducted by Fletcher Markle. Available on the Walt Disney Classic Caballeros Edition DVD release of *Saludos Amigos* and *The Three Caballeros* and on YouTube.

Walt & El Grupo (2008), produced by Kuniko Okubo; written and directed by Theodore Thomas.

INDEX

Page numbers in *italics* indicate illustrations.

Abbott and Costello, 135

ABC radio, 194–195, 196

Academy Awards. *See also specific award winners*
1929 ceremony, ix
1942 ceremony, 62, *64*, 65, 102, 153, 154
1943 ceremony, *153*, 153–155
1944 ceremony, 154, 155
1945 ceremony, 152, 187–188
plaques, *64*, *153*, 155
statuettes, *64*, *153*, 154, *154*, 155

Across the Pacific (film), 48, *61*, 61–62, 67–68, 98, *98*, 99

Act of Violence (film), 193

"The Adventure of the Dancing Men" (Conan Doyle), 133–134

Advise & Consent (film), 97

African-American actors. *See also specific actors and films*
all-Black musicals, 140, *142*, 142–145, *144*
discrimination against, 8, 181, 194
federal mandate, 69
postwar abandonment, 194, 201
prewar, x
war effort, *71*, 71–72, *72*

African-American servicemen, 68–72, *80*
Battle of the Bulge, 183
discrimination against, 181
Horne and, 180
The Negro Soldier, 69–70, 145
number of, 145

postwar discrimination against, 194–195
segregation, 68, 140
761st Tank Battalion, 183
standing guard over Nazi soldiers, *183*
Tuskegee Airmen, 68, 140, *141*, 182
violence against, 140, 180, 194–195

After the Thin Man (film), 41

Ahn, Philip, 10, *10*, 99, *99*

Air Force (film), *66*, 66–67

Alabama Drydock and Shipbuilding Company, 143

Aleutian Islands, Battle of the, 82, 92, 191

Algiers (film), *3*

Alice in Wonderland (Carroll), 89

Alison, Joan, 48

Alleborn, Al, 118

All Quiet on the Western Front (film), 139

All Through the Night (film), 52, 95–96

Altman, Robert, 188, 202

The Amazing Dr. Clitterhouse (film), *14*

Ameche, Don, 84

America First movement, 19, 39–40

American Legion Magazine, 197

American Red Cross, 21, *169*

Anchors Aweigh (film), *168*, *179*, 187, *187*

Anchors Aweigh (Navy radio program), *124*

Anderson, Eddie "Rochester," 142, *142*, 143, 181, *182*

Anderson, Judith, 139

Andrews, Dana, 192

Andy Hardy film series, 5, 99, 148

Andy Hardy's Blonde Trouble (film), 99

Angel Face (film), 97

Anschluss, 3, 6, 95

Antheil, George, 108

anti-Fascism, 8

anti-miscegenation rules, 9–10

anti-Nazi voices, xii, 5, 6, 13–14, 197

anti-Semitism, 4–6, 15, 19, 21, 197, 199–200

Aquacade (swimming show), 178

Arco, Louis V., 117

Arizona, USS, *44*, 46

Armed Forces Radio, 72, *80*, 121, 145, 155, 174

Armed Forces (US). *See also specific branches and servicemen*
pinup girls and, 158, 160
segregation, 68, 140
size, 54, 56

Armstrong, Louis, 142

Army Air Forces. *See also specific battles and servicemen*
airplane "nose art," 160, *196*
filmmaking unit, 127
recruitment needs, 68
stress, 165, 167

Army Signal Corps, 49

Arnaz, Desi, 73, 75

Arnold, "Hap," 129, 185

Arnold, "Pop," 123

Arsenic and Old Lace (film), 49–50, 51, 57

Asian-American actors, 9–10, 62, 98–101

Astaire, Fred, 5, 61, *73*, *189*

Astor, Mary, 61–62, *64*

atomic bombs, 188, 196

Attu, Battle of, 191

Auschwitz concentration camp, 185

Aventure Malgache (film), 163

Ayres, Lew, 149

Babbitt, Art, 33–34

Babes on Broadway (film), 31

Back to Bataan (film), 99, *99*

Baer, Max, *182*

Ball, Lucille, *front endpapers*, *73*, *82*, 145

Bambi (film), 36, 161

Bartlett, Sy, 49

Bataan Death March, 74–75

Bataan (film), 125

Bathing Beauty (film), 178

The Battle of Midway (film), 95

The Battle of Russia (film), 137, 155

Bauernhaus und Grafenschloß (film), 117

Beach Jumpers, 126

Beery, Wallace, 57, 153

Benamou, Catherine L., 86

Benchley, Robert, 35

Bennett, Joan, 21–22, *22*, 73, 75

Benny, Jack, 57, 59–60, 105, 152, 155, 179, 181

Berg, A. Scott, 4

Bergen-Belsen concentration camp, 185, 194

Bergman, Ingrid, 111, *113*, 118, 154, *154*

Berkeley, Busby, 135

Berlin, Germany, 6, 11, 13

Berlin, Irving, 45, 48, 61, *120*, 120–121, 154–155

Berlin Diary (Shirer), 49

Berliner, Trude, 117

Berman, Pan, 4, 86

Bernstein, Sidney, 185–186

The Best Years of Our Lives (film), 191–192, *192*, 193, 199, 201, 202

Betrayal from the East (film), 99

"Between Americans" (Corwin), 47

Beverly Hills Script, 9

Bickford, Charles, *82*

The Big Wheel (film), 194

Black Americans. *See* African-American actors; African-American servicemen

Black Legion (film), 15, 144

blacklisted actors, 197, 199, 201, 202

Blondell, Joan, 73, *75*

Blood on the Sun (film), 99

The Blue Angel (film), 11

Bogart, Humphrey
    Across the Pacific, 61–62, 68
    All Through the Night, 95–96
    Casablanca, 95, 113, *113*, 114, 118, 155
    Hollywood Victory Caravan, 73, 76
    The Maltese Falcon, 68, 160

Bois, Curt, 117

Boles, Robert, 127

Bombs Over Burma (film), 99, 101

Bonavita, Rosina, 108

Bon Voyage (film), 163

Boom Town (film), 107

Born to Dance (film), 41

Borzage, Frank, 21

Bottome, Phyllis, 20

Boyer, Charles, xii, *xii*, 3, 18, 57, 73, 75

Boyle, Robert, 47

Boys Town (film), *4*, 5

Brackett, Charles, *2*

Brady, Fred, *82*

Breen, Joseph, 15, 39

Briskin, Samuel, 1, 4, 86

Bronson, Charles, 184

Brooks, Louise, 145

Brooks, Mel, 26

Brooks, Richard, 200

Brown, Clarence, 147

Brown, Joe E., 172

Bruce, Nigel, 133, *133*

Bruckner, Robert, 138

Bulge, Battle of the, 183

Buñuel, Luis, 23

Burnett, Murray, 48

Buzzell, Edward, 157

The Cabinet of Dr. Caligari (film), 96, 117

Cabin in the Sky (film), x, 140, *142*, 142–145, *143*, 180, 197, 201

Cagney, James, *front endpapers*, 13, 61, 73, *73*

Cagney, William, 61

Cain, James M., 1

Calloway, Cab, 144

Cantor, Eddie, 105

Cape Fear (film), 49

Capra, Frank

anti-Fascism, 13, 14, 49

Army Pictorial Service, 166

Army Signal Corps films, 17, 49–52, 69, 137

Arsenic and Old Lace, 49–50

character traits, 50, 52

directing career, *49*, 49–50

as Directors Guild of America president, 49

Hollywood Anti-Nazi League, 13

as immigrant, 49, 52

It's a Wonderful Life, 193

Liberty Films, 193

Lost Horizon, 139

Meet John Doe, 49

motivation, 130

The Name Above the Title (autobiography), 49

The Negro Soldier, 69

Prelude to War, 50, 51

war's damage to career, 193

Why We Fight series, 17, 51–52, 137

Carmen Jones (film), 201

Carroll, John, *37*

Carson, Robert, 62

Casablanca Conference, 119

Casablanca (film)
    Academy Award, 119, 155
    as collective effort, 118
    as *Everybody Comes to Rick's*, 48, 51–52
    Golden Globe Awards, 155
    legacy, 202
    opening narration, 123
    plot, xi
    refugees as cast members, 95, *113*, 113–119, *115*, *116*, *119*
    release, 118–119

Catholic Legion of Decency, ix

Caught in the Draft (film), *78*, 79

Cavallaro, Carmen, 76

CBS Radio, 45, 47, 48, 84, 121

Chamberlain, Neville, 6, 15

Chan, Spencer, 98

Chaplin, Charlie, 15, *23*, 23–27, *26*, 49, 59, 197

Chapman, Marguerite, *82*

A Charlie Brown Christmas (TV special), 36

Chennault, Claire Lee, 37–38, 101

China, 8–10, 29, 37–38, 98

Chinese-American actors, 62, 98–101

Churchill, Winston, 119, 131, 132, 163

Citizen Kane (film), 16, 38–39, 47, 65, 84, 87, 106

City Lights (film), 24, 26

Civil Liberties Act (1988), 62

Clair, René, 23

Clark, Bennett, 40

Clark, Dane, *171*, 172

Clarke, Thurmond, 194

Cohan, George M., 61

Cohan, Steven, 202

Cohn, Harry, 1, 49, 170, 196

Colbert, Claudette, 57, 73, *75*, 105, 111, 145

Cold War, 196–201

Colman, Ronald, 57, 70–71

Colonna, Jerry, 81

Columbia, 6–7, 49, 170, 193, 196

Colvin, Ian, 131–132

Combat America (film), 129, 184

Come Live with Me (film), 41

Command Performance (Armed Forces Radio Service show), *80*

Conan Doyle, Arthur, 133–134

concentration camps, 185–186, 194, 200

Confessions of a Nazi Spy (film), 15–20, *19*
    as anti-Nazi statement, 15–17, 40
    cast, 14, 16, *16*, 17, 18, 96
    dissection of Nazi mindset, 17, 18–19, 25–26
    efforts to stop release, 15, 18, 25
    legacy, 202
    Litvak as director, 14, 17–18, 51
    Prelude to War comparisons, 50

Cooper, Gary, *43*, 57, *64*, 65, 105

Cooper, Merian C., 37–38, 188

Coral Sea, Battle of the, 76, *77*, 93, 94

Cornered (film), 193, 197

Corwin, Norman, 47

Cotton, Joseph, 84, 106

Coughlin, Father Charles, 6, 15

Courage of Lassie (film), *190*, 191

Craig, James, 147

Crawford, Joan, *171*, 178

Crisp, Donald, *64*

Cromwell, John, 152

Crosby, Bing
    Academy Award, 152, *154*
    Going My Way, 151–152, *152*
    Holiday Inn, 45, *45*, 61, 151
    Hollywood Victory Caravan, 73–74, 76
    Kraft Music Hall, 58, 120
    "Song of Freedom," 61
    "White Christmas," 45, *45*, 58, 120–121, 151

Crossfire (film), 197, 200

Crossroads (film), 158

Crowther, Bosley, 119

Curtis, Tony, 188

Curtiss, USS, 125, 188

Curtiz, Michael, 61, 114, 118, 138, 155

Dachau concentration camp, 185, 200

Dalio, Marcel, 114, 116–117

Daly, John Charles, 45, 47, 48

Dantine, Helmut, 90, *91*, 95, 113

Darnell, Linda, 106

Darrieux, Danielle, 18

Daughter of Shanghai (film), *10*

Daves, Delmer, 172

Davies, Joseph E., 138

Davis, Bette
    as AMPAS president, 65, 102
    film career, 102, 169, 172
    Hollywood Canteen, 102, 104–105, *105*, 106, *106*, 169, 202
    Hollywood Hall of Honor, 169
    Hollywood Victory Committee, 57
    McDaniel's all-Black revue, 182
    Red Cross work, *169*
    war bonds effort, 102, 169

Day, Laraine, 29

Days of Glory (film), 111, 139, 149, *150*, 151

D-Day (Operation Overlord), 146, 164–167, *167*

Death Mills (film), 186

Debs, Eugene V., 36

December 7th (film), 50, 65, 99, 155

Deering, John, 16

de Havilland, Olivia, 67–68, 199

del Rio, Dolores, 106

Der Fuehrer's Face (Disney short), *161*, 161–162

Desert Victory (film), 155

Desperate Journey (film), 62, 151

Destination Tokyo (film), 188

The Diary of Anne Frank (film), 200

Dies, Martin, 6, 13, 15, 61, 197

Dietrich, Elisabeth, 194

Dietrich, Marlene
    Armed Forces Radio, 174
    awards, 174
    background, 11, 173
    entertaining troops, 166
    family, 194
    film career, 11, 12, *170*, 174
    frontline entertainment, *173*, 174
    on Hitler, 11–12
    Hollywood Canteen, 105–106, 173
    "Lili Marleen," 174
    The Mercury Wonder Show, 170, 173
    postwar years, 194
    US citizenship, 12
    USO shows, *173*, 174
    war bonds sales, 173–174

"Die Wacht am Rhein" (German march), 114

Directors Guild of America, 49

Disney, Elias, 35–36

Disney, Walt. See also Walt Disney Studios
    Chaplin and, 25
    HUAC testimony, 199
    labor problems, 33–34, 36, 199
    Motion Picture Alliance for the Preservation of American Ideals, 199
    The New Spirit, 161
    propaganda films, 160–162
    as Red Cross ambulance driver, 161
    Riefenstahl and, 13
    South American diplomacy, 32–36, *34*, *36*, 85, 88
    Victory Through Air Power, *163*, 163–164
    Why We Fight films, 161

Disney bombs, 163

Disney-Pixar, 162

Dmytryk, Edward, 193, 197

Dönitz, Karl, 185

Donovan, William "Wild Bill," 39, 65

Doolittle, James, *74*, 75–76, 149, 181

Dorsey, Tommy, 120, 156

Double Indemnity (film), 1, 2, 186

Douglas, Kirk, 125, 202

Down Argentine Way (film), 31, 84

Dr. Gillespie movies, 99

Dr. Kildare film series, 149

draft, 30, 54, 79

Dragon Seed (film), 101

Dumbo (film), 36, 48

Dunne, Irene, 57, 111, 149

Duprez, June, *70*

Ecstasy (film), 2–3, *3*

Edens, Roger, 145

Edge of Darkness (film), 111, 139, 151

Education for Death (propaganda film), 162

Eforgan, Estel, 132

Eisenhower, Dwight D., 118–119, 165

Eisenstein, Sergei, 13, 137

El Alamein, Second Battle of, 118

Ellington, Duke, 144

"enemy aliens," 108, 114, 118, 172, 173

Enigma code, 132

Enola Gay (B-29 bomber), 188

Epstein, Julius and Philip, 51–52, 118

Escape (film), 96

Esquire magazine, 196

Evans, George, 157

Evans, Redd, 108

Everybody Comes to Rick's (play), 48, 51–52. *See also Casablanca*

Eyman, Scott, 175

Fairbanks, Douglas, Jr., 12, 35, 126, *126*, 183

Falkenburg, Jinx, *82*

A Family Affair (film), 5

Fantasia (film), 13, 32, 35, 161

Faye, Alice, *83*

Feldman, Charles, 199

Field, Connie, 55

The Fighting Lady (film), 125

Film Weekly, 9

Fine, Larry, *27*

The First of the Few (film), 130

Fitzgerald, Barry, 151–152, *152*, *154*

Five Graves to Cairo (film), 139

Flash Gordon (comic book), 158

Fleischer brothers, 33

Fleming, Ian, 90, 132

Fleming, Peter, 90

Fletcher, Frank, 94

Flying Tigers, 101, 188

Flying Tigers (film), *37*

Flynn, Errol, 151

Follow the Boys (film), *170*

Fonda, Henry, x, 22, 41, *53*, 58, *124*, 124–125, 188

Fonda, Jane, 58

Fong, Benson, 99

Fontaine, Joan, *64*

Ford, John
  Academy Awards, 22, 39
  The Battle of Midway, 95
  D-Day, 166, 167
  December 7th, 50, 65
  Doolittle Raid, 75
  The Grapes of Wrath, 38
  Hollywood Anti-Nazi League, 13, 14
  Hollywood Canteen, 104
  How Green Was My Valley, 39, 50, 65
  The Informer, 22
  La Grande Illusion, 22
  The Long Voyage Home, 39
  motivation, 130
  Navy Field Photo unit, 38–39, 52, 65, 93, 124–125
  New York Film Critics Circle prize, 65
  Pearl Harbor attack and, 47–48
  Stagecoach, 13
  They Were Expendable, 187

Ford, Mary, 47–48, 104

Foreign Correspondent (film), 29, *29*

49th Parallel (film), 130

For Whom the Bell Tolls (film), 111

Foster, Norman, 84, 85

Four Jills in a Jeep (film), 177, *178*, *179*

Fox. *See* 20th Century Fox

Francis, Kay, 172, 177, *178*

Franco, Francisco, 8, 130, 132

Franz Joseph, Emperor (Austria-Hungary), 114

Freed, Arthur, 142, 145

frontline entertainment, 173–179

Der Fuehrer's Face (Disney short), *161*, 161–162

Gable, Clark
  Army Air Forces, ii, *vi*, x, 59, *60*, *122*, 127–129, *128*, 184
  autograph's value, 158
  film career, 57, 58–59, 76, 127, 129, 184
  grief over Lombard's death, x, 59, 60
  Hollywood Victory Committee, 57
  House Un-American Activities Committee, 13
  marriage to Lombard, 57–59, *58*
  McDaniel and, 194
  MGM contract, 184
  "Show Business at War," *127*
  Turner and, 59

The Gang's All Here (film), 135, *137*

Garbo, Greta, ix

Gardner, Ava, 148, 197

Garfield, John, 57, *66*, 102, 104, 172, 199–202

Garland, Judy, *front endpapers*, 57, *73*

Garson, Greer
  Academy Award, 95, *153*, *154*
  Goodbye, Mr. Chips, 89
  Hollywood Victory Caravan, *73*
  Mrs. Miniver, 89, *89*, *93*, 95, 111–112, 154
  war bonds tour, *front endpapers*

Gaslight (film), 154

Gavin, James, 181

Gentleman Jim (film), 151

Gentleman's Agreement (film), 199–200

George VI, King (Britain), 126

German American Bund, 5, 6, *16*, 18, *19*, 27

German Concentration Camps Factual Study (film), 186

Germany. *See also* Hitler, Adolf
  Afrika Korps, 118
  ban on Warner Bros. films, 18
  Blitz, 29
  declaration of war on United States, 48
  Dietrich and, 11–12
  film industry, 114 (*See also* Goebbels, Joseph; Riefenstahl, Leni)
  Holocaust, 185–186, *200*
  invasion of Poland, 18, 25
  invasion of Soviet Union, 39, 137, 139
  market for Hollywood film, 6
  nonaggression pact with Soviet Union, 137
  occupation of Italy, 146
  persecution of Jews, 2–3, 5, 11
  surrender, 185

GI Bill, 191

Gilda (film), 193, 196

Gladstone, Kay, 186

Goddard, Paulette, 25, *79*

God Is My Co-Pilot (film), 98

Goebbels, Joseph
  ban on Warner Bros. films, 18
  Dietrich and, 11, 174
  Howard's death and, 132
  Jannings and, ix
  Lang and, 2
  on *Mrs. Miniver*, 92
  "racial questionnaire," 96
  Veidt and, 114

Going My Way (film), 151–152, *152*, 202

Golden Gate Quartet, 104

Golden Globe Awards, 155

Goldwyn, Samuel, 4, 199

Gone with the Wind (film), x, 32, 57, 72, 92, 118, 129, 130

Goodbye, Mr. Chips (film), 89

The Good Earth (film), 9–10

Good Neighbor Policy, ix, *28*, 30, 31, 83–87, *85*

Göring, Hermann, 160

Grable, Betty, 111, 158, 160, *160*, 180

Graham, Martha, 149

La Grande Illusion (film), 22, 116, 139

Grant, Cary, 57, 73, 188

Grant, Joe, 162

The Grapes of Wrath (film), 22, 26, 38, 41, 65, 137

Grauman's Chinese Theatre, 84, 155

The Great Dictator (film), *23*, 23–27, *24*, *26*, 59, 202

Greenstreet, Sydney, 62, 117

Greenwich Village (film), 193

Greenwood, Charlotte, 75

Grinde, Nick, 10

Grüning, Ilka, 117

Guadalcanal campaign, 102, 126

Guilaroff, Sydney, 145

Gulf Screen Guild Theater (CBS Radio), 47, 84

Guthrie, Woody, 194

A Guy Named Joe (film), 111, 149

Gwynne, Anne, *82*

Gyssling, Georg, 15

Hair Styles for Safety (film), 111

Hall, Charles B., 140

Hallelujah (film), 140

Hampton, Lionel, *182*

HANL (Hollywood Anti-Nazi League), 13–14, 197

Harbou, Thea von, 96

Hardwicke, Cedric, *82*

Hardy, Oliver, 73, 75

Hart, Larry, 61

Harvey, Lillian, 186

Hatcher, William, 129

Hawks, Howard, 37, 66–67

Hayworth, Rita
  Columbia contract, 170, 193, 196
  film career, 193, 196
  Hollywood Canteen, *102*, 105, 106
  The Mercury Wonder Show, 106, 169–170
  as pinup, 158, *159*, 160, *196*
  signing autographs, *157*
  USO show, *201*
  Welles and, 88, 106, 169–170, 193

Hearst, William Randolph, 47, 65, 106

Heflin, Van, *153*

Henie, Sonja, 135, *136*

Henreid, Lisl, 114

Henreid, Monika, 114, 118, 172

Henreid, Paul, *73*, 113, *113*, 114, 118, 172

Hernried, Karl, 114

Herrmann, Bernard, 87

Herr Meets Hare (cartoon), 160

Hess, Rudolf, 12

Hintze, Herbert, 131

Hiroshima, Japan, 188

Hitchcock, Alfred, 29, *29*, 47, 163, 186, 193

Hitler, Adolf
  as ardent film watcher, 6, 27, 49
  Chamberlain's appeasement efforts, 6
  Chaplin parallels, 23
  death, 185
  declaration of war on United States, 48

Dietrich infatuation, 11–12

film bans, 3

film satires, 15

Gable's capture as priority, 129

German film industry purge of Jews, 96

The Great Dictator and, 27

Holocaust, 185

invasion of Soviet Union, 137

Mandl and, 2–3

Mussolini and, 146

Nuremberg Laws, 5

Pickford on, 6

proposed invasion of Britain, 63

ruling through fear, 162

transfer of troops to Italian border, 126

use of mass media, 26

violence against Jewish people, 13

Hold Back the Dawn (film), 1, 2

Holden, Gloria, *124*

Holiday Inn (film), 45, *45*, 61, 74, 120, 151

Hollywood Anti-Nazi League (HANL), 13–14, 197

"Hollywood at War" (*Look* magazine), 123

Hollywood Canteen, x, *102*, 102–106, *104*
  attire, 178
  closure, 188
  Davis's role, 102, 104–105, *105*, 106, *106*, 202
  legacy, 202
  McDaniel's donation, 182
  one-year anniversary party, 169
  racial integration, 104, 172, 180
  studio talent nights, 170, 172

Hollywood Canteen (film), *103*, 104, *171*, 172

Hollywood Foreign Correspondents Association, 155

The Hollywood Reporter, 18, 83

Hollywood Ten, 197

Hollywood Victory Caravan, *73*, 73–76, *75*, 81

Hollywood Victory Caravan (film), 76, 79

Hollywood Victory Committee, 53, *53*, 56–59, 71, 194

Holocaust, 185–186, *200*

home front films, 89, 146–149, 151–152. See also *Mrs. Miniver*

Homer, Tom, 123

Hope, Bob
  as Academy Awards host, 65, 188
  film career, *78*, 79, *80*, 97, 151
  Hollywood Canteen, 105
  Hollywood Victory Caravan, 73–74, 76, 79
  Hollywood Victory Committee, 57
  military fan letters, 177
  radio routine, 179
  on rationing, 153
  USO shows, 79–81, *81*, 175, 177
  Victory Golf Tournament, 79

Hopkins, Harry, 25

Horne, Lena
  blacklisted, 197, 199
  Cabin in the Sky, x, 142, *142*, 145, 180, 197
  Cotton Club, 145
  daughter, 201
  entertaining troops, 179–181
  hairdressers, 145
  Hollywood Canteen, 180
  Jubilee, 180, *182*
  live performances, *198*, 199

Horne, Lena (*continued*)
McDaniel's all-Black revue, 182
as pinup, 180, *180*
postwar military outreach, *xi*
racial discrimination against, 181
Stormy Weather, x, *144*, 145, 180
V-E Day show, *181*
Hornet, USS, *74*, *75*, 93
House Un-American Activities Committee (HUAC), 6, 13, 15, 61, 197, 199, 200
housing discrimination, 194
Howard, Leslie, x, *129*, 129–132, *131*
Howard, Moe, *27*
Howard, Ronald, 131–132
How Green Was My Valley (film), 39, *40*, 50, 65
"How the Reds Made a Sucker Out of Me" (Robinson), 197
HUAC. *See* House Un-American Activities Committee
Hughes, Howard, 107
Hull, Cordell, 7
The Human Comedy (film), *147*, 147–149, *148*, 166
Hunt, Marsha, *82*, 105, 147–148
Huston, John, 15, 48, 61, 67–68, 82, 190–191
Huston, Walter, 51
Hutton, Betty, *front endpapers*, *73*, 76, *177*
Hutton, Robert, 172

Iceland (film), 135, *136*
I'd Rather Be Right (Broadway musical), 61
Immortal Sergeant (film), 124
The Informer (film), 22

Ingram, Rex, *70*, 70–71, 104, 142, 143, *143*
Inside Out (film), 162
International Pictures, 193
internment camps, 62
In This Our Life (film), 67–68
Invisible Agent (film), 96
Israel, Wilfred, 132
Italy, 6, 29, 126, 140, 146, 166, 182
It Can't Happen Here (Lewis), 20
It Happened One Night (film), 49
It's All True (film), 65, 85, 86, *86*, *87*, 87–88, *88*, 193
It's a Wonderful Life (film), 193
I Wake Up Screaming (film), 158
Iwo Jima, Battle of, 183, 184

James, Dan, 25
James, Harry, 160
Jane Eyre (film), 170
Jannings, Emil, *viii*, ix, 11
Japan
Allied invasion of, 188
Battle of Midway, 92–94, *94*
China incursions, 8–9, 29, 98
Doolittle Raid, *74*, 75
Oregon attacks, 66
Pearl Harbor attack, ix, *44*, 45–47, *46*
Philippines, invasion of, 63, 74–75, 76
propaganda aimed at African-Americans, 70
submarines off California, 63
surrender, 188
Japanese-Americans, 62
Jewish heritage. *See also* anti-Semitism

actors, 3–4, 96
assimilation, 4
film characters, *4*, *5*
Hollywood assistance to refugees, 6–7, 12
Hollywood moguls, 4
ignored or erased by Hollywood, 3–4, 6
writers and directors, 1–2
Jews Are Looking at You (Nazi propaganda book), 24
Jezebel (film), 102
The Jimmy Durante Show, 193–194
Johnson, Van, 111, 147, *147*, 149, *149*, 157, 202
Johnston, Ollie, 33
Jones, Chuck, 33
Jones, Gail, 201
Journey into Fear (film), 84
Joyce, William "Lord Haw Haw," 133
Juarez (film), 15, 102
Jubilee (Armed Forces Radio Service show), 72, 145, 180, *182*

Karloff, Boris, 79
Kaufman, Phil, 6
Kazan, Elia, 199, 200
Kelly, Gene, 149, *168*, *176*, *179*, 187, *187*
Kennedy, Joseph P., 6
The Keys of the Kingdom (film), 151
Kiesler, Hedwig. *See* Lamarr, Hedy
Kindertransport, 132
King Kong (film), 37
King of Chinatown (film), 10, 99
Kippen, Manart, *138*
Kismet (film), 174
Knight Without Armour (film), 12

Knox, Frank, 65
Koch, Howard, 118
Koerner, Charles, 86, 87
Korda, Alexander, 12, 24, 25
Korean-American actors, 98–101
Kraft Music Hall (NBC radio show), 58, 120
Kresa, Helmy, 121
Krier, Mae, 111
Krims, Milton, 15
Kristallnacht, 5, 13
Kruger, Otto, 22
Kuhn, Fritz J., 18
Ku Klux Klan, 15, 144
Kung Fu (TV series), 99
Kursk, Battle of, 126
Kushner, Barak, 70
Kwajalein, Marshall Islands, 125
Kyle, Tiny, 145
Kyser, Kay, *73*, 108

Ladd, Alan, 154
Lady Be Good (film), 65
Lady from Chungking (film), 101
The Lady from Shanghai (film), 193
Laemmle, Carl, 6–7
Lagergren, Nina, 132
La Grande Illusion (film), 22, 139
Lake, Veronica, *110*, 111, *112*
Lamarr, Hedy (Hedwig Kiesler), 2–4, *3*, 105–108, *107*, 158
"La Marseillaise" (French national anthem), 114, 116
Lamour, Dorothy, 97
Landis, Carole, ii, 177–178, *178*, *back endpapers*
Landry, Bob, 158
Lang, Fritz, 2, *2*, 39, 96

Langford, Frances, 73, 81

Lassie films, 134, 190, *190*, 191

Laughton, Charles, 139

Laura (film), 97

Laurel, Stan, 73, 75

Lawford, Peter, 134

Lawrence, Eddie, 184

Lear, Norman, 184, 202

Lebeau, Madeleine, 114, *115*, 116–117

Lederer, Francis, 17, *17*, 21–22, *22*, *82*, 96

Lee, Anna, *37*

Leisen, Mitchell, 1

LeRoy, Mervyn, 96

Leslie, Joan, 103, *146*, 172

Leslie Howard (Eforgan), 132

Lessing, Gunther, 33

Let There Be Light (film), 190–191

Lewis, Joseph H., 101

Lewis, Sinclair, 20

Lexington, USS, 76, *77*

Liberty Films, 193

The Life and Times of Rosie the Riveter (film), *55*

Life magazine, 63, 83, 88, 106, 111, 158

Lindbergh, Charles, 19

Lischka, Karl, 15

Little Caesar (film), 13

Litvak, Anatole, xii, *xii*, 14, *14*, 17–18, 51, 137

Liu Liangmo, 8

Loder, Anthony, 107, 108

Loeb, John Jacob, 108

Lombard, Carole, x, *57*, 57–60, *58*, 73, 84, 129

The Lone Ranger (serialized radio drama), 158

The Long Voyage Home (film), *39*

Loo, Beverly Jane, 98–99

Loo, Richard, 98–99

Look magazine, *123*, 200

Looney Tunes, 33, 160

Lorre, Peter, 96, 117

Los Angeles, California, 63, 65, 144

Lost Horizon (film), 139

The Lost Weekend (film), 187

Lottery Lover (film), 1

Love Laughs at Andy Hardy (film), 148

Loy, Myrna, 57, 134

Lubitsch, Ernst, 26, 59–60

Luce, Claire Booth, 97

Lukas, Paul, 17, 19

Luke, Keye, 99

Lumet, Sidney, 201–202

lynchings, 69, 70

MacArthur, Douglas, 76

MacDonald, Jeanette, 154

Madison Square Garden, New York City, 5, 6, 27

The Magnificent Ambersons (film), 84, 85, 86–87, 193

Mahin, John Lee, 127

Majdanek concentration camp, 185

The Major and the Minor (film), *2*

The Maltese Falcon (film), 61, 67, 68, 160

Manchester, William, 156

Mandl, Fritz, 2–3

Man Hunt (film), 39, 40, 89

The Man I Married (film), 21–22, *22*, 40, 96, 197

Mankiewicz, Herman J., 65

Mann, Thomas, 6, 11

Mannix, Eddie, 59, *60*, 84, 148

Marathon Man (film), 117, 202

"The March of Time" (newsreel series), *127*

Margin for Error (film), 97

"La Marseillaise" (French national anthem), 114, 116

Marshall, George, 50

Marshall, Herbert, *29*

Martin, Nora, 105

Marx, Groucho, 73

Marx, Harpo, *73*

Masaharu, Sato, 70

Matthau, Walter, 184

Matzen, Robert, 165, 167

Mayer, Louis B.
filmmaking philosophy, 5
German film market, 6, 7
Jewish heritage, 4
Lamarr and, 3
Lombard's death and, 59
as MGM chief, 4
The Mortal Storm, 20–21
Mrs. Miniver, 89, 90
not letting top stars join military, 127, 148
Somewhere I'll Find You, 58–59

Mayerling (film), xii, 18

Mayfair, Mitzi, 177, *178*

MCA (mega-agency), 102, 199

McCarey, Leo, 152

McCrea, Joel, 29, *29*

McDaniel, Hattie
all-Black revue, 181–182
discrimination against, 194
film career, 72, 152, 182, 194
war effort, *71*, 71–72, *72*, 181–182, 194

McDowall, Roddy, 134

McGuire, Dorothy, 124

McHugh, Frank, 75

McIntyre, Andrew J., 127

McQueen, Butterfly, 72, 145

Meet John Doe (film), 49

Melendez, Bill, 36

Mellett, Lowell, 69, 140

Mercury Productions, 86

Mercury Theatre, 84

The Mercury Wonder Show, 106, 169–170, 173

Meredith, Burgess, 125, 186–187

Merrie Melodies shorts, 160

Merry Macs, 121

Methot, Mayo, 155

MGM (Metro-Goldwyn-Mayer). *See also* Mayer, Louis B.; *specific films*
African-American actors and, 197
American Red Cross rally for war relief efforts, 21
Army Air Forces filmmaking unit, 127
Gable's return, 184
German film market, 6, 7
hairdressers, 145
Hollywood Victory Committee Christmas party, 57–58
Horne as "Negro Ambassador" for war effort, 180
Lamarr hired by, 3
not letting top stars join military, 127, 148, 175
Thalberg as production chief, 6
twentieth anniversary class photograph, 124

Micheaux, Oscar, 140

Midway, Battle of, 92–94, *94*, 125

Mildred Pierce (film), 178

Milestone, Lewis, 139

Miller, J. Howard, 111

Miller, Sidney, 4

Minnelli, Vincente, 142

The Miracle of Morgan's Creek (film), 160

Miranda, Carmen, *28*, 30–31, *31*, 34, *83*, 84, 135, 193–194

Mission to Moscow (film), *138,* 138–139, 199

Mitchell, R. J., 130

Mitchum, Robert, 149, *148*

Mobile, Alabama, 143

Modern Times (film), 23–24, 26

Mog, Aribert, *3*

Monroe, Rose Will, 108

Montagu, Ivor, 24

Montalbán, Ricardo, *xi*

Montgomery, Bernard, 118, 146, 165

Montgomery, Robert, 21, 41, 126, 165, 166, *166,* 188

Morgan, Frank, 21, 191

Morris, Leland B., 48

The Mortal Storm (film), *20,* 20–21, 35, 40

Moscovich, Maurice, 25

Moss, Carlton, 145, 180

Motion Picture Alliance for the Preservation of American Ideals (MPA), 199

Motion Picture Producers and Distributors of America, 40

Mountbatten, Lord Louis, 50, 126

Mowbray, Alan, *53*

MPA (Motion Picture Alliance for the Preservation of American Ideals), 199

Mr. Smith Goes to Washington (film), 41, 52

Mrs. Miniver (film), 48, 69, *89,* 89–92, *90, 91, 93,* 95, 111–112, 119

Muni, Paul, 9

Music in the Air (film), 1, 2

Mussolini, Benito, 3, 6, 13, *24,* 29, 126, 146, 185

Mussolini, Vittorio, 13

MUZAK radio broadcasts, 174

My Friend Bonito (film), 85

NAACP, *69,* 140, 142, 143, 194, *195*

Nagasaki, Japan, 188

Nagumo, Chūichi, 46, 92

The Name Above the Title (Capra autobiography), 49

Nanjing Massacre, 98

National Catholic Community Service, 81

National Inventors Council, 108

National Jewish Welfare Board, 81

National Socialist German Actors' Guild, 114

National Travelers Aid Association, 81

Navy Relief, 120

Navy (US), 108. *See also specific sailors*

Nazi Agent (film), 95, 96

Nazi Germany. *See* Germany

Nazi supporters
  German American Bund, 5, 6, *16,* 18, *19,* 27
  Jannings, ix, 11
  Pickford, 6
  Silver Legion of America "Silver Shirts," 6, 48

NBC Blue, 85

NBC radio, 58, *72*

The Negro Soldier (film), 69–70, 145

Nesbit, Meg, 106

New China Recipes (cookbook), 101

Newman, Paul, 188

The New Spirit (film), 51, 161

New York Film Critics Circle, 65, 137

The New York Times, 23–24, 61, 98–99, 119, 135

Ney, Richard, 89

Nicholas Brothers, 144

A Night at the Garden (film), 5

Night Train to Munich (film), 113

Nimitz, Chester, 94

Niño, Marcelo, 35

Ninotchka (film), 139

Niven, David, 129

Noack, Frank, ix

Normandie (ship), xii, *xii,* 3

Northern Pursuit (film), 151

The North Star (film), 139, 199

Notorious (film), 193

Nuremberg trials, 6, 27

Nye, Gerald P., 39–40

Nye Committee, 40, 65, 197

Oakie, Jack, *24*

Oberon, Merle, 73, 76

Objective, Burma! (film), 151

Office of Strategic Services (OSS), 39

Office of the Coordinator of Inter-American Affairs (OCIAA), 30, 31, 34, 84

Office of War Information, 125, 137–138, 145

O'Hara, Maureen, 139

Okinawa, Battle of, 187, 188

Oliveira, José, 34

Olivier, Laurence, 117

Olympia (film), 13

O'Neil, Brian, 30

O'Neill, Eugene, 39

O'Neill, Henry, *82*

One Million B.C. (film), 177

Only Angels Have Wings (film), 37

On the Waterfront (film), 200

Operation Husky, 126

Operation Overlord (D-Day), 146, 164–167, *167*

Operation Torch, 118–119

Orson Welles Commentaries (ABC radio series), 194–195, 196

Osborn, Frederick, 50

Osborne, Robert, 138

Oscars. *See* Academy Awards

OSS (Office of Strategic Services), 39

Otto, Elinor, 108, 111

Owen, Reginald, *82*

Page, Joy, 113

Pal (collie), 134–135, 191

Palfi, Lotte, 117

Pal Joey (film), 149

The Palm Beach Story (film), 111

Palmer, Maria, 111

Panama Hattie (film), 145

Paramount, 4, 10, 11, 15, 26, 199. *See also specific films*

Paris, liberation of, 174

Parsons, Louella, 24, 93

Partridge, Derek, 130

Patton, George S., 174, 181, 183

Payne, John, 135

PCA. *See* Production Code Administration

Pearl Harbor attack, *44,* 45–47, *46*
  films about, *66,* 66–67
  impact on films, 61–62
  Los Angeles fears, 63, 65
  radio reports, ix, 45, 47, 84
  US ships, 125
  vengeance, 166–167

Peck, Gregory, 149, *150,* 151, 199

Pelley, William Dudley, 48

Perón, Juan, 193

Peters, Susan, 139

The Philadelphia Story (film), 26, 41

Philippines, 63, 74–75, 76, 183

Philippine Sea, Battle of the, 166–167

Pichel, Irving, 22, 197

Pickens, Andrew, 47–48

Pickford, Mary, 6, 105

Pidgeon, Walter, 39, *82*, 89, *89*, 108

The Pied Piper (film), 96–97

"Pimpernel" Smith (film), 130, 132, 133

Pinocchio (film), 32, 161

Pin-Up Girl (film), 158

pinups, 158–160, *159*, *160*

Poland, German invasion of, 18, 25

Porgy and Bess (film), 201

Porter, Jean, 158

post-traumatic stress disorder (PTSD), 190–192

Pot o' Gold (film), 41

Powell, Dick, *73*

Powell, Eleanor, 57, 73, 75

Powell, Michael, 130

Powell, William, 134, 158

Power, Tommy, *67*

Power, Tyrone, 57, *124*, 154, 184, 188

Powolny, Frank, photo by, *160*

Poynter, Nelson, 137–138

Prager, Ilona, 96

Prelude to War (film), *50*, 51, *52*, 95

Preminger, Otto, 97, *97*, 201

A Present with a Future (patriotic short), 169

The Producers (film), 26, 202

Producers Releasing Corporation, 101

Production Code Administration (PCA), 9–10, 11, 15–16

propaganda, 161

PTSD (post-traumatic stress disorder), 190–192

The Purple Heart (film), 98

Pyle, Ernie, 187

"Quarantine Hitler" (HANL rally), 13

Queen Mary (ship), 164

"race riots" (1943), 143–144

Radosevic, Nikola, 27

Rains, Claude, 15, 113

Rand, Ayn, 199

Rathbone, Basil, 133, *133*

rationing, *146*, 147, 153

Rationing (film), 153

Raye, Martha, 177, *178*

Reagan, Ronald, 62, 184

The Rear Gunner (training film), 125

Reason and Emotion (film), 162, *162*

Rebel Without a Cause (film), 36

Red Cross, 21, *169*

Red Scares, 197

Reed, Carol, 113

Reed, Donna, *148*

refugees, 6–7, 12, *113*, 113–119

Reinhardt, Max, 15

Reinhardt, Wolfgang, 15

The Reluctant Dragon (film), 35

Renoir, Jean, 22, 116, 139

Report from the Aleutians (film), 82, 155, 191

Republic Pictures, 37

Reville, Alma, *47*

Reynolds, Adeline De Walt, *152*

Ribbentrop, Joachim von, 48

Richard, Alfred Charles, Jr., 88

Riefenstahl, Leni, 13, 23, 51

Riley, Lewis A., 106

Rio Bravo (film), 36

Rio de Janeiro, Brazil, 30, 31, 34, 83–85, *85*, 88

Rio Rita (film), 135

RKO. *See also specific films*
  Berman as chief of, 4
  Cooper's career, 37
  Disney films, 161, 163
  Hollywood Canteen, 172
  Welles and, 84, 86–88, 170

Roach, Hal, 13

Road movies, 151

Robeson, Paul, 8, *8*, 71, 197

Robinson, Bill "Bojangles," 144, *144*

Robinson, Casey, 118

Robinson, Edward G.
  The Amazing Dr. Clitterhouse, 14
  Confessions of a Nazi Spy, 14, 16, 17, *17*, 137, 193
  Hollywood Anti-Nazi League, 13–14, 197
  "How the Reds Made a Sucker Out of Me," 197
  Little Caesar, 13
  radio broadcasts, 137
  screen persona, 13–14
  The Stranger, 193
  USO shows, *197*

Rockefeller, Nelson, 30, 31, 34, 84, 86

Rockwell, Francis W., *124*

Rodzinski, Artur, 45

Rogers, Ginger, 5, 47, 57

Romano, Tony, 81

Rooney, Anne, *82*

Rooney, Mickey
  Academy Award nomination, 147, 148
  film career, 31, *147*, 147–148
  frontline entertainment, 174–175, *175*
  Gardner and, 148
  Hollywood Victory Caravan, *73*

Hollywood Victory Committee Christmas party, 57

military service, ii, 148, 174, 175, 188

war bonds tour, *front endpapers*

war's damage to career, 193

Roosevelt, Eleanor, 8, 73

Roosevelt, Franklin D.
  Casablanca Conference, 119
  China air support, 38
  Dietrich and, 173–174
  draft, 30, 79
  on entertainment as national asset, 73
  expansion of production capacity, 54, 56
  fireside chats, 63
  Gable and, 58
  Good Neighbor Policy, ix, 30, 83
  The Great Dictator (film), 25
  inauguration, 104
  internment camps, 62
  Mellett as liaison for, 69
  Miranda and, 31
  Mrs. Miniver, 92
  OCIAA, 30
  OSS, 39
  USO shows, 81
  Victory Through Air Power (film), 163
  war bonds, 56, 173–174

Rope (film), 186

Rose, Helen, 145

Rose Marie (film), 41

Rosen, Jody, 121

Rosie the Riveter (women in the workforce)
  hair safety, 111
  The Life and Times of Rosie the Riveter, 55
  movies as escape for, 112

Rosie the Riveter (*continued*)
  number of, 108
  onscreen combat roles, 111
  onscreen fashion and
    hairstyles, ix, 111–112, *112*
  real-life Rosies, 108, 111
  Rosies in Hollywood, *107*,
    107–112
  "We Can Do It!" poster,
    109, 111
Roxie Hart (film), 47
Rubinstein, Arthur, 45
The Rules of the Game (film),
  116
Rumrich, Guenther Gustave
  Maria, 15, 17
Russell, Harold, 192, *192*
Russell, Rosalind, 57
Russian War Relief, 137

Saboteur (film), *47*
Sabu, *70*
Sahara (film), 143
Sakall, S. Z. "Cuddles," *116*, 117
Saludos Amigos (film), 35,
  88, 161
Salvation Army, 81
Sandrich, Mark, 61, 74
San Juan, Olga, 76
Saroyan, William, 147, 166
Saturday Evening Post, 62
The Scarlet Pimpernel (film),
  130
Schaefer, George, 86
Schlesinger, Leon, 33
Schlosberg, Richard T., 50
Schulberg, Budd, 6, *7*, 27
Screen Cartoonist's Guild, 33,
  33, 36
Selective Training and Service
  Act (1940), 30
Selznick, Daniel Mayer, 5
Selznick, David O., 118

Selznick International
  Pictures, 30, 37, 47
Sergeant York (film), 43, 65,
  67
Seversky, Alexander P. de,
  163, 184
Sex Hygiene (training film), 38
Shanghai Express (film), 11
Shaw, Irwin, 166
Sheridan, Ann, 111
Sherlock Holmes films, *133*,
  133–134
Sherman, Vincent, 68
Shirer, William L., 49
The Shop Around the Corner
  (film), 20
Shostakovich, Dimitri, 138
Show Boat (film), 8, 197
"Show Business at War"
  (newsreel), *127*
Shubert, Lee, 30–31, 84
Shull, Lynwood, 194–195
Sicily invasion, 126, 140, 146
Sikeston, Missouri, 69
"Silent Night" (Christmas
  carol), 121, 169
Silver Legion of America
  "Silver Shirts," 6, 48
Sinatra, Frank
  Anchors Aweigh, *168*, *179*,
    187
  4-F status, 149, 156, 157
  as heartthrob, 79, *156*,
    156–157
  Hollywood Canteen, 105
  "I'll Never Smile Again,"
    47, 156
  as most hated man of
    World War II, 156
  Pearl Harbor attack and, 47
Sinatra, Nancy, 157
Since You Went Away (film),
  152, 194
Siodmak, Robert, 1

Skelton, Red, 57
Smith, Joseph B., 132
*Snow White and the Seven
  Dwarfs* (film), 32
Something for the Boys (film),
  193
Somewhere I'll Find You (film),
  58–59, 76, 127
The Song of Bernadette (film),
  155
Song of Russia (film), 139, 199
Song of the South (film), 194
Son of Lassie (film), 134, *134*
Soong Mei-ling (Madame
  Chiang Kai-shek), 37–38
So Proudly We Hail! (film),
  111, *112*
Soviet Union, 39, 126, 137,
  139, 188, 197, 199
Spanish Civil War, 8
Spartacus (film), 202
Spellbound (film), 151
The Spider Woman (film), 134
Spiegel, Sam, 193
Spigelgass, Leonard, 52,
  157–158
Springtime in the Rockies
  (film), 135
Spruance, Raymond, 94
Stagecoach (film), 13
Stage Door Canteen, 102
Stage Fright (film), 186
Stalin, Joseph, 137, 138, *138*,
  160, 197
Stalingrad, Soviet Union, 126
Stanwyck, Barbara, 73
Starr, Kevin, 1, 111
Stars and Stripes newspaper,
  157
stars in uniform, 122–126, 154,
  169. *See also specific people*
"The Star-Spangled Banner"
  (national anthem), 29, 71
Stein, Jules, 102

Steiner, Max, 118
Stephenson, Sir William, 132
Sternberg, Josef von, 11
Stevens, George, 70–71, 158,
  166, 185, 200, *200*
Stevens, Risë, 73, *75*, *152*
Stewart, Alex, 41
Stewart, Jimmy
  Academy Award, 41
  Academy Awards
    ceremonies, 154, 188
  Army Air Force service, ii,
    vi, x, 41–43, *42*, *43*, 48,
    123, 123–124, 126, *164*,
    164–167, 184–185
  autograph's value, 158
  film career, 20, *20*, 41, 68,
    123
  Fonda and, 41, 58
  Meredith and, 125
  return from war, 188
  war relief radio broadcast,
    67
Stormy Weather (film), x, *144*,
  144–145, 180, 201
The Story of G.I. Joe (film),
  186–187
Stössel, Ludwig, 95, 117
The Stranger (film), 192–193,
  202
The Streets of Paris (Broadway
  show), 31, 135
Stroheim, Erich von, 139
Sullivan, Margaret, 20
Surovy, Walter, *152*
Swanson, Gloria, 2, 7
Sweden, film bans, 132
Sweet Rosie O'Grady (film),
  160

The Talk of the Town (film),
  70–71, 104, 166
Tanner, Peter, 186
Tarawa, Battle of, 165

Tarkington, Booth, 86–87

Tashlin, Frank, 36

Taylor, Elizabeth, 191

Taylor, Robert, 13, *125*, 125–126, 139, 199

Temple, Shirley, 13

Terrell, Edward, 163

Thalberg, Irving, 1, 6, 9–10

Thank Your Lucky Stars (film), 182

That Night in Rio (film), 84

They Got Me Covered (film), 97

They Were Expendable (film), 187

They Were Expendable (radio performance), *124*

The Thief of Bagdad (film), 70

The Thin Man Goes Home (film), 134

Thirty Seconds Over Tokyo (film), 74, 149, *149*, 187, 202

This Gun for Hire (film), *110*

This Is the Army (Broadway musical), *120*

This Is the Army (film), 120

This Land Is Mine (film), 139

Thomas, Frank, 33, 34

Thomas, Jeanette, 34

Thomas, Patty, 81

Thomson, David, 90

The Three Caballeros (film), 35

Three Stooges, 26, *27*

Time magazine, *157*

Tiomkin, Dimitri, 137

To Be or Not to Be (film), 26, 57, 58, 59–60, 202

Tokyo, firebombing of, 184

Toland, Gregg, 38–39, 65, 99

Tora! Tora! Tora! (film), 47

Toti, Mario, 127

Toumanova, Tamara, 139

Tracy, Spencer, 5, 105, 149

Triumph of the Will (film), 23, 26, 51

Trumbo, Dalton, 202

Turner, Lana, x, *x*, 47, 59, 76, 79, 160

Tuskegee Airmen, 68, 140, *141*, 182

Twardowski, Hans Heinrich von, 117

20th Century Fox, 4, 145, 155, 158. *See also specific films*

Two-Faced Woman (film), ix

UFA (German studio), 1, 11, 114

Uncertain Glory (film), 151

Under Capricorn (film), 186

United Artists, 6–7, 25, 163, 177

United China Relief, 8, 10, 101

United Service Organizations. *See* USO

Universal, 6–7, 133, 139

USO
    Astaire, Fred, *189*
    Dietrich, Marlene, *173*, 174
    Hayworth, Rita, *201*
    Hope, Bob, 79–81, *81*, 175, 177
    Horne, Lena, 180
    Hutton, Betty, *177*
    member organizations, 81
    Robinson, Edward G., *197*
    Wayne, John, 175
    Williams, Esther, 179

The Valley of Decision (film), 151

Vargas, Getúlio, 35, 85, 88

Variety, 120

V-E Day and aftermath, 184–188

Veidt, Conrad, *95*, 95–96, 114, 119, *119*

Victor Emmanuel III, King (Italy), 126

Victory Committee. *See* Hollywood Victory Committee

Victory Gardens, *107*

Victory Golf Tournament, *79*

Victory Through Air Power (film), *163*, 163–164

Victory Through Air Power (Seversky), 163, 184

Vietnam War, 190

V-J Day, 188

von Stroheim, Erich, 139

Voss, Howard, 127

"Die Wacht am Rhein" (German march), 114

Wake Island (film), 98

Walburn, Raymond, *82*

Wallace, Henry, 105

Wallace, Oliver, 161

Wallenberg, Raoul, 132

Waller, Fats, 144

Wallis, Hal, 48, 66–67, 117, 118

Walsh, Raoul, 68

Walt Disney Studios. *See also specific films*
    financial problems, 32–33, 36, 48
    management-labor divide, 13, *33*, 33–34, 36
    propaganda films, 161–163
    US Army garrison, 48, 51
    as wartime industrial plant, 51, 161

Walter, Rosalind P., 108

War Assistance League, 170

war bonds, x, 56, 58–59, 72, 76, 102, 169, 173–174, *176*

Warner, Harry, 4, 13, 18

Warner, Jack, 4, 6, 15, 102

Warner Bros. *See also specific films*
    anti-Fascism, 6, 102
    employment lawsuit against, 199
    German ban on films, 18
    Hollywood Canteen, 170
    live-action art department, 36
    Looney Tunes, 33, 160
    studio chiefs, 4

Waters, Ethel, 142, 182

Watson, Bobs, 4

Watts, Steven, 51

Wayne, John, *37*, 175, 199

"We Can Do It!" poster, *109*, 111

Week-End in Havana (film), *83*, 84

Weidler, Roberta, 200–201

Weidler, Virginia, 158

A Welcome to Britain (film), 125

Welles, Orson
    Academy Award, 65
    Brazil trip, 83–88, *85*, 86
    Citizen Kane, 38–39, 47, 65, 84, 106
    del Rio and, 106
    Follow the Boys, 170
    Gulf Screen Guild Theater, 47, 84
    Hayworth and, 88, 106, 169–170, 193, 196
    It's All True, 65, 85, *86*, 87–88, 193
    Jane Eyre, 170
    Journey into Fear, 84
    The Lady from Shanghai, 193
    The Magnificent Ambersons, 84, 85, 86–87, 193
    The Mercury Wonder Show, 106, 169–170
    Orson Welles Commentaries, 194–195, 196
    on Pearl Harbor attack, 47, 84
    "President Vargas's Birthday," 85
    RKO and, 84, 86–88, 170

Welles, Orson (*continued*)
  The Stranger, 192–193
  war's damage to career,
    193
Wellman, William, 186–187
Wenders, Wim, 117
White, Walter Francis, 140
White Cargo (film), 158
Whitman, Ernie "Bubbles," 72
Whitney, John Hay, 30, 84
Whitty, Dame May, 89, *90*
Why We Fight (film series),
    51–52
  Academy Awards, 95, 137
  as anti-Nazi statement, 17,
    51, 92
  The Battle of Russia, 137,
    155
  budget, 52
  Disney and, 161
  Litvak as co-director, 17, 51
  ongoing power of, 193
  Prelude to War, *50*, 51, *52*,
    95
  writers, 51–52, 157
Wilcoxon, Henry, 92
Wilcoxon, Robert, 92
The Wild Bunch (film), 36
Wilder, Billy, 1–2, 12, 117, 139,
    186, 187
Wilder, Eugenia, 1
Williams, Esther, 178–179, *179*
Williams, Spencer, 140
Willkie, Wendell, 40, 65
Wilson, Dooley, 113
Wilson, Marie, *front endpapers*
Wings of Desire (film), 117
Winning Your Wings (short
    film), 68, 123
Winter Line, 146
Wise, Robert, 84, 85, 86–87
The Wiz (film), 201
women in the workforce. *See*
  Rosie the Riveter

Wong, Anna May, 8–11, *9*, *10*,
    99, *100*, 101, 104
Wong, Tyrus, 36
Woodard, Isaac, 194–195, *195*
Woolley, Monty, 96–97
World War I, 5, 38, 64, 130,
    161
World War II. *See also specific
    battles*
  American opposition to, 5,
    21, 29–30
  financing, 53–54, 56
Wright, Cleo, 69
Wright, Teresa, 89, *90*, 92, 95,
    111, *153*, 154
Wyler, Talli, 48
Wyler, William
  The Best Years of Our Lives,
    192
  Mrs. Miniver, 48, 69, *90*,
    92, 138
  The Negro Soldier, 69, 145
  Pearl Harbor attack and,
    48
Wyman, Jane, 111

X-Day, 188
Ximena, José Rey, 132

Yamamoto, Isoroku, 47
Yamamura, Sô, 47
Yankee Doodle Dandy (film),
    13, 61, 172
Y-Day, 188
YMCA, 81
Yorktown, USS, 93–94, 125
You Nazty Spy! (film), 26, *27*
The Youngest Profession (film),
    52, 157–158
Your Hit Parade (CBS radio
    show), 121
Yung, Victor Sen, *61*, 62, 98,
    98, 99
YWCA, 81

Zanuck, Darryl F.
  Academy Award, 50
  as Academy of Motion
    Picture Arts and
    Sciences' Research
    Council chair, 38
  in Army Signal Corps
    reserve, 38, 39, 40, 50
  Gentleman's Agreement,
    199–200
  Good Neighbor Policy, 84
  The Grapes of Wrath, 22, 38
  heritage, 4
  How Green Was My Valley,
    40, 50, 65
  Nye Committee testimony,
    40
  Preminger and, 97
  Production Code
    Administration and, 22
Zanuck, Richard, 199
Zé Carioca, 34
Ziegfeld Girl (film), 41
Zilzer, Wolfgang, 117
Zinnemann, Fred, 1, 193
Zoot Suit Riots, 144
Zukor, Adolph, 4, 40